LAW FIRM BREAKUPS

LAW FIRM BREAKUPS
The Law and Ethics of Grabbing and Leaving

ROBERT W. HILLMAN

Professor of Law
University of California, Davis

LITTLE, BROWN AND COMPANY
Boston   Toronto   London

Library of Congress Catalog Card No. 89-85737

ISBN 0-316-36379-0

HC

Published simultaneously in Canada
by Little, Brown & Company (Canada) Limited

Printed in the United States of America

To Olympia Ilona

SUMMARY OF CONTENTS

TABLE OF CONTENTS

Chapter 3
TORT AND AGENCY LAW
PERSPECTIVES   45

Chapter 4
LAW FIRMS AS PARTNERSHIPS   61

Chapter 5
THE RELEVANCE OF
INCORPORATION   113

FOREWORD

Hell hath no fury like a lawyer entoiled in a law firm breakup. One lawyer is jilted by departing colleagues who vanish with key client files, leaving no capital behind to pay ongoing firm expenses. Another is flung out the door by disenchanted colleagues. A third sits working feverishly and unrewarded in a cramped office, chafing under the yoke of a tyrannical senior lawyer and yearning to break into the bright light of opportunity in a new situation. A fourth is bound by a partnership agreement to much less compensation than what, according to the lawyer's own calculations, the lawyer is bringing into the firm.

Until recently, none of those lawyers (or their opposing numbers in the firm) could find much guidance in the law. ("Guidance"—the lodestar that a lawyer tries to set in every client's firmament—becomes even more desirable when the lawyer's own legal problems raise the questions.) The general law of partnership and agency provides only the most general and incomplete compass. Fitting lawyer's problems only into general partnership and agency molds also ignores the special claims of clients and the special responsibilities of lawyers under the lawyer codes and other law specifically regulating lawyers. Turning to the lawyer codes, unfortunately, gives little further by way of specific guidance, although there is much general language there that may be of consequence.

The few general textual treatments of the law of lawyers give only partial and perfunctory treatment to the many issues involved in law firm breakups. I feel more confident slighting the treatment in C. Wolfram, Modern Legal Ethics (1986)[1] than I do saying that G. Hazard and W. Hodes, The Law of Lawyering (1985)[2] is a sketch at best. Perhaps I have missed something in the Hazard-Hodes index, but I doubt it. Keyed, as that excellent treatise is, to only those areas covered by the ABA's Model Rules of Professional Conduct, it is inevitable that the work would omit most of the interesting and important issues involved in law firm breakups.

Now, however, we have Professor Robert W. Hillman's Law Firm Breakups: The Law and Ethics of Grabbing and Leaving. This volume solves the problem of finding the definitive written resource. Professor Hillman brings to his work all that an anxious reader would wish to find. His academic background combines expertise in both business organization law and the law of partnerships. His treatment reflects a well researched grounding in all other relevant areas of the law.

Many law-trained authors approaching one of the outlands peopled by lawyers and their legal/ethical problems have foundered on uncharted shoals of exotic doctrine or mysterious legal institutions or become lost in the murk of vague and confusing lawyer code language. Professor Hillman shows, on the whole, a sure and confident knowledge of this important area. (I withhold complete agreement solely out of academic conservativism.) Where many others have gone astray, Professor Hillman keeps to the path. Where others would confidently state what the law demands or prohibits, he urges a cautious approach. To boot, he writes in a tight and interesting style.

The book deals with the classical problem of lawyers' leaving firms and taking clients with them. It builds upon and very usefully enlarges Professor Hillman's earlier treatment of the subject in a lead

---

[1] See pp. 879-880 (sale of law practice), 885 (restrictive convenant—in one sentence), 887-889 (law firm dissolution).
[2] See pp. 885-887 (restrictive covenants).

article in a volume of the Texas Law Review.[3] While this central problem inspired the book and provides its title, it hardly circumscribes its coverage. Lawyers will also find much that is useful concerning advertising, relationships with clients, constructing a firm partnership agreement, and the like.

In the ill remembered days of a mythical lawyering past, lawyers all exuded virtue, practiced with an eye solely on the public interest, and were altruistic and endlessly generous in their dealings with firm colleagues. Today, most firms strive to realize the best aspects of that ideal, when they can make a profit. Occasional cosmic flare-ups remind us that the virtues of kindness and forbearance among firm colleagues are atrophying, if they were ever accurately reported as universally vigorous.

Firms are becoming larger and, necessarily, more impersonal. Lawyers are becoming more candid in their interest in their incomes. Reflecting the restless society of the larger world in which they practice, lawyers no longer espouse constancy in firm associations. Increasingly, lawyers at all levels of seniority dart off to new firms in lateral moves, perhaps under the tutelage of a professional head-hunter from a lawyer-placement service. The bottom-line mentality expressed in greater and more open pursuit of additional client fee-income through aggressive marketing also finds occasional correlative expression in drastic measures to cut costs. Many law firms were once operated as private-sector socialist paradises, with cradle-to-grave security and a steadily rising income offered to any lawyer who had managed to climb into the feather bed of a partnership position. That security is also unraveling, sometimes with rude abruptness. The economic pyramid on which all but very few law firms are modeled has required, and always will require, that young associates either be stalled indefinitely in their lower-paying positions or be cycled out of the firm to be replaced by younger, and cheaper, laborers. That young associates and other departing lawyers would wish to take firm clients with them to ease their way into another practice is unremarkable. That their former colleagues and

---

[3] Hillman, Law Firms and Their Partners: The Law and Ethics of Grabbing and Leaving, 67 Tex. L. Rev. 1 (1988).

bosses, occupying the lucrative top of the pyramid, should regret the loss of firm clients is also no cause for surprise.

In short, the forces that lead to law firm breakups on less than congenial terms are endemic in the social structure and economics of the modern firm. Conflict is a natural and robust outgrowth. As lawyers, we tend to think first of law and legal methods to resolve conflicts of all sorts, including our own. In Professor Hillman's book, we have a vade mecum for any lawyer drawn into such conflicts as combatant/participant, advisor, or mediator.

Charles W. Wolfram

Bayville, Maine
August 1989

PREFACE

This book describes and evaluates the restraints imposed upon lawyers who withdraw from law firms and take with them the major assets of their firms—clients. Even a brief perusal of ongoing media accounts reveals the extent to which the "grabbing and leaving" activities of law firm members have destabilized law firms of all sizes. The tumult will continue for some time to come.

The book began rather modestly as I assembled materials for a short chapter on law firms in a treatise on breakups of closely held business and professional associations. I was struck by the absence of literature offering an integrated view of legal principles affecting lateral movements by lawyers and of the relative "rights" of firms and their lawyers to clients. The chapter grew into an article published in the November 1988, issue of the Texas Law Review. The response to the article and developments subsequent to its completion prompted me to expand, revise, and update my commentary. This book is the product of that effort.

Although the focus of the book is not insolvent firms or those undergoing reorganization, I have included an appendix section on this subject. Additional appendices provide primary sources on both partnership law and legal ethics. Legal and ethical norms relevant to grabbing and leaving, however, are far from static. Readers should stay alert to changes in partnership law that will come about as a result of the National Conference of Commissioners' planned revision of the Uniform Partnership Act. Moreover, the American Law Institute has undertaken to prepare a Restatement of the Law Governing Lawyers; tentative drafts of a chapter on confidentiality have already appeared. And the lawyer codes regulating such matters as the sale of law firm goodwill are in a state of flux and bear close watching.

I owe much to many people. Keith Flaum, Todd Baran, Don Bradley, Peter Feinberg, Cindy Shepard, Roberto Berry, and Susan Firtch provided valuable research support. The editors of the Texas Law Review did a fine job in editing the 1988 article I published in their journal. Dean Florian Bartosic and my colleagues at King Hall were most supportive and helpful throughout this project, as were Monte Van Norden, Jay Boggis, and Shana Wagger at Little, Brown. Professors Harry Haysnworth of the University of South Carolina School of Law and Donald Weidner of Florida State University College of Law offered many helpful comments. And most especially, my wife tolerated my long absences and irritability with the grace, understanding, and good humor I have come to expect, but do not necessarily deserve.

Robert W. Hillman

Davis, California
May 1989

ACKNOWLEDGMENTS

The author gratefully acknowledges permission to reprint the following appendix materials.

The American Bar Association. The Model Code of Professional Responsibility.

The American Bar Association. The Model Rules of Professional Conduct.

The American Bar Association. Selected Ethics Opinions.

The above materials are excerpted from the Model Rules of Professional Conduct, Model Code of Professional Responsibility and Ethics Opinions, copyright by the American Bar Association. All rights reserved. Reprinted with permission.

N. Feinstein, S. Feldman, A. Olick & M. Temin, Materials Concerning the Insolvency and Reorganization of Professional Associations and Corporations: Legal, Practical, and Ethical Considerations. Reprinted with permission.

The Uniform Partnership Act. This act has been printed through the permission of the National Conference of Commissioners on Uniform State Laws, and copies of the act may be ordered at a cost of $5.00 each from them at 676 North St. Clair Street, Suite 1700, Chicago, IL 60611.

LAW FIRM BREAKUPS

Chapter 1
INTRODUCTION

§1.1 *The Setting*

Law firms are under siege. The traditional view of the law firm as a stable institution with an assured future is now challenged by an awareness that even the largest and most prestigious firms are fragile economic units facing a myriad of risks in their quests to survive and prosper. No longer can the law graduate join a major firm with the sanguine assumption that the firm will not experience major upheavals, turnover in lawyers, or, in extreme cases, receivership.[1] As

---

§1.1 [1] See, e.g., Cox, A "Lifeboat" for Firms Going Under, Natl. L.J., Sept. 5, 1988, at 8, col. 1 [hereinafter Cox, *"Lifeboat" for Firms*] (discussing the activities of a receiver for five Los Angeles firms); Cox, End Comes at Last to L.A. Firm, Natl. L.J., Feb. 16, 1987, at 3, col. 1 (describing the dissolution of a large Los Angeles firm that entered receivership); Stille, The Fall of the House of Herrick, Natl. L.J., Feb. 24, 1986, at 6, col. 1 (reporting the sudden demise of a prominent and longstanding Boston firm of 79 lawyers); Weingarten, Breaking Up: Requiem for a Heavyweight Law Firm, Natl. L.J., June 1, 1981, at 1, col. 2 (describing the breakup of a major New York patent and trademark firm).

the unseemly and well publicized demise of the nation's fourth largest law firm aptly illustrates,[2] partnership in seemingly successful firms is a prospect to be approached with, to say the least, a measure of caution.

Law firms, in short, are in turmoil, and many of their problems arise from within the firms themselves. Firms are increasingly but temporary resting places for their partners. Lateral hiring, once confined largely to junior lawyers, now extends through all levels of a partnership.[3] The partner who can transport clients and revenues to another firm is a particularly attractive candidate for lateral move-

---

[2] The firm of Finley, Kumble, Wagner, Underberg, Manley, Myerson & Casey had 245 partners and approximately 2000 associates and staff members prior to its breakup. Jensen, Scenes from a Breakup, Natl. L.J., Feb. 8, 1988, at 1, col. 1. The press and the legal community closely monitored the demise of the firm. See, e.g., Jensen & Wise, Finley Kumble: The Firm's Final Days, Natl. L.J., Dec. 21, 1987, at 3, col. 1; Jensen & Wise, Finley Kumble: The End of an Era, Natl. L.J., Nov. 23, 1987, at 1, col. 1; Shipp, The Splintering of Finley Kumble, N.Y. Times, Nov. 15, 1987, §3, at 1, col. 2.

[3] In a column entitled Lateral Moves, the National Law Journal regularly reports the movement of partners. See, e.g., Lateral Moves, Natl. L.J., Aug. 15, 1988, at 2, col. 3. Changing economic conditions, however, may affect the frequency of lateral movements. See Zeldis, Lateral Frenzy Over?, Natl. L.J., Feb. 8, 1988, at 2, col. 2.

Various aspects of the problems attendant to lateral moves are beginning to generate law review commentary. See, e.g., Gilson & Mnookin, Sharing Among the Human Capitalists: An Economic Inquiry into the Corporate Law Firm and How Partners Split Profits, 37 Stan. L. Rev. 313, 338-339 (1985) (describing grabbing and leaving as a means of opportunism that can cause problems in determining a firm's profit sharing arrangements); Hillman, Law Firms and Their Partners: The Law and Ethics of Grabbing and Leaving, 67 Texas L. Rev. 1 (1988); Johnson, Solicitation of Law Firm Clients by Departing Attorneys: Tort, Fiduciary, and Disciplinary Liability, 50 U. Pitt. L. Rev. 1 (1988); Terry, Ethical Pitfalls and Malpractice Consequences of Law Firm Breakups, 61 Temp. L. Rev. 1055 (1988); Comment, Barefoot Shoemakers: An Uncompromising Approach to Policing the Morals of the Marketplace When Law Firms Split Up, 19 Ariz. St. L.J. 509 (1987) (discussing the respective rights and liabilities of the firm and departing lawyers when firm members grab and leave); Comment, Lateral Moves and the Quest for Clients: Tort Liability of Departing Attorneys for Taking Firm Clients, 75 Calif. L. Rev. 1809 (1987) (discussing tests for determining the tort liability of departing attorneys who grab and leave); Comment, Winding Up Dissolved Law Partnerships: The No-Compensation Rule and Client Choice, 73 Calif. L. Rev. 1597 (1985) (discussing the inequities of the no-compensation rule in partnership dissolutions and proposing an alternative for postdissolution compensation of partners).

ment,[4] a fact evidenced by the advertisements of firms and their agents seeking partners with substantial client "portfolios."[5] For each firm that gains a partner and a new basket of clients, another firm loses an important source of revenues and gains an incentive to do its own lateral hiring.[6] The ripple effect is obvious.

There are a number of reasons for the destabilization of American law partnerships.[7] One of the more important is the inability of

---

[4] See, e.g., Adams, Shea & Gould's Merger Man, Am. Law., Oct. 1985, 15, at 15 ("It was a coup for Shea & Gould. Goldstein brought with him more than half the real estate department from his former firm . . . in addition to an office in Miami and several prize clients."); Pollock, Till a Better Deal Do Us Part, Am. Law., Oct. 1985, 1, at 1 ("For eight partners at two New York firms . . . this has not been a good year. . . . No, they hadn't been kicked out of their firms. . . . It's just that the majority of their partners — including those responsible for the core of each firm's business — had left as a group to become partners at other firms, leaving their now-former partners little more than the lease, a tattered letterhead, and best wishes."); Burrough, Bialkin, Top Securities Lawyer, To Leave Willkie Farr over Conflict with Partners, Wall St. J., Jan. 15, 1988, §1, at 2, col. 3 (describing a lateral move following a conflict among partners and observing that the "move is considered a coup for Skadden Arps and could be a blow to Willkie Farr, which might lose business if clients loyal to Mr. Bialkin follow him to Skadden Arps"); Effron, Dramatic Exodus in Philadelphia, Natl. L.J., Mar. 24, 1986, at 2, col. 1 (quoting the chairman of a firm laterally hiring two partners to the effect that the partners' "tobacco, coal, insurance, financial services and other [clients] plan to move with them, greatly enhancing the firm's presence and competitive posture statewide").

[5] For examples of such classified ads targeted at partners, see N.Y.L.J., Feb. 8, 1988, at 12, col. 1 ("Senior Partner — Any Art with Portfolio for Major Firm"); id. at 10, col. 7 ("A very well-regarded mid-sized mid-town full service firm with a strong real estate reputation seeks a senior real estate partner. Clientele in the area of $500,000 a plus."); see also Jones, The Challenge of Change: The Practice of Law in the Year 2000, 41 Vand. L. Rev. 683, 688 (1988) (commenting that "[t]he concept of the 'portable practice' and the increasing willingness of lawyers to leave their current firms to work for the highest bidding competitors have created a whole new growth industry in legal recruitment services").

[6] Cf. Riley, Lateral Movement Works Both Ways, Natl. L.J., Mar. 10, 1986, at 2, col. 2 (describing reciprocal lateral hires by two firms).

[7] Professors Gilson and Mnookin wonder why lawyers ever have to leave:

The new firm is presumably prepared to pay the departing lawyer his real marginal product. But why is not the old firm prepared to match the bid? . . . One would suppose that the new firm must know that the original firm has better information concerning the actual marginal product of the lawyer who is leaving. Thus, any time the new firm is successful in hiring the winner, there is an implication that a party with better information concerning the lawyer's real value would not bid that high.

Gilson & Mnookin, supra note 3, at 338 n.43.

law partners to develop an acceptable mode of dividing the income pie. The compensation problem was comparatively minor in the era of restricted lateral movement between firms. Lockstep compensation schemes, which allocated income principally on the basis of seniority, prevailed in larger firms.[8] Although some lawyers chafed at a system that rewarded age over productivity, they had few options when inter-firm movements by partners were difficult.[9] But increased mobility has permitted lawyers with the ability to transport clients and revenues to demand a larger share of firm income.[10] Bolstering the unsatisfied partner's demands is the ever present threat of the lawyer's leaving and "grabbing" what many regard as the firm's assets — its clients.[11]

There are several answers to this question. The lawyer may have greater value to another firm. Cf. Robinson, The Best Offense, Natl. L.J., July 27, 1987, at 2, col. 2 (reporting that the movement between firms of a prominent criminal defense attorney enhanced the white collar crime practice of the new firm). Personality conflicts and friction (which often are exacerbated by the prospect of grabbing) may cause a partner's current firm to bid less than another firm. Lawyers may also leave firms because of disgruntlement over management policies. See, e.g., Middleton, Aggression Pays off for Chicago Firm, Natl. L.J., Oct. 6, 1986, at 1, col. 1 (describing how operating policies of the new firm proved critical in a lawyer's decision to move).

[8] See Gilson & Mnookin, supra note 3, at 315–316. Professors Gilson and Mnookin argue that lockstep systems can prove more profitable to partners than alternatives outside their firms. Id. at 341–345.

[9] The spinoff was, and still is, an alternative to changing firms. See, e.g., Seigle, Gibson, Dunn's Costly Defections, Am. Law., July-Aug. 1987, 9, at 9 (describing the establishment of a new firm by 17 lawyers who withdrew from a large firm).

[10] See, e.g., Galante, Partner Leads Mass Exodus from L.A. Firm, Natl. L.J., Dec. 19, 1983, at 3, col. 1 ("Other observers from within and without point to the defection of Mr. Pircher's department as the latest symptom of a growing problem in large firms over the last ten years: senior partners who aren't producing enough to justify their high draws."). Some prestigious firms, most notably Cravath, Swaine & Moore, Wilmer, Cutler & Pickering, and Covington & Burling, apparently continue to operate successfully under compensation schemes geared to sharing rather than production, however defined. See Gilson & Mnookin, supra note 3, at 341. Nevertheless, the trend is away from such systems. See, e.g., Frey, Ups and Downs at White & Case, Am. Law., Jan.-Feb. 1986, at 116, 117 (presenting an account of a major firm abandoning the lockstep system in favor of incentive compensation, with the observation of the managing partner that "Cravath can do lockstep. . . . We need the incentive feature for our partners").

[11] "Grabbing" is used here to refer to the taking of clients from a firm rather than a demand for a reallocation of firm profits. See Comment, Lateral Moves and

4

§1.2 Sources of Restraints on Grabbing and Leaving

A number of areas of law affect to one degree or another the ability
of lawyers to grab and leave, as well as the potency of their firms'
responses to this activity. Partnership law defines the rights and
duties of lawyers as business associates. Agency law defines the
loyalty obligations of those who work on behalf of others. Tort law
establishes certain expectancy interests in existing or prospective
contractual relationships with clients. And norms of legal ethics
define the responsibilities owed by lawyers, and to a lesser extent
their firms, to the consumers of their services.[1]

There is thus an abundance of "law" dealing with the subject of
grabbing and leaving. The difficulty is that the relevant sources of
law are disparate and fail to provide an integrated regime for regulating the activity. Exploring only the ethical perspective yields one set
of conclusions, while an examination of the law firm as a partnership
or a corporation leads to quite different, and often contradictory,
results. For example, fiduciary duties grounded in agency law and
partnership law may give rise to loyalty obligations to the firm.
Similarly, the firm might look to tort law for relief in the event that
one of its present or former members interferes with the firm's
contractual relations with its clients. Notions of loyalty to the firm
and contractual expectancies, however, stand in tension with the

---

the Quest for Clients: Tort Liability of Departing Attorneys for Taking Firm
Clients, 75 Calif. L. Rev. 1809, at 1603 n.29 (1987). This definition is somewhat
different from that espoused by Professors Gilson and Mnookin; they define "grabbing" as "a partner's extraction of a larger than previously agreed share of firm
profits by threatening to depart" and "leaving" as "a partner's departure from the
firm with clients and business in tow." Gilson & Mnookin, Sharing Among the
Human Capitalists: An Economic Inquiry into the Corporate Law Firm and How
Partners Split Profits, 37 Stan. L. Rev. 313, 321 (1985).

§1.2 [1] Although partnership law, agency law, tort law, and legal ethics are the
primary sources of law regulating grabbing and leaving, other areas of law are also
relevant. For example, constitutional law may limit the use of ethics standards to
restrict the solicitation activities of lawyers. See §2.2.1. Rules affecting the insolvency and reorganization of professional associations are of importance when law
firms fall into receivership. See Appendix E. And in the case of the professional
corporation, corporate law becomes important in identifying the rights and duties
of members of a firm. See chapter 5.

norm of legal ethics enabling clients to discharge their lawyers at any time, with or without cause. Considered separately, legal ethics, tort law, partnership law, and agency law provide only a distorted view of the duties of lawyers to each other and to their clients. Considered together, they yield the law and ethics of grabbing and leaving.

§1.3 A Vocabulary Primer

The words we use to describe activities and actors shape our thinking and evoke particular responses. This observation is particularly true in discussions of the issues raised by law firm breakups.

There is a "firm" — an entity — even though the law under which it is organized might deny its existence.[1] A lawyer "departs," "withdraws," or "leaves" the firm. Other lawyers "stay," and the firm "continues" after the lawyer's withdrawal. If the departing lawyer "takes" a client, the client's "file" is "transferred" from the firm to the lawyer; this event represents, from the perspective of the departing lawyer, successful "grabbing and leaving." Unsuccessful grabbing and leaving means that the client "stays" with the firm. This vocabulary implies that it is withdrawing lawyers, not the firms they leave, who engage in "grabbing."

These words express value judgments about the relative rights and interests of lawyers competing for clients. "Grabbing," for example, suggests exploitative behavior that may require regulation. The more neutral "leaving" takes on a pejorative tone when combined with "grabbing." The idea that a partner "leaves" while others "stay" tips the analysis towards a view that the partner "taking" clients is, in effect, looting the firm.

Consider the plight of the hypothetical *ABC* firm, composed of the three name partners and seven additional partners. The seven junior partners leave the partnership to form a firm, *XYZ*, located on another floor of the building. Which of the two groups now constitutes *ABC*, and which lawyers should the law favor in the compe-

---

§1.3   [1] See infra §4.2.

tition for the clients of the original, ten-lawyer firm? Which group of lawyers, the group of three or the group of seven, truly "withdrew" from the firm? Is the continuity or change of name, location, and telephone number dispositive? These questions are more difficult, and the issues they implicate more subtle, than the jargon associated with lawyers' movements might suggest.[2]

The vocabulary's bias may present less difficulty in examining splinters from much larger firms. If *ABC* is a firm of three hundred lawyers, the departure of seven presumably has little effect on the continuity of the enterprise. The firm and its clients might reasonably characterize the event as one in which seven lawyers "left" the firm. If accepted uncritically, however, this description may prescribe the incorrect treatment of the consequences attending the attorney's departure. Assume, for example, that the seven had brought a group of clients into the firm and had provided the legal services those clients required. Both the firm and the seven may now compete for the clients, but only the efforts of the departing lawyers prompt the label "grabbing."

Case law, codes, partnership agreements, and commentary are so imbued with the bent of this language that any attempt to develop more neutral descriptive terms would be futile. Although this book employs the terms commonly used by others, the vocabulary's prejudice is an unfortunate impediment to the analysis.

---

[2] In a case involving a small professional corporation, one court noted that the "law should simply recognize that the lawyers once practiced together and are now practicing separately on the same cases as before, and no good purpose is served by characterizing one entity as the members who left and the other entity as the members who remained." Fox v. Abrams, 163 Cal. App. 3d 610, 616, 210 Cal. Rptr. 260, 265 (1985).

Chapter 2
THE ROLE OF ETHICS CODES IN REGULATING GRABBING AND LEAVING

§2.1 In General

If, as Roscoe Pound suggested, an organized profession is not "the same sort of thing as a retail grocers' association,"[1] the distinction is enforced largely through codes of professional responsibility. Compared to other professionals, lawyers developed their codes of trade relatively late. The American Bar Association (ABA) did not pro-

---

§2.1 [1] R. Pound, The Lawyer from Antiquity to Modern Times 7 (1953).

mulgate the Canons of Professional Ethics (Canons)[2] until 1908. The Model Code of Professional Responsibility (Model Code)[3] followed the Canons in 1969; in turn, the 1983 Model Rules of Professional Conduct (Model Rules)[4] are rapidly replacing the Model Code.

The codes are as important for the changing circumstances they reflect as for the rules they enunciate. This reflection of changing attitudes within the legal profession is particularly apparent with respect to the quest for clients. The Canons, for example, reflected a different era for the legal profession. Their message on competition was clear: "Efforts . . . in any way to encroach upon the professional employment of another lawyer, are unworthy of those who should be brethren at the Bar."[5] Not surprisingly, the Canons condemned the solicitation of employment "not warranted by personal relations."[6]

The Canons may well have been a product of an era in which clients came to lawyers unsolicited and competition was an activity of merchants rather than professionals. A legal career was a "cherished tradition, the preservation of which is essential to the lawyer's reverence for his calling."[7] Whether such a world ever existed is

---

[2] Canons of Professional Ethics (1908) (superseded 1970) [hereinafter Canons].

[3] Model Code of Professional Responsibility (1969) (amended 1980) [hereinafter Model Code].

[4] Model Rules of Professional Conduct (1983) (amended 1987 and 1989) [hereinafter Model Rules]. In a process that is still underway, 31 states have adopted the Model Rules (as of March 1989): Arizona, Arkansas, Connecticut, Delaware, Florida, Idaho, Indiana, Kansas, Louisiana, Maryland, Michigan, Minnesota, Mississippi, Missouri, Montana, Nevada, New Hampshire, New Jersey, New Mexico, North Carolina (borrows from both the Model Rules and the Model Code), North Dakota, Oklahoma, Oregon, Pennsylvania, South Dakota, Utah, Virginia, Washington, West Virginia, Wisconsin, and Wyoming. See Law. Man. on Prof. Conduct (ABA/BNA) 01:3-4 (Mar. 15, 1989). A number of these adopting states, however, have modified certain provisions of the Model Rules. California has its own rules. See California Rules of Professional Conduct (adopted 1988, effective 1989) [hereinafter California Rules].

[5] Canons, Canon 7.

[6] Id. Canon 27. This canon even limited the sending of seasonal greetings. See ABA Comm. on Professional Ethics, Informal Op. 522 (1962) in App. D.

[7] H. Drinker, Legal Ethics 211 (1953).

debatable,[8] but it was clearly the dream of those who articulated and enforced the Canons' ethical standards.[9] And it still may be. The guidelines of the more contemporary Model Code and Model Rules are somewhat less restrictive, but neither is a mandate for competition among lawyers.[10] This chapter examines whether attorneys' codes of conduct restrict grabbing through such rules as restrictions on solicitation; it then investigates how those codes might operate conversely in curbing law firms' efforts to squelch grabbing by attorneys leaving their ranks.

---

[8] One commentator has observed:

[A] lawyer who actively seeks out prospective clients is engaged in a practice that has a long, if disreputable, history and in this century has been flatly prohibited by professional rules. Abraham Lincoln solicited clients unabashedly. In several notable instances in the nation's legal history — including the Peter Zenger case, the Aaron Burr case, the Dred Scott case, and others — prominent lawyers, without the prior invitation of the client, approached a person in legal trouble and offered their services. Despite very stern measures taken for decades by bar associations, the practice continues, perhaps thrives.

C. Wolfram, Modern Legal Ethics §14.2, at 785-786 (1986).

[9] Bar associations devoted considerable efforts to restraining competition under the Canons. See G. Hazard & D. Rhode, The Legal Profession: Responsibility and Regulation 289-290 (1985); J. Hurst, The Growth of American Law: The Law Makers 331 (1950); C. Wolfram, Modern Legal Ethics, §2.6.1, at 48 n.87.

[10] The Model Code provides that a "lawyer shall not . . . recommend employment as a private practitioner, of himself, his partner, or associate to a layperson who has not sought his advice regarding employment of a lawyer." Model Code, supra note 16, DR 2-103(A) (footnotes omitted). It also states:

A lawyer who has given in-person unsolicited advice to a layperson that he should obtain counsel or take legal action shall not accept employment resulting from that advice, except that:
(1) A lawyer may accept employment by a close friend, relative, former client (if the advice is germane to the former employment), or one whom the lawyer reasonably believes to be a client.

Id. DR 2-104(A) (footnote omitted). The Model Rules likewise prohibit "in-person or live telephone contact [soliciting] professional employment from a prospective client with whom the lawyer has no family or prior professional relationship when a significant motive for the lawyer's doing so is the lawyer's pecuniary gain." Model Rules, Rule 7.3.

§2.2 Competition and Solicitation: Ethical Rules as Restraints on Grabbing and Leaving

§2.2.1 Constitutional Considerations

The once prevalent attitude that competition for clients is inherently unethical has changed since the promulgation of the Canons. To a considerable extent, this change was forced upon the segment of the profession that supported the use of ethical norms to restrain competition. In Bates v. State Bar of Arizona,[1] for example, the Supreme Court eviscerated the advertising prohibitions of the original Model Code by according first amendment protection to commercial speech by lawyers and by sharply limiting the scope of permissible state regulation of advertisements. While paying lip service to the dignity of the legal profession, the Supreme Court recognized the changing times:

> It appears that the ban on advertising originated as a rule of etiquette and not as a rule of ethics. . . . Eventually, the attitude toward advertising fostered by this view evolved into an aspect of the ethics of the profession. But habit and tradition are not in themselves an adequate answer to a constitutional challenge. In this day, we do not belittle the person who earns his living by the strength of his arm or the force of his mind. Since the belief that lawyers are somehow "above" trade has become an anachronism, the historical foundation for the advertising restraint has crumbled.[2]

Bates seems noncontroversial, at least in retrospect. The newspaper advertisements prompting the disciplinary proceedings only informed prospective clients of the lawyers' availability and standard charges for routine legal work. Subsequent Court opinions, however, have extended similar constitutional protections to more targeted and specific written communications. In In re R.M.J.,[3] the Supreme Court held that advertisements that included information not in conformity with state-court rules were constitutionally pro-

---

§2.2   [1] 433 U.S. 350 (1977).
[2] Id. at 371-372.
[3] 455 U.S. 191 (1982).

tected, as were the attorney's mailings of notices to announce the opening of a law office. The Court thus expanded its protection of communications to include those transmitted to a much broader group of addressees than the category of "lawyers, clients, former clients, personal friends, and relatives" set out by the state supreme court's rules.[4] Similarly, in Zauderer v. Office of Disciplinary Counsel,[5] the Court held that an attorney was engaging in constitutionally protected commercial speech when he placed newspaper advertisements offering to represent individuals charged with "drunk driving" and women who had used the Dalkon Shield Intrauterine Device.[6] Although neither of these cases denied states the right to regulate communications to protect consumers of legal services from deception or to advance another "substantial governmental interest,"[7] each rejected overly broad restrictions on written communications directed at prospective clients.

The regulation of more personal solicitation activities stands on a different footing. In contrast to written communications, solicitation involves direct, targeted, and personal contact with a prospective client. Invasion of privacy, overreaching, the exercise of undue

---

[4] Id. at 204. The Supreme Court observed:

Mailings and handbills may be more difficult to supervise than newspapers. But again we deal with a silent record. There is no indication that an inability to supervise is the reason the State restricts the potential audience of announcement cards. Nor is it clear that an absolute prohibition is the only solution. For example, by requiring a filing with the Advisory Committee of a copy of all general mailings, the State may be able to exercise reasonable supervision over such mailings. There is no indication in the record of a failed effort to proceed along such a less restrictive path.

Id. at 206 (footnote omitted). Although R.M.J. addressed audience rather than content restrictions, its reasoning is applicable to both.

[5] 471 U.S. 626 (1985).

[6] The Court observed:

Print advertising may convey information and ideas more or less effectively, but in most cases, it will lack the coercive force of the personal presence of a trained advocate. In addition, a printed advertisement, unlike a personal encounter initiated by an attorney, is not likely to involve pressure on the potential candidate for an immediate yes-or-no answer. . . . Thus, a printed advertisement is a means of conveying information about legal services that is more conducive to reflection. [Id. at 642.]

[7] Id. at 647; see R.M.J., 455 U.S. at 203.

influence, and the lack of opportunity for public scrutiny of a lawyer's actions are among the dangers of in-person contacts that justify greater state regulation.[8] Accordingly, the Supreme Court held in Ohralik v. Ohio State Bar Association,[9] a classic ambulance-chasing case, that a state's interest in protecting consumers and maintaining standards of licensed professionals justifies a ban on in-person solicitation for the purpose of pecuniary gain. The opinion makes clear that courts tolerate far more when the solicitation is in writing than when it is in person.[10]

How much more courts will tolerate is outlined in a 1988 decision on the subject of solicitations by lawyers, Shapero v. Kentucky Bar Association.[11] In *Shapero,* a lawyer sought approval from a state attorney advertising commission to send a letter soliciting the business of individuals who were in danger of losing their homes through foreclosures. The letter was neither false nor misleading, but in format and tone, it was far more targeted, personalized, and

---

[8] Commentators have advanced a number of arguments to justify prohibitions on solicitation, including claims that solicitation (1) stirs up litigation; (2) entices lawyers or clients to falsify claims; (3) corrupts other parties, such as physicians, hospital attendants, and police officers; (4) injures the legal profession's reputation and permits a small number of lawyers to gain a disproportionate amount of business; and (5) harms the client. See Comment, A Critical Analysis of Rules Against Solicitation by Lawyers, 25 U. Chi. L. Rev. 674, 675-684 (1958); see also Ohralik v. Ohio State Bar Assn., 436 U.S. 447, 457 (1978) (Stating, "Unlike a public advertisement, which simply provides information and leaves the recipient free to act upon it or not, in-person solicitation may exert pressure and often demands an immediate response, without providing an opportunity for comparison or reflection").

[9] 436 U.S. at 447.

[10] In contrast to *Ohralik* is In re Primus, 436 U.S. 412 (1978), which the Supreme Court decided the same day. In *Primus,* the Court accorded broader first amendment protection to an American Civil Liberties Union lawyer who had given a speech advising a group of women about legal recourse available for sterilizations performed as preconditions to receiving public medical assistance. The lawyer also wrote a letter informing one of the women that the ACLU would file a lawsuit on her behalf. Id. at 415-416 & 416 n.6. Distinguishing *Ohralik,* the Court noted that the solicitation was neither in-person nor for the purpose of pecuniary gain but instead was in the nature of political expression. Id. at 422. Furthermore, the Court held that broad antisolicitation rules were unconstitutional when applied to the lawyer's conduct and that the state could only regulate such activities in a specific manner. Id. at 438.

[11] 108 S. Ct. 1916 (1988).

pressing than the communications deemed protected in *Zauderer* and *R.M.J.*[12] Nevertheless, the Court rejected as "facile" the argument that "this case is merely '*Ohralik* in writing.'"[13] After noting that "the mode of communication makes all the difference," the Court observed:

> [M]erely because targeted, direct-mail solicitation presents lawyers with opportunities for isolated abuses or mistakes does not justify a total ban on that mode of protected commercial speech. The State can regulate such abuses and minimize mistakes through far less restrictive and more precise means, the most obvious of which is to require the lawyer to file any solicitation letter with a state agency, giving the State ample opportunity to supervise mailings and penalize actual abuses.[14]

Shapero clears the way for virtually unrestricted *written* communication with prospective clients. Indeed, commentators described the case as one that "effectively places at the disposal of lawyers some of the same large-scale direct-mail marketing techniques currently employed by purveyors of goods and services from credit cards and magazines to automobiles and real estate."[15] *Shapero* conceded that states may regulate some written communications, but its suggestion that they might require lawyers to file their solicitation letters with a state agency is impractical. The high volume of letters submitted for clearance would overwhelm any agency charged with the task of overseeing direct mailings.[16]

---

[12] The letter read as follows:

It has come to my attention that your home is being foreclosed on. If this is true, you may be about to lose your home. Federal law may allow you to keep your home by *ORDERING* your creditor [*sic*] to STOP and give you more time to pay them.

You may call my office anytime from 8:30 A.M. to 5:00 P.M. for *FREE* information on how you can keep your home.

Call *NOW*, don't wait. It may surprise you what I may be able to do for you. Just call and tell me that you got this letter. Remember it is *FREE*, there is *NO* charge for calling. [Id. at 1919.]

[13] Id. at 1922 (quoting Respondent's Brief in Opposition at 10 (No. 87-16)).

[14] Id. at 1923 (citations omitted).

[15] Stewart & Nelson, Hawking Legal Services, A.B.A.J., Aug. 1, 1988, at 44.

[16] See id. at 49.

Shapero represents a logical extension of the Court's earlier decisions concerning written communications by attorneys seeking clients. Although the opinion reaffirmed the reasoning of these same opinions — that in-person solicitation activities are a different matter and may be categorically banned by the states — the Court's refusal to treat highly targeted mailings as the equivalent of face-to-face solicitations represents a significant defeat for continuing attempts by state bars to control competition among lawyers.[17]

§2.2.2 Grabbing and Leaving as Solicitation

The constitutional debate on the permissible scope of state regulation of solicitation has centered largely on lawyers who pursue clients they have not previously represented. Whether grabbing by departing law partners is or should be regulated as solicitation is a different question.

"Solicitation" is a vague term usually employed to describe contact with prospective, as opposed to existing, clients. Paying taxi cab drivers in a "divorce haven" state to bring clients from the airport to a lawyer's office, giving gratuities to ambulance drivers or doctors for tips on lucrative personal injury cases, providing commissions to bail bond writers, and general "ambulance chasing" are among those activities commonly regarded as solicitation.[18] In these situations, the antisolicitation rules check, at least theoretically, readily apparent abuses.

Grabbing, on the other hand, typically involves clients for

---

[17] Cf. id. at 48 ("The significance of *Shapero* is thus not so much that it departs from the Court's previous decisions [on advertising] as that it rejects the attempts of some state bars and courts, backed by the ABA, to limit the Court's decisions on advertising by drawing a clear line between permissible general circulation advertising and impermissible targeted-mail solicitation."). For an account of the Kentucky bar's activities to restrict mailings by Mr. Shapero even after the Court's decision, see He Can Advertise — But Only in Principle?, Wall St. J., Aug. 30, 1988, at 21, col. 1. For a pre-*Shapero* discussion of this topic, see J. Nowak, R. Rotunda & J. Young, Constitutional Law §16.31, at 915-920 (3d ed. 1986); Calavani, Langenfeld & Shuford, Attorney Advertising and Competition at the Bar, 71 Vand. L. Rev. 761, 763-764 (1988).

[18] See C. Wolfram, Modern Legal Ethics §14.2 at 786 (1986).

whom the lawyer has previously worked. Although grabbing may present some of the abuses of solicitation, it also may effectuate a client's educated and considered choice of a lawyer.[19] Broad regulation of grabbing through ethical standards targeted at solicitation reflects the assumption that a firm "owns" clients and has a prior claim on their "files." A logical extension of this view is that grabbing by "departing" lawyers should be regulated but that grabbing by firms attempting to "retain" clients does not present the same dangers. In a particular case, the actual relationships between a firm, its lawyers, and its clients may or may not justify the presumption favoring the firm in a battle for clients. When applied generally to all cases, however, treatment of grabbing as solicitation is little more than an uncritical extension of the vocabulary's biases.[20]

If it is assumed that grabbing is solicitation within the ethics codes, those norms may well affect the ability of partners to transport clients from firm to firm. Ethics standards once presented significant obstacles to grabbing and leaving. More recently, however, they have proven far less effective in providing an edge to firms in their attempts to "retain" clients.

§2.2.3 The Model Code

§2.2.3.1 Withdrawal Notices

The Model Code sets a negative tone for grabbing and leaving by flatly prohibiting lawyers from making an unsolicited recommendation of their own employment.[21] Moreover, the Model Code

---

[19] Cf. Johnson, Solicitation of Law Firm Clients by Departing Partners and Associates: Tort, Fiduciary, and Disciplinary Liability, 50 U. Pitt. L. Rev. 1, 31-32 (1988) ("The dearth of controlling authority concerning the professional relationship exception is perhaps due in part to the fact that the practice of 'soliciting' one's present or former clients is so well-engrained into the lore of law practice, and takes so many subtle forms, as to give rise to little comment.").

[20] See supra §1.3.

[21] "A lawyer shall not, except as authorized [in rules concerning advertising], recommend employment as a private practitioner, of himself, his partner, or associate to a layperson who has not sought his advice regarding employment of a lawyer." Model Code, supra note 16, DR 2-103(A) (footnotes omitted).

prohibits a lawyer from accepting employment following in-person, unsolicited advice concerning the need for counsel or the desirability of legal action.[22]

Excepted from this rule is employment obtained after advising "a close friend, relative, former client (if the advice is germane to the former employment), or one whom the lawyer reasonably believes to be a client."[23] This exception regarding advice given to existing or former clients again raises the "client of whom" question, but the Model Code's restrictive and specific guidelines covering the mailing of formal announcement cards following a withdrawal may provide something of an answer:

> A brief professional announcement card stating new or changed associations, addresses, change of firm name, or similar matters . . . may be mailed to lawyers, clients, former clients, personal friends, and relatives. It shall not state biographical data except to the extent reasonably necessary to identify the lawyer or to explain the change in association, but it may state the immediate past position of the lawyer. It may give the names and dates of predecessor firms in a continuing line of succession.[24]

Because of recent Supreme Court decisions concerning constitutionally impermissible regulation of communications in writing to prospective clients,[25] and because of the growing acceptance of the Model Rules as a replacement for the Model Code, the Model Code's restrictions on withdrawal announcements are of little consequence. They do reveal, however, the biases of the recent past and reflect an attitude that a law firm should be able to protect its interest in its clients by restricting the methods by which departing lawyers can grab them.

The apparent strictness of the Model Code's withdrawal announcement restriction was softened in a 1980 opinion of the ABA's ethics committee.[26] The opinion approved a lawyer's proposed let-

---

[22] See id. DR 2-104.
[23] See id. DR 2-104(A)(1) (footnote omitted).
[24] Model Code, DR 2-102(A)(2) (footnotes omitted).
[25] See supra §2.2.1.
[26] See ABA Comm. on Ethics and Professional Responsibility, Informal Op. 1457 (1980).

ter, to be sent to clients "for whose active, open, and pending matters he was directly responsible." The letter read:

> Effective [date], I became the resident partner in this city of the *XYZ* law firm, having withdrawn from the *ABC* law firm. My decision should not be construed as adversely reflecting in any way on my former firm. It is simply one of those things that sometimes happens in business and professional life.
> I want to be sure that there is no disadvantage to you, as the client, from my move. The decision as to how the matters I have worked on for you are handled and who handles them in the future will be completely yours, and whatever you decide will be determinative.

The committee, however, limited its opinion to the case presented, which included showings that (1) the notice was mailed; (2) the notice was sent *only* to persons with whom the lawyer had "an active lawyer-client relationship immediately before the change in the lawyer's professional association"; and (3) the notice did not urge the client to sever the relationship with the lawyer's former firm, although it did indicate the lawyer's willingness to work on the client's matters.[27] A recent Massachusetts decision accepted this opinion as "the standard for general guidelines as to what partners are entitled to expect from each other concerning their joint clients on the division of their practice."[28]

---

[27] Id.; see also ABA Comm. on Ethics and Professional Responsibility, Informal Op. 1466 (1981) (applying similar reasoning to a case involving an associate).

[28] Meehan v. Shaughnessy, 404 Mass. 419, 535 N.E.2d 1255, 1265 (1989).

Ethics opinions have varied in their interpretations and enforcement of formal announcement restrictions. Compare Ethics Comm. of the Kentucky Bar Association, Op. 317, digested in Law. Man. on Prof. Conduct (ABA/BNA) 901:3902 (Nov. 1986) (holding that upon withdrawal, a lawyer may contact the firm's clients that she had represented previously and advise them that they are free to choose between the firm and the lawyer) and Comm. on Professional Ethics of the Illinois State Bar Association, Op. 86-16, digested in Law. Man. on Prof. Conduct (ABA/BNA) 901:3005 (May 13, 1987) (same) with Comm. on Professional and Judicial Ethics of the State Bar of Michigan, Op. CI-1133, digested in Law. Man. on Prof. Conduct (ABA/BNA) 901:4753 (Apr. 2, 1986) (holding that an associate who changes firms may not send announcements to his former firm's clients, even if he had substantial personal contact, unless the clients were "clearly his own clients and not the firm's").

§2.2.3.2 In-Person Contacts

Despite the erosion of the Model Code's restriction on withdrawal announcements, it may restrict other activities associated with grabbing. Mailed communications are but one means of attracting clientele. Lawyers may communicate with actual or prospective clients in countless other ways, ranging from a casual and brief conversation over lunch to an extended campaign designed to "secure the business."[29] In-person contacts for the purpose of grabbing may present some of the dangers attendant to general solicitations by lawyers. Although grabbing is normally distinguishable from more standard solicitation, a few courts have interpreted the Model Code's solicitation provisions as sharply limiting the ability of former associates to communicate with clients they earlier served.[30]

In some ways, in-person contacts present greater dangers than mailed communications and thus may generate a stronger argument for regulation under the Model Code. Grabbing effectuated through personal contacts may involve elements of coercion and undue influence. Furthermore, the regulation of abusive private contacts is more problematical than that of mailings because of the inherent difficulty in monitoring lawyers' private actions.

---

[29] See, e.g., Blodgett, Client Development: Lawyers Enlist Research Data Bases in Marketing Efforts, A.B.A.J., Aug. 1, 1986, at 22 (describing how attorneys are using information in research data bases to acquire new clients); Curtis, Marketing Through Seminars, A.B.A.J., Jan. 1, 1986, at 62, 63 (listing steps recommended in a seminar to secure new clients).

[30] See, e.g., Pratt, P.C. v. Blunt, 140 Ill. App. 3d 512, 520, 488 N.E.2d 1062, 1068 (1986) (relying on the Model Code to enjoin attorneys from further communications with clients of their former firm); Adler, Barish, Daniels, Levin & Creskoff v. Epstein, 482 Pa. 416, 428, 393 A.2d 1175, 1181 (1978) (prohibiting lawyers from contacting clients of their former firm except by use of formal announcement as permitted by the Model Code). See also Michigan State Bar Comm. on Professional and Judicial Ethics, Informal Op. CI-1133 (1986), summarized in Law Man. on Prof. Conduct (ABA/BNA) 901:4753 (1986) (forbidding associate from sending notices of new affiliations to even those clients with whom he had substantial personal contact, but allowing the notices if the client was "clearly" the associate's). But see Illinois State Bar Assoc. Comm. on Professional Ethics, Op. 86-16, summarized in Law Man. on Prof. Conduct (ABA/BNA) 901:3005 (1987). See generally Johnson, Solicitation of Law Firm Clients by Departing Attorneys and Associates, 50 U. Pitt. L. Rev. 36-41 (1988).

Yet a policy effectively restricting in-person communications is questionable on several grounds. First, disfavoring in-person grabbing communications may deprive the client of the very information needed to make an intelligent choice of counsel.[31] Second, grabbing is most likely to succeed when the client knows the lawyer well and is satisfied with the quality of her work;[32] in such cases, restricting in-person contacts as improper solicitation does little more than restrain competition among lawyers. Finally, restrictions on grabbing assume a vulnerability and naiveté on the part of clients that may not exist. The sophistication of clients, especially that of larger institutions, may easily match that of their lawyers,[33] in which case the abuses targeted by the antisolicitation provisions simply do not exist.

A strict application of the Model Code's antisolicitation rules to grabbing gives an advantage to law firms in their battles with grabbing lawyers and may ill serve the interests of clients. Judicial decisions sanctioning grabbing as solicitation under the Model Code assume that firms have a prior "right" to their clients and that regulation of firms' attempts to "retain" clients by fending off grabbing is unnecessary. The application of this double standard also conflicts with other tenets of legal ethics, most particularly the principle of client choice and the ban on restrictive covenants, that provide an edge to grabbing partners.[34] The permissible scope of state regulation of grabbing activities remains an open question, but the increasing acceptance of the more liberal Model Rules may render the issue moot and thereby further sharpen the competition of lawyers for "their" clients.

---

[31] See Perschbacher & Hamilton, Reading Beyond the Labels: Effective Regulation of Lawyer's Targeted Direct Mail Advertising, 58 U. Colo. L. Rev. 255, 268-269 (1987) (noting that advertising provides prospective clients with information about cost and availability of attorney services).

[32] See Seigle, supra note 9, at 9 (explaining that a corporate client followed an attorney to his new firm because of the "good working relationship with its lawyer").

[33] See Morris, Power and Responsibility Among Lawyers and Clients: Comment on Ellman's Lawyers and Clients, 34 UCLA L. Rev. 781, 798-799 (1987).

[34] See infra §2.3.

§2.2.4 The Model Rules

Like the Model Code, the Model Rules prohibit false or misleading statements by lawyers about their services.[35] Unlike the
Model Code, however, the Model Rules do not directly restrict the
content and audience of formal announcements of withdrawal. Prior
to its amendment in 1989, rule 7.3 provided that "[a] lawyer may
not solicit professional employment from a prospective client with
whom the lawyer has no family or prior professional relationship, by
mail, in-person or otherwise, when a significant motive for the
lawyer's doing so is the lawyer's pecuniary gain." In Shapero v.
Kentucky Bar Assn.,[36] the Supreme Court held unconstitutional the
application of rule 7.3 to categorically prohibit lawyers from sending letters to potential clients known to be in need of legal service. In
response to *Shapero,* the president of the American Bar Association
issued the following statement:

> The ABA has a continuing obligation to the consuming public
> to advance professional rules of conduct which will protect the public
> from the overreaching and undue influence of counsel seeking to
> solicit legal work. We will undertake promptly to develop the most
> effective standard we can devise to protect the consumer consistent
> with today's ruling.[37]

The promised action took the form of an amended rule 7.3, which
was approved by the House of Delegates early in 1989.[38] Gone are

---

[35] See Model Code, DR 2-101; Model Rules, Rule 7.1.
[36] See supra §2.2.1.
[37] Hengstler, ABA Responds to *Shapero,* A.B.A.J., Aug. 1, 1988, at 17.
[38] The relevant parts of the amended rule read:

(a) A lawyer shall not by in-person or live telephone contact solicit
professional employment from a prospective client with whom the lawyer has
no family or prior professional relationship when a significant motive for the
lawyer's doing so is the lawyer's pecuniary gain.
(b) A lawyer shall not solicit professional employment from a prospective client by written or recorded communication or by in-person or telephone contact even when not otherwise prohibited by paragraph (a), if:
(1) the prospective client has made known to the lawyer a desire not to
be solicited by the lawyer; or

the prohibitions on targeted mailing. The rule retains, however, restrictions on in-person contacts[39] with prospective clients with whom the lawyer has no family or prior professional relationship, when a significant motive for the communication is the lawyer's pecuniary gain.[40] The rule also requires written or recorded communications to prospective clients with whom the lawyer has no family or prior professional relationship to include the words, "Advertising Material."[41] The comment elaborates:

> There is far less likelihood that a lawyer would engage in abusive practices against an individual with whom the lawyer has a prior personal or professional relationship or where the lawyer is motivated by considerations other than pecuniary gain. Consequently, the general prohibition [against solicitation is] not applicable in those situations.

The "prior professional relationship" qualification in both the pre-amended and present versions of rule 7.3 is a hole through which most grabbing activities will slide. The drafters of the Model Rules justified harsh treatment of most solicitation because of the "abuse inherent" in direct contacts, which subject the "lay person to the private importuning of a trained advocate, in a direct interpersonal encounter."[42] On the other hand, the drafters perceived advertising as less abusive because it does not subject the client "to direct personal persuasion that may overwhelm the client's judgment."[43] Although grabbing is not in public view, which prevents scrutiny and therefore might justify regulation under the drafters' reasoning,

---

(2) the solicitation involves coercion, duress or harassment.

(c) Every written or recorded communication from a lawyer soliciting professional employment from a prospective client known to be in need of legal services in a particular matter, and with whom the lawyer has no family or prior professional relationship, shall include the words "Advertising Material" on the outside envelope and at the beginning and ending of any recorded communication. [Model Rules, Rule 7.3.]

[39] This includes communication by telephone.
[40] Id. Rule 7.3(a).
[41] Id. Rule 7.3(c).
[42] Id. Rule 7.3 comment 1.
[43] Id. Rule 7.3 comment 3.

it is, with one potentially important exception, virtually unregulated under the Model Rules.[44]

The exception is found in the rule's explicit statement of what would otherwise be implicit: under no circumstances may a lawyer use coercion, duress, or harassment in the solicitation of clients.[45] Not surprisingly, this restriction applies even to those lawyers with prior professional relationships with the individuals they are soliciting. Although the comment to rule 7.3 undoubtedly is correct in observing that abusive conduct is less likely when there has existed a prior professional relationship between the lawyer and the client, abuse is not unheard of in these circumstances.

§2.3 Attorney and Client Freedoms: Ethical Rules as Aids to Grabbing and Leaving

§2.3.1 Client Choice

The freedom of clients to discharge their lawyers at any time, with or without cause, greatly facilitates competition among lawyers.[1] Because the lawyer-client relationship is personal in nature and dependent on the client's trust in the lawyer,[2] both the Model Code[3] and the Model Rules[4] mandate lawyer withdrawal upon

---

[44] Rules relating to information disclosure and conflicts of interest, however, may restrict some grabbing and leaving activities. See id. Rules 1.6-.10. For example, Model Rule 1.9 makes leaving less attractive by restricting the lawyer's representation of his or her new firm's clients in "the same or related matter in which that [client's] interests are materially adverse to the interests of the former client." Id. Rule 1.9(a). The Rules also proscribe use of "information relating to the representation to the disadvantage" of a former client. Id. Rule 1.9(c).

[45] Id. Rule 7.3(b).

§2.3 [1] "It is now uniformly recognized that the client-lawyer contract is terminable at will by the client. For good reasons, poor reasons, or the worst of reasons, a client may fire the lawyer." C. Wolfram, Modern Legal Ethics §9.5.2, at 545 (1986).

[2] See Comment, Winding Up Dissolved Law Partnerships: The No-Compensation Rule and Client Choice, 73 Calif. L. Rev. 1597, 1604 (1985) ("[W]ithout complete confidence in the attorney, the client's decision to follow the attorney's instructions or to execute the prepared documents is impaired.").

[3] Model Code, DR 2-110(B)(4).

[4] Model Rules, Rule 1.16(a)(3).

discharge by a client.[5] For purposes of grabbing, the client's power to choose, discharge, or replace a lawyer borders on the absolute.

Even a contract purporting to bind the client to a lawyer or a firm is terminable at the will of the client.[6] Lawyers and clients most frequently litigate this issue when the contract involves a contingent fee and the client discharges the attorney prior to the occurrence of the contingency.[7] From the discharged lawyer's perspective, removal without cause under these circumstances may seem harsh and unfair. Fairness to lawyers, however, is a policy consideration subordinated to the right of clients to choose and change their legal representatives.[8] The only issue is that of determining reasonable compensation for the fired lawyer.[9] Although discharge may terminate the lawyer's claim to a contractually based contingent fee,[10] quantum meruit recovery for the value of services rendered prior to removal has emerged as the governing principle of compensation.[11]

The ease with which clients can change lawyers or firms sets the stage for grabbing and leaving. If constraints on grabbing exist, the principle of client choice requires that they be founded on a premise other than the right of lawyers to "possess" their existing clients.

---

[5] Curiously, the California rules omit client discharge as a reason for mandatory withdrawal. See California Rules, Rule 3-700(B). One commentator has called this inexplicable. See C. Wolfram, Modern Legal Ethics §9.5.2 at 546 n.43 (1986).

[6] C. Wolfram, Modern Legal Ethics §9.5.2, at 545-546 (1986).

[7] Id. §9.5.2 at 546-547.

[8] See, e.g., Fracasse v. Brent, 6 Cal. 3d 784, 790, 494 P.2d 9, 13, 100 Cal. Rptr. 385, 389 (1972) (stating that the interests of clients are superior to the interests of attorneys).

[9] See id. at 792-793, 494 P.2d at 14-15, 100 Cal. Rptr. at 390-391; Kaushiva v. Hutter, 454 A.2d 1373, 1375 (D.C.), cert. denied, 464 U.S. 820 (1983).

[10] See C. Wolfram, Modern Legal Ethics §9.5.2 at 546 (1986) ("The rule, which is now recognized in almost every state that has passed on the question in the last decade, is that a client's discharge of a lawyer ends the lawyer's right to recover on the contract of employment."). A possible exception arises when a cause for discharge is not present and the contract has been substantially performed. See, e.g., Kaushiva, 454 A.2d at 1374 (allowing an attorney to recover the full contingent fee when the contract had been substantially performed); Salem Realty Co. v. Matera, 384 Mass. 803, 804, 426 N.E.2d 1160, 1161 (1981) (denying recovery on the contract but indicating factors that would permit such a recovery, including the degree to which the performance had been completed).

[11] See C. Wolfram, Modern Legal Ethics §9.5.2 at 546 (1986); see also Note, Limiting the Wrongfully Discharged Attorney to Quantum Meruit — Fracasse v.

§2.3.2 The Curious Demise of Restrictive Covenants

Because attorneys cannot bind clients to their services by contract, an enforceable agreement precluding competition by a partner who withdraws from a firm would prove an effective alternative restraint on grabbing and leaving. Such an agreement would not only discourage withdrawals but would also deny clients the ability to choose between the firm and the withdrawing partner who previously represented them.

Legal ethics, however, clearly preclude the use of restrictive covenants as antigrabbing devices. In 1961, the American Bar Association's Committee on Professional Ethics declared improper an anticompetition covenant in a firm's employment agreement with an associate.[12] The committee's Formal Opinion 300 notes that attorneys can neither buy nor sell clients, adding that a restrictive covenant represents an attempt to "barter in clients."[13] This language, standing alone, might suggest the committee's principal concern was to facilitate a client's free choice of a lawyer. Further statements in the opinion, however, reveal a contrary intention. Relying upon the Canons' prohibitions against "encroachment" on employment and solicitation,[14] the opinion concludes that a "former employee of a lawyer or a law firm would be bound by these

---

Brent, 24 Hastings L.J. 771, 771-774 (1973) (describing the right to recover on the basis of quantum meruit as the majority rule). There remain a number of questions concerning the discharged attorney's right to recover under the theory of quantum meruit or unjust enrichment. Most importantly, case law is split on whether quantum meruit recovery is still conditioned upon the happening of the contingency in the contract. An important decision of the California Supreme Court suggests that it is. See *Fracasse,* 6 Cal. 3d at 792, 494 P.2d at 14, 100 Cal. Rptr. at 391. Other courts have agreed. See, e.g., Rosenberg v. Levin, 409 So. 2d 1016, 1021 (Fla. 1982) (limiting quantum meruit recovery to the agreed fee); Plaza Shoe Store, Inc. v. Hermel, Inc., 636 S.W.2d 53, 60 (Mo. 1982) (limiting recovery to the lesser of the contracted fee or the reasonable value of the services). But see Tillman v. Komar, 259 N.Y. 133, 136, 181 N.E. 75, 76 (1932) (holding that the attorney's cause of action accrues immediately upon discharge).

[12] ABA Comm. on Professional Ethics, Formal Op. 300 (1961) in App. D.

[13] Id.

[14] See Canons, Canon 7 (stating that any efforts "to encroach upon the professional employment of another lawyer . . . are unworthy of those who should be brethren at the Bar").

canons to refrain from any effort to secure the work of clients of his former employer.[15] Thus, according to the opinion, restrictive covenants are improper because they are not needed; clients cannot be bartered between a firm and its attorneys because the Canons presume that they belong to the firm. Grabbing and leaving, in short, was unethical, a point the committee reaffirmed the following year in an informal decision that termed unethical a restrictive covenant preventing a departing associate from working for his former firm's clients.[16]

Although Formal Opinion 300 concerned restrictive covenants applicable to associates, the committee's later informal decision hinted that restrictive covenants may be permissible in partnership agreements, because partners stand "on an equal footing"[17] In 1967, the committee repudiated this suggestion in Informal Opinion 1072 and ruled that restrictive covenants involving partners are also improper.[18] Even though this opinion's conclusion has important implications for grabbing and leaving, its underlying reasoning may have even greater significance. After stating that Formal Opinion 300 had "like application" to partnerships, the committee went on to quote "from so much more of [the opinion] as we believe here applicable."[19] Included in this quotation are comments condemning bartering in clients, but excluded is the statement that the Canons preclude postwithdrawal competition for a firm's clients. The opinion concluded that "attorneys should not engage in an attempt to barter clients, nor should their practice be restricted. *The attorney must remain free to practice when and where he will and to be available to prospective clients who might desire to engage his services.*"[20]

This represents a significant shift in reasoning over a seven-year period. Formal Opinion 300 implies that grabbing is unethical, while Informal Opinion 1072 emphasizes the client's freedom of choice. The later opinion is thus much less critical, and perhaps even

---

[15] ABA Comm. on Professional Ethics, Formal Op. 300 (1961) in App. D.
[16] ABA Comm. on Professional Ethics, Informal Op. 521 (1962) in App. D.
[17] Id.
[18] ABA Comm. on Professional Ethics, Informal Op. 1072 (1968) in App. D.
[19] Id.
[20] Id. (emphasis added).

supports, grabbing. Both the Model Code and the Model Rules adopt this ban on restrictive covenants,[21] and case law further supports this position.[22] Thus, the proscription against restrictive covenants, a doctrine that originated entirely from within the bar and

---

[21] Both the Model Code and the Model Rules prohibit a lawyer from making or offering an employment or partnership agreement that restricts the rights of a lawyer to practice after termination of the relationship; excepted are agreements concerning benefits on retirement or those that are made as part of a claim settlement for a client. See Model Code, DR 2-108(A); Model Rules, Rule 5.6.

California follows a somewhat different approach. It also prohibits restrictive covenants in nonretirement situations, but provides an exception for a covenant that "[i]s a part of an employment, shareholders', or partnership agreement among members provided the restrictive agreement does not survive the termination of the employment, shareholder or partnership relationship." California Rules, Rule 1-500(B).

In adopting the Model Code, the Illinois Supreme Court did not accept DR 2-108 and instead adopted the following rule: "In connection with the settlement of a controversy or suit, a lawyer shall not enter into an agreement that restricts his right to practice law." Ill. Code Prof. Responsibility DR 2-108. See also Hicklin v. O'Brien, 11 Ill. App. 2d 541, 138 N.E.2d 47, 52 (1957) (upholding a restrictive covenant in an agreement for the sale of a law practice and commenting "[i]t is not necessary for us to determine whether the contract violates some canon of professional ethics").

[22] See, e.g., Dwyer v. Jung, 137 N.J. Super. 135, 136, 348 A.2d 208, 208 (App. Div. 1975) (holding a restrictive covenant void as against public policy); In re Silverberg, 75 A.D.2d 817, 819, 427 N.Y.S.2d 480, 482 (1980) (holding that restrictive covenants are incompatible with the professional status of attorneys). State and local ethics opinions also support the ban on restrictive covenants. See, e.g., Comm. on Professional Ethics of the Illinois State Bar Association, Op. 86-16, summarized in Law. Man. on Prof. Conduct (ABA/BNA) 901:3005 (May 13, 1987). Agreements that seek to impose economic sanctions against a competing lawyer do not fare better. See, e.g., Gray v. Martin, 63 Or. App. 173, 182, 663 P.2d 1285, 1290 (1983) (holding that loss of benefits because of grabbing and leaving is the equivalent of a restrictive covenant); Legal Ethics Comm. of the District of Columbia Bar, Op. 65 (1979) (forbidding a requirement that a departing attorney share fees because it deterred the attorney from accepting work from clients of the former firm by making such work less profitable); Comm. on Professional Ethics of the Illinois State Bar Association, Op. 628 (1978), reprinted in 67 Ill. B.J. 380 (1979) (declaring improper a partnership agreement provision that required a "former employee" to pay the partnership one-half of fees received from clients who were clients of the partnership and for whom the former employee performed services within two years of separation from the partnership); Ethics Comm. of the Kentucky Bar Association, Op. 326, summarized in Law. Man. on Prof. Conduct (ABA/BNA) 901:3903 (Sept. 1987) (holding that a partnership agreement may not condition the withdrawing partner's right to an account settlement on a covenant not to compete).

that is now a basic, but perhaps little known,[23] tenet of legal ethics, eliminates what might otherwise have been a common provision in law partnership agreements.

This prohibition against anticompetition clauses sets lawyers apart from members of other professions. Accountants and physicians, for example, regularly enter into covenants not to compete.[24] The reasons for distinguishing lawyering from other professions in this context are vague, and it is questionable whether the availability of choice for the client is any less critical when the professional engaged is a physician, for example, rather than a lawyer. In any event, the demise of the contract as a means of restricting competition marked the destruction of what would have proven a potent weapon in a firm's battle against partners who grab and leave.

§2.3.3 Agreements Discouraging Competition

It is one thing to conclude that covenants restricting future competitive activities of lawyers within a firm are unethical. It is quite another to define the types of covenants governed by this restraint. The issue arises with agreements that discourage, rather than prohibit, post-withdrawal competition by the lawyer. The common theme in these agreements is an economic disincentive, often in the form of discounted account valuations for the partners

---

[23] See, e.g., Brill, The Partner Breakup Follies, Am. Law., Mar. 1988, at 3, 102 (revealing that half of the firms interviewed had covenants restricting competition and that 18 out of 20 partners had not read the Model Code all the way through, including two who had served on "important" bar ethics committees).

[24] See, e.g., Perry v. Moran, 109 Wash. 2d 691, 700, 748 P.2d 224, 229 (1987) (stating that [a] covenant prohibiting the former employee from providing accounting services to the firm's clients for a reasonable time is a fair means of protecting that client base"). For a discussion of the approaches of other professions to restrictive covenants and an argument that the legal profession's per se ban on restrictive covenants is unreasonable, see Kalish, Covenants Not to Compete and the Legal Profession, 29 St. Louis U.L.J. 423, 424-425, 450-456 (1985). For a discussion of the enforceability of restrictive covenants in partnership agreements generally, see S. Williston, A Treatise on the Law of Contracts §§1633-1644 (W. Jaeger ed. 1972). Many jurisdictions that limit or prohibit such agreements provide an exception for certain covenants drafted in anticipation of partnership dissolutions. See, e.g., Cal. Bus. & Prof. Code §16602 (West 1964); Fla. Stat. §542.33 (1987).

who compete with their former firms. For the most part, such agreements share the fate of restrictive covenants, although some recent opinions have shown more tolerance in balancing the interests of the firm against the principal of client choice.

§2.3.3.1 Agreements Not Enforced

The agreement contested in Gray v. Martin,[25] an Oregon case, included a typical disincentive to competition. Under the agreement, the withdrawing partner was entitled to a share of profits for two years after his withdrawal unless he resumed during that time the active practice of law in the area, in which event he would get nothing. The continuing partners sought to distinguish the agreement from a restrictive covenant by arguing it did not restrict the withdrawing partner's right to practice law. The court disagreed and concluded that an economic disincentive restricts the ability of clients to choose their lawyers in much the same way that a restrictive covenant inhibits the exercise of choice by clients. Similar conclusions have been reached by ethics committees in a number of jurisdictions.[26]

---

[25] 63 Or. App. 173, 182, 663 P.2d 1285, 1290 (1983).

[26] See, e.g., Legal Ethics Comm. of the District of Columbia Bar, Op. 65 (1979) (forbidding a requirement that a departing attorney share fees because it deterred the attorney from accepting work from clients of the former firm by making such work less profitable); Legal Ethics Comm. of the District of Columbia Bar, Op. 181, summarized in Law. Man. on Prof. Conduct (ABA/BNA) 901:2307 (undated) (rejecting an agreement that, in part, prevented a withdrawing lawyer from continued association with the firm's employees and required the lawyer to keep confidential any and all information acquired during the course of employment); Legal Ethics Comm. of the District of Columbia Bar, Op. 194 (1988) (rejecting an agreement that reduced payouts to withdrawing partners who practiced law in competition with the firm within twelve months after their withdrawal); Comm. on Professional Ethics of the Illinois State Bar Association, Op. 628 (1978), reprinted in 67 Ill. B.J. 380 (1979) (declaring improper a partnership agreement provision that required a "former employee" to pay the partnership one-half of fees received from clients who were clients of the partnership and for whom the former employee performed services within two years of separation from the partnership); Ethics Comm. of the Kentucky Bar Association, Op. 326, summarized in Law. Man. on Prof. Conduct (ABA/BNA) 901:3903 (Sept. 1987) (holding that a partnership agreement may not condition the withdrawing partner's right to an account settlement on a covenant not to compete); Texas State Bar Prof.

A recent California case presented a variation on the typical economic disincentive to post-withdrawal competition. In Champion v. Superior Court,[27] the partnership agreement provided that, upon withdrawal of a partner, all clients and client files remained the "property" of the firm and that, if firm clients elected to have the withdrawing partner represent them, all fees from the post-withdrawing work would be the property of the firm. This arrangement was particularly onerous for the withdrawing partner, for it meant that the partner would receive only that percentage of the fee for his work allocable under the partnership agreement; at the same time, he had no claim to post-withdrawal fees from clients who elected to stay with the firm. The affected partner illustrated his distress with the example of one case in which he performed significant post-withdrawal activities and, out of a total fee of $50,088, would be entitled to only $912. The court had little difficulty in finding that the agreement constituted an "unconscionable" infringement on the client's freedom of choice. It added, however, that the result might be different if both the firm and the withdrawing partner shared fees derived from work unfinished at the time of withdrawal.

§2.3.3.2 Disincentives Enforced

Although the prevailing opinion is that a discounted account settlement for those who compete is tantamount to a restrictive covenant, and therefore is impermissible, this view is not universally accepted. In Cohen v. Lord, Day & Lord,[28] a New York case, the partnership agreement provided for a sharing of profits for three years after a withdrawal of a partner who had been a member of the firm for at least ten years. It also provided a disincentive to competition:

Ethics Comm., Op. 459, summarized in Law. Man. on Prof. Conduct (ABA/BNA) 901:8307 (1988) (reaching the same conclusion with respect to an agreement requiring departing associates to share fees). See also In re Silverberg, 75 A.D.2d 817, 427 N.Y.S.2d 480, 482 (1980) (striking down an agreement requiring a post-withdrawal sharing of fees and observing, "Lawyers should not traffic in clients . . . , nor make payments by one partner to another in a law firm depend on a percentage of legal fees to be earned after dissolution of the partnership without any professional responsibility for handling the cases").
[27] 201 Cal. App.3d 777, 247 Cal. Rptr. 624 (1988).
[28] 534 N.Y.S.2d 161 (App. Div. 1988).

[I]f a Partner withdraws from the Partnership and without the prior written consent of the Executive Committee continues to practice law in any state or other jurisdiction in which the Partnership maintains an office or any contiguous jurisdiction, either as a lawyer in private practice or as a counsel employed by a business firm, he shall have no further interest in and there shall be paid to him no proportion of the net profits of the Partnership collected thereafter, whether for services rendered before or after the withdrawal. There shall be paid to him only his withdrawable credit balance on the books of the Partnership at the date of his withdrawal, together with the amount of his capital account, and the Partnership shall have no further obligation to him.[29]

A partner withdrew, taking with him a number of clients, and joined a competing firm. Rather than seeking monetary or injunctive relief to redress what it undoubtedly viewed as a "raid" of its clients, Lord, Day & Lord simply invoked the above quoted clause of the partnership agreement and denied that the partner had any interest in post-withdrawal profits. The court upheld the validity of the agreement, offering little analysis other than the observation that the ban on restrictive covenants is designed to protect clients, not their lawyers.[30]

The shortcoming of *Cohen's* rationale is its failure to recognize that an economic incentive for the lawyer may operate to the benefit of the client, and, conversely, an economic disincentive for the lawyer may operate to the detriment of the client. Faced with a choice of taking a share of the firm's profits or some of its clients, a partner may well choose the former if it yields a net economic benefit. In that case, the clients' freedom of choice has been bargained away just as effectively as if the partnership agreement contained a bald restrictive covenant.

---

[29] *Cohen,* 544 N.Y.S.2d at 162.

[30] "[The agreement] prevents departing partners who are likely to cause potential economic injury to the firm from either reaping the . . . windfalls or from eating into what could be shrinking profits due to loss of business." Id. at 163. See also Standing Comm. on Legal Ethics of the Virginia State Bar, Op. 985, summarized in Law. Man. on Professional Conduct (ABA/BNA) 901:8715 (1987) (value of stock of a professional corporation held by a withdrawing shareholder may be reduced if clients are taken because agreements that affect only the termination of the relationship are not prohibited).

A recent Massachusetts decision required significant and one-sided fee sharing on the partners of lawyers *unfairly* taking cases from a firm. In Meehan v. Shaughnessy,[31] the court found withdrawing partners had unfairly removed cases from their firm and required the lawyers to remit to their former firm 89.2 percent of the profits on these cases. It rejected the argument that this would impede the free exercise of client choice:

> We agree that punitive measures may infringe on a client's right to adequate representation, and to counsel of his or her own choosing. . . . We believe, however, that the remedy we impose does not suffer from the MBC attorneys' claimed defects. Under the constructive trust we impose, Meehan and Boyle will receive a share of the fruits of their efforts in the unfairly removed cases which is the same as that which they would have enjoyed at Parker Coulter. We note, moreover, that incentives other than profit motivate attorneys. These incentives include an attorney's ethical obligations to the client and the profession, and a concern for his or her reputation.
>
> Furthermore, the MBC attorneys' argument would provide us with no mechanism to enforce the partners' fiduciary duties. Imposition of a narrowly tailored constructive trust will enforce the obligations resulting from a breach of duty and will not harm the innocent clients.[32]

Two associates who were part of the cabal fared even worse. They were required to turn over to the firm all of the profits they derived from unfairly removed cases: "Although the associates were not parties to the partnership agreement, and thus were not contractually bound to remove cases fairly, we believe their fiduciary duties require this result.[33]

Since *Meehan* is a case involving a breach of fiduciary duties, it does not provide support for including in partnership agreements disincentives activated by mere withdrawal and competition. The case is noteworthy, however, because of the court's seeming lack of concern over the denial of economic incentives caused by its remedy.[34]

---

[31] 404 Mass. 419, 535 N.E.2d 1255 (1989).
[32] Id. at 447, 535 N.E.2d at 1270-1271.
[33] Id. at 448, 535 N.E.2d at 1271.
[34] *Meehan* is discussed more fully in §4.5.

§2.3.4 Restrictive Covenants as Conditions to the Payment of Retirement Benefits

Both the Model Code and the Model Rules permit restrictive covenants that are conditions to retirement benefits. Retirement, however, is not defined, which leaves open the possibility that a firm might seek to circumvent the ban on restrictive covenants by defining *any* departure from the firm as a retirement. This argument was rejected in Gray v. Martin:[35]

> If retirement has the same meaning as withdrawal in DR2-108 (A), then the disciplinary rule has no meaning. Every termination of a relationship between law partners would be a retirement, and agreements restricting the right to practice would always be allowed. We conclude that Paragraph 25 of the partnership agreement violates DR2-108 (A).[36]

Gray's analysis is correct but provides no guidance for determining the type of withdrawal that qualifies as a retirement. A recent ethics opinion from Virginia provides somewhat more direction on this problem.[37] The opinion draws a distinction between benefits that amount to deferred compensation and benefits funded by the firm or a third party and concludes only the latter qualify as retirement benefits. A letter from the chair of the ethics committee to the firm requesting the opinion explains:

> It is our opinion that a plan containing a clause which would prohibit a lawyer from withdrawing compensation already earned in the event that attorney engaged in the practice of law in a geographically competitive radius to his old firm, would be in violation of the Disciplinary Rule, but only to the extent that the plan involved

---

[35] 63 Or. App. 173, 663 P.2d 1285 (1983).

[36] Id. at 1290. See also Ethics Comm. of the Kentucky State Bar Association, Op. 326, Law. Man. on Professional Conduct (ABA/BNA) 901:3903 (1987) (noncompetition clause that does not distinguish between termination, withdrawal, and retirement is in conflict with disciplinary rules).

[37] See Standing Comm. on Legal Ethics of the Virginia State Bar, Op. 880, summarized in Law. Man. on Professional Conduct (ABA/BNA) 901:8715 (1987).

deferred compensation. To the extent that the benefits from such a plan came from funding by the employer corporation or partnership or third parties, then the exception to the basic rule should prevail and the restriction on the right to practice within a "reasonable radius" should be acceptable.[38]

The difficulty with this analysis is its assumption that the source of benefits is easily traceable. In a law firm, partners "fund" their own post-withdrawal benefits by accepting less in the way of present compensation in exchange for payments in the future. Any benefit paid to a withdrawing partner is a form of deferred compensation. This is true even of those plans basing benefits to a former firm member on a percentage of the firm's current profits. The profits allocable to the remaining partners are reduced, a consequence they accept in the hope they will enjoy similar benefits when they leave the firm.

A better approach is to define retirement as the cessation of the practice of law.[39] This definition conforms with widely held notions of the meaning of retirement and, at least when compared with the opinion of the Virginia ethics committee, offers ease of administration. It is not, however, without its own interpretive difficulties. Will accepting an occasional case, or working for the law department of a corporation, or accepting a position as a lawyer in the public sector annul retirement status? The interpretive difficulties are not overwhelming and can be resolved on a case by case basis in the relatively few situations where they are likely to arise.

§2.4 Conflict of Interest

Two broad principles underlie the conflict rules governing lawyers — lawyers owe a duty of loyalty to their clients, and lawyers must maintain in confidence information acquired in the course of representing their clients.[1] Balanced against these client interests are the

---

[38] Letter from Colin J.S. Thomas (Mar. 11, 1987).

[39] See Johnson, Solicitation of Law Firm Clients by Departing Partners and Associates: Tort, Fiduciary, and Disciplinary Liability, 50 U. Pitt. L. Rev. 1, 115 (1988) (reaching the same conclusion).

§2.4 [1] See C. Wolfram, Modern Legal Ethics §7.1.3 (1986).

lawyers' interests in career mobility and building a stable and diverse portfolio of clients.[2]

In the setting of law firm breakups, conflict rules may limit the mobility of lawyers by restricting the clients that they, and their new firms, may represent. An obvious problem arises when a lawyer withdraws from a firm and takes to a new firm a client with interests materially adverse to those of another client at the new firm. A more subtle but equally serious conflict problem develops when the client *stays* with the first firm. In this case, conflict of interest considerations may disable not only the lawyer but also the new firm from representing a client with interests adverse to those of a client in the lawyer's former firm.

§2.4.1 The Former-Client Conflict Problem

For obvious reasons, lawyers are barred from simultaneously representing parties with interests that conflict significantly. Nor may they represent parties with interests adverse to those of former clients if the present and previous subjects of representation are substantially related.[3] Concerns over confidentiality and loyalty un-

---

[2] See id. §7.1.3 (1986).

[3] The standard was set forth in T.C. Theatre Corporation v. Warner Brothers Pictures, Inc., 113 F. Supp. 265, 268 (S.D.N.Y. 1953):

> [W]here any substantial relationship can be shown between the subject matter of a former representation and that of a subsequent adverse representation, the latter will be prohibited. [T]he former client need show no more than that the matters embraced within the pending suit wherein his former attorney appears on behalf of his adversary are substantially related to the matters or cause of action wherein the attorney previously represented him, the former client.

The literature on this and the related subject of the imputed disqualification of law firms is vast. See, e.g., C. Wolfram, Modern Legal Ethics §§7.4 and 7.6; Goldberg, The Former Client's Disqualification Gambit: A Bad Move in Pursuit of an Ethical Anomaly, 72 Minn. L. Rev. 227 (1987); Liebman, The Changing Law of Disqualification: The Role of Presumption and Policy, 73 N.W.U.L. Rev. 996 (1979); Morgan, Conflicts of Interest and the Former Client in the Model Rules of Professional Conduct, 1980 Am. B. Found. Res. J. 993; Talley, Toward Chinese Walls: The Seventh Circuit Debates Rebuttable Presumptions in Vicarious Disqualification Cases, 11 S. Ill. U.L.J. 59 (1986); Terry, Ethical Pitfalls and Malpractice

derlie these restrictions. Clients would be reluctant to share information with their lawyers if they know it might be used against them later. Moreover, the adverse use of a former client's confidential information is a form of "treachery" repugnant to the notion that lawyers owe a duty of loyalty to those whom they serve.[4] The disloyalty risk is not limited to the former client, for confidentiality and loyalty obligations to that client may impede the lawyer's willingness and ability to represent with vigor the succeeding client when interests conflict.[5]

§2.4.2 Imputed Disqualification of a Firm

The imputed disqualification doctrine extends the disqualification of one member of a firm to all members of the firm.[6] In an era of lawyer mobility, this is a matter of some importance both to

---

Consequences of Law Firm Breakups, 61 Temp. L. Rev. 1055, 1101-1104 (1988); Note, Motions to Disqualify Counsel Representing an Interest Adverse to a Former Client, 57 Tex. L. Rev. 726 (1979); Comment, Disqualification of Counsel: Adverse Interests and Revolving Doors, 81 Colum. L. Rev. 199 (1981); Comment, The Chinese Wall Defense to Law-Firm Disqualification, 128 U. Pa. L. Rev. 677 (1980).

[4] C. Wolfram, Modern Legal Ethics §7.4.2 at 361 (1986).

[5] Id. at 362. In an attempt to avoid imputed disqualification because of the taint of a single lawyer, some firms employ a screening device commonly referred to as the "Chinese Wall." See, e.g., id. §7.6.4 (1986); Talley, Toward Chinese Walls: The Seventh Circuit Debates Rebuttable Presumptions in Vicarious Disqualification Cases, 11 S. Ill. L. Rev. 59 (1986); Comment, The Chinese Wall Defense to Law-Firm Disqualification, 128 U. Pa. L. Rev. 677 (1980). The notion behind this stratagem is that if the disqualified lawyer is screened from all discussion and information about a case as well as any profits generated by the case, there is no need to employ the radical measure of disqualifying the entire firm. With the exception of cases where the conflict arises because of a lawyer's former government service, screening as a means of avoiding imputed disqualification has not achieved widespread judicial acceptance, at least in reported opinions.

[6] A leading commentator has described the imputed disqualification presumption as follows:

> The presumption is the legal mechanism by which an imputed disqualification is customarily imposed by courts. Once the moving party makes the necessary showing of primary conflict on the part of a firm lawyer and demonstrates the conditions for the imputed disqualification, it is presumed that all the firm's lawyers are secondarily disqualified. [Id. §7.6.3 at 398.]

lawyers who change firms and to the firms they join. An important early case illustrates the breadth of the doctrine. In Laskey Bros. v. Warner Bros. Pictures,[7] Isacson, while employed by his previous firm, obtained confidential information about Warner Brothers. He left and formed a partnership with Malkan. The firm of Malkan and Isacson was then retained to pursue an antitrust action against the motion picture industry. Warner Brothers was one of the defendants. Although Isacson left the firm, the defendants moved to disqualify the Malkan firm. The district court granted the motion, and the Second Circuit affirmed, noting "all authorities agree that all members of a partnership are barred from participating in a case from which one partner is disqualified.[8] In short, the presumption that Isacson shared information with his partner was irrebuttable.[9]

A strict application of the imputed disqualification doctrine eventually would either sharply restrict the ability of lawyers to move between firms or require massive disgorgements of clients by their firms. Fortunately, some courts take a "realistic" view of the problem. Silver Chrysler Plymouth, Inc. v. Chrysler Motors Corporation[10] is a leading case in which a firm was not disqualified even though one of its lawyers had, while at another firm, represented a party it was suing. While a junior associate at a large corporate firm, the lawyer had worked on several matters for Chrysler Motors. He then became a partner at another firm. A client of his new firm filed a claim against Chrysler much like the type of claim the lawyer's previous firm regularly defended. The Second Circuit held that the lawyer had made a sufficient showing that the work he had done for Chrysler at the first firm was not substantially related to the present litigation and that there was no "realistic chance" disqualification was necessary to protect the confidences of a client.[11] After that showing, the burden shifted to Chrysler to prove that the lawyer had had access to confidential information.

---

[7] 224 F.2d 824 (2d Cir. 1955), *cert. denied,* 350 U.S. 932 (1956).

[8] Id. at 826.

[9] Fearing the chain of disqualification would never end, the court did not disqualify Malkan from a second and identical case accepted by his firm after Isacson left.

[10] 518 F.2d 751 (2d Cir. 1975).

[11] Id. at 757.

Silver Chrysler's attempt to deal with imputed disqualification in a "realistic" fashion was prompted by the court's view of the "importance of not unnecessarily constricting the careers of lawyers who started their practice of law at large firms."[12] Most circuits follow *Silver Chrysler's* lead and permit an associate who changes firms to rebut the presumption that confidential information was acquired while at the former firm.[13] The decision, while undeniably important,[14] does not represent a major assault on the imputed disqualification doctrine as it is applied to lawyers changing firms, for if the associate's firm had been smaller, or if the associate had been a partner at the firm,[15] the outcome would likely have been different.[16]

§2.4.3 The Model Code and Model Rules

Strangely, the Model Code fails to address expressly the former client conflict problem. Ethical considerations preclude use by a lawyer of "information acquired in the course of the representation of a client to the disadvantage of the client"[17] and oblige the terminated lawyer to maintain the confidences of a former client.[18] The Code does not prescribe, however, loyalty duties independent of

---

[12] Id. at 754.

[13] See, e.g., Freeman v. Chicago Musical Instrument Co., 689 F.2d 715, 723 (7th Cir. 1982); Gas-A-Tron v. Union Oil Co., 534 F.2d 1322, 1324 (9th Cir. 1976), *cert. denied*, 429 U.S. 861 (1976); Goldberg, The Former Client's Disqualification Gambit: A Bad Move in Pursuit of an Ethical Anomaly, 72 Minn. L. Rev. 227, 243-251 (1987).

[14] *Silver Chrysler* has been cited in nearly two hundred federal and state reported opinions.

[15] See C. Wolfram, Modern Legal Ethics §7.6.3 at 396 (1986) ("Certainly *partners* are normally assumed to share confidential information about all of a firm's clients, subject to possible rebuttal in a particularly strong case. *Associates* in large firms, on the other hand, are less likely to be exposed to confidential information about clients for whom they perform no work.") (Emphasis in original.)

[16] See id. at 400. See also Bicas v. Super. Ct., 116 Ariz. 69, 567 P.2d 1198, 1202 (Ariz. Ct. App. 1977) ("Leonard was not merely an employee or associate of a large law firm but was a partner in a firm with approximately 12 lawyers.").

[17] Model Code, EC 4-5. See also ABA Comm. on Prof. Ethics, Informal Op. 428 (1961) in App. D.

[18] See id. EC 4-6.

confidentiality requirements that would restrict the ability of a lawyer to represent a client with interests materially adverse to those of a former client.[19]

On the subject of imputed disqualification, the Code takes a more specific, and sweeping, stance:

> [I]f a lawyer is required to decline or to withdraw from employment under a Disciplinary Rule, no partner, or associate, or any other lawyer affiliated with him or his firm, may accept or continue such employment.[20]

The Model Rules deal more specifically with conflict of interest and imputed disqualification issues. Rule 1.7 provides that a "lawyer shall not represent a client if the representation of that client will be directly adverse to another client" unless each client consents to the representation and the lawyer believes the representation will not adversely affect the relationship with the other client. Rules 1.9 and 1.10 directly address the situation where a lawyer changes firms and represents a client with interests materially adverse to those of a client of the lawyer's former firm. Rule 1.9, sets forth the unsurprising precept that a lawyer who represented a client while at the former firm is barred from representing the new client in the same or a substantially related matter, unless the former client consents. If the lawyer had not previously represented the client of the former firm, the lawyer may represent the new client unless the lawyer had obtained confidential information about the client while at the former firm.[21] The comment to this rule reflects the difficulty of devising ethics rules in an era of lawyer mobility and intense competition for clients:

> When lawyers have been associated within a firm but then end their association, the question of whether a lawyer should undertake representation is . . . complicated. There are several competing con-

---

[19] See generally C. Wolfram, Modern Legal Ethics §7.4.2 at 363-364.

[20] Model Code DR 5-105D.

[21] See Model Rules, Rule 1.9(b). The lawyer may represent the new client, however, in the unlikely event the former client consents. Id. Without regard to who represented the client at the former firm, the lawyer may not normally use any information relating to the representation to the disadvantage of the client. See id. Rule 1.9(c).

siderations. First, the client previously represented by the former firm must be reasonably assured that the principle of loyalty to the client is not compromised. Second, the rule should not be so broadly cast as to preclude other persons from having reasonable choice of legal counsel. Third, the rule should not unreasonably hamper lawyers from forming new associations and taking on new clients after having left a previous association. In this connection, it should be recognized that today many lawyers practice in firms, that many lawyers to some degree limit their practice to one field or another, and that many move from one association to another several times in their careers. If the concept of imputation were applied with unqualified rigor, the result would be radical curtailment of the opportunity of lawyers to move from one practice to another and of the opportunity of clients to change counsel.

Rule 1.10 establishes imputed disqualification rules for law firms. If lawyers are associated in a law firm, no member of the firm may knowingly represent a client if any other member of the firm would be disqualified to do so on conflict of interest grounds.[22] Once a lawyer leaves a firm, the firm may represent a client with interests adverse to those of a client previously represented by the departed lawyer unless the representation pertains to a matter that is the same or substantially related to the subject of the previous representation *and* any lawyer remaining in the firm has confidential information protected under rules 1.6 and 1.9 (c).[23]

§2.4.4 Anticipating the Problem: Information Considerations

Ideally, a lawyer who changes firms will take to the new firm complete information on the clients presently and previously represented by the former firm.[24] Particularly when the former firm is large, it may be impossible for the lawyer's new firm to assess the

---

[22] See Model Rules, Rule 1.10(a).

[23] See id. Rule 110(b).

[24] See Terry, Ethical Pitfalls and Malpractice Consequences of Law Firm Breakups, 61 Temp. L. Rev. 1055, 1103-1104 (1988).

potential for conflicts without this information. Practical considerations, however, limit the usefulness of this suggestion. The acrimony surrounding the departure of a lawyer may render this form of cooperation impossible, and even if the information is made available, confidentiality considerations and the overwhelming burden of evaluating and processing the information may prove significant obstacles to identifying conflict problems prior to the filing of motions to disqualify.

§2.5 Additional Ethical Considerations

§2.5.1 Diligent and Competent Representation

Disciplinary proceedings based upon inadequate representation of clients as a result of a breakup are comparatively rare, but they do exist. In the present environment of grabbing and leaving, the problem is more often one of intense competition for, rather than neglect of, clients. Nevertheless, the disruptive impact of a breakup sometimes does result in malfeasance or nonfeasance in the handling of certain client's affairs.[1] Moreover, the partnership law principle that partners are not entitled to additional compensation for completing the unfinished business of a dissolved partnership may produce situations in which partners attempt to shed cases requiring substantial additional work but little in the way of economic incentives.[2]

The fear of direct of vicarious liability for malpractice following a breakup is a more effective inducement for diligent and competent representation than ethics norms. This is discussed in the later analysis of post-withdrawal liability for malpractice claims.[3]

---

§2.5 [1] See, e.g., Grievance Committee v. Lempesis, 248 S.C. 147, 148 S.E.2d 869 (1966).
[2] See infra §4.4.3.
[3] See infra §4.6.

§2.5.2 Fee Splitting

After a partner withdraws from a firm, there is often a sharing of fees by the former partner and the firm for some period of time following the withdrawal. The status of a law firm as a partnership or professional corporation is relevant in evaluating the ethical implications of such fee splitting, and a complete discussion of this issue is provided in later sections of this book.[4]

---

[4] See infra §§4.4.1 and 5.8.

Chapter 3
TORT AND AGENCY
LAW PERSPECTIVES

§3.1 Tortious Interference with Existing or Prospective Contractual Relations

§3.1.1 In General

The typical response to a lawyer's breach of legal ethics is a disciplinary proceeding conducted by the attorney's licensing bar.[1] Although the bar's role in restraining competition through the enforcement of ethical norms has diminished in recent years, that development has not helped to resolve the question addressed by

---

§3.1   [1] C. Wolfram, Modern Legal Ethics §2.3 at 34 (1986).

this chapter: whether a lawyer or firm losing a client to another lawyer may seek relief or recompense through a private action alleging a violation of legal ethics.

In order to seek private relief, an aggrieved firm might package its ethics grievance with the wrappings of tort law. One possible theory for relief is that convincing a client to change lawyers or firms constitutes tortious interference with prospective or existing contractual relations. Although the parameters of the tort are unclear,[2] the Restatement (Second) of Torts outlines the principle that a party is liable for pecuniary losses for interference either with the performance of a contract[3] or with prospective contractual relations.[4] Among the considerations relevant to establishing tortious interference is the nature of the actor's conduct.[5] The commentary to the applicable Restatement provision offers the following guidance:

Business Ethics and Customs

Violation of recognized ethical codes for a particular area of business activity or of established customs or practices regarding disapproved actions or methods may also be significant in evaluating the nature of the actor's conduct as a factor in determining whether his interference with plaintiff's contractual relations was improper or not.[6]

---

[2] See Comment, Lateral Moves and the Quest for Clients: Tort Liability of Departing Attorneys for Taking Firm Clients, 75 Calif. L. Rev. 1809, 1811 (1987). For a general discussion of tortious interference with contractual relations, see W. Keeton, D. Dobbs, R. Keeton & D. Owen, Prosser and Keeton on the Law of Torts §§129-130 (5th ed. 1984). The development of the tort cause of action for interference dates back to Lumley v. Gye, 2 El. & Bl. 216, 118 Eng. Rep. 749 (Q.B. 1853). A singer under contract with one theatre was induced to breach her contract and sing at a rival theatre. Despite the fact that there was no fraud, violence, or defamation in the inducement, the court decided against the defendant rival theatre. Id. at 269, 118 Eng. Rep. at 769.

[3] Restatement (Second) of Torts §766 (1977).

[4] Id. §766B.

[5] Id. §767. Other considerations include the actor's motive, the interests of the other with which the actor's conduct interferes, the interests sought to be advanced by the actor, the social interests in protecting the freedom of contract and the contractual interests of the other, the proximity or remoteness of the actor's conduct to the interference, and the relations between the parties. Id.

[6] Id. §767 comment c.

If grabbing does constitute a legal ethics violation, the ethics codes may thus lay the groundwork for a private cause of action.

When the cause of action is for tortious interference with contractual relations, however, the client's right of discharge may again limit the action's use as an antigrabbing device.[7] Terminable-at-will contracts pose special problems under tortious interference law. A comment to the Restatement describes such arrangements as "valid and subsisting" and accordingly concludes that they are protected from interference.[8] But the Restatement lessens the degree of protection accorded such fragile relationships in two ways. First, the fact that a contract is terminable at will is relevant to the computation of damages.[9] Second, if the interfering party is a competitor and "does not employ wrongful means," interference with an existing terminable-at-will contract or with a prospective contractual relation is not improper.[10]

§3.1.2 Application to Grabbing and Leaving

Courts have long recognized that improper third-party interference with attorney-client relations is actionable as tortious interference with contractual relations.[11] An extension of this theory to the grabbing activities of lawyers changing firms, however, awaited a

---

[7] See supra §2.3.

[8] Restatement (Second) of Torts §766 comment g (1977).

[9] Id.; see also id. §774A (discussing damages).

[10] Id. §768. The party interfering with the terminable-at-will contract also must not create or continue an unlawful restraint of trade and must act "at least in part to advance his interest in competing with the other." Id.

[11] A large number of the cases involve efforts by insurance companies to persuade claimants to abandon their attorneys. See, e.g., Employers Liab. Assurance Corp. v. Freeman, 229 F.2d 547, 548-549 (10th Cir. 1955); Herron v. State Farm Mut. Ins. Co., 56 Cal. 2d 202, 204-205, 363 P.2d 310, 311, 14 Cal. Rptr. 294, 295-296 (1961); Lurie v. New Amsterdam Casualty Co., 270 N.Y. 379, 380-381, 1 N.E.2d 472, 472-473 (1936). See generally Note, The Attorney as Plaintiff: Tortious Interference with Contract and the Attorney-Client Relationship, 55 Ky. L.J. 682 (1967) (noting that courts consider a number of policies in an attorney's tortious interference claim, including a client's "near absolute right" to dismiss the attorney, the need to protect the client from dismissing necessary legal advice at the insistence of another, and a policy "slightly disfavoring" contingent fee contracts).

comparatively recent decision of the Pennsylvania Supreme Court. In Adler, Barish, Daniels, Levin & Creskoff v. Epstein,[12] a group of Adler, Barish associates who had been working on cases assigned to them by partners decided to leave and establish their own firm. They hoped to grab clients for whom they had worked and, on the basis of projected fees, were able to secure a bank line of credit shortly before leaving the firm. Immediately after terminating their employment, the associates contacted the clients concerning their choice of counsel.[13]

Some of these contacts were in person or by phone, but most were by letter. A sample letter appended to the court's opinion (1) confirmed a recent conversation, (2) indicated that the lawyer had terminated association with the firm, (3) advised the client of his or her right to select counsel, (4) confirmed the client's desire expressed in the previous conversation to retain the letter's author, and (5) identified enclosed documents to be mailed to Adler, Barish and to the author to implement the choice of counsel.[14] The letter included a contingent fee agreement for the client to execute and a self-addressed, stamped envelope.[15]

The grabbing efforts proved so productive that Adler, Barish sought and obtained injunctive relief. Rejecting claims that the quest for clients was constitutionally protected, the court condemned the associates' conduct as "improper" and potentially damaging to both the firm and its clients.[16] Because the associates acted in a manner inconsistent with the "rules of the game,"[17] the court enjoined them from further communications with the Adler, Barish clients other

---

[12] 482 Pa. 416, 393 A.2d 1175 (1978), *cert. denied,* 442 U.S. 907 (1979).

[13] Id. at 421, 393 A.2d at 1177-1178.

[14] Id. at 421, 393 A.2d at 1178.

[15] Id.

[16] Id. at 433, 393 A.2d at 1184. The court commented that the associates' actions "adversely affected more than the informed and reliable decisionmaking of Adler Barish clients with active cases. *Their conduct also had an immediate impact upon Adler Barish.* Adler Barish was prepared to continue to perform services for its clients and therefore could anticipate receiving compensation for the value of its efforts. Moreover, . . . Adler Barish's fee agreements with clients were a source of anticipated revenue protected from outside interference." Id. at 434, 393 A.2d at 1184 (emphasis added).

[17] Id.

than by means of formal announcements permitted by the Model Code.[18]

The "rules of the game" to which the *Adler, Barish* court referred are indefinite standards for regulating attorney conduct.[19] There are no rules proscribing all competition among attorneys or prohibiting an attorney from leaving a firm and, in the process, taking its clients. Nevertheless, some rules do prohibit certain forms of solicitation by lawyers[20] and define the duties of employees to their employers.[21] Although *Adler, Barish* is muddled on the precise nature of the "rules of the game" violated by the associates, it drew from two disparate sources purportedly restricting the competitive activities of lawyers: ethical standards imposed by the Model Code and fiduciary responsibilities owed by agents to their principals.[22]

§3.1.3 Ethical Standards

The court felt that the *Adler, Barish* associates had violated the Model Code's ethical norm prohibiting solicitation by self-recommendation.[23] The associates presumably broke the "rules" when they did more than send the formal announcement permitted by the Model Code and actively expressed an interest in representing clients that, in the court's view, were the firm's property:[24]

---

[18] See Model Code, DR 2-102 (A) (2).

[19] Cf. Comment, Lateral Moves and the Quest for Clients: Tort Liability of Departing Attorneys for Taking Firm Clients, 75 Calif. L. Rev. 1809, 1831, (1987) (also criticizing use of vague standards such as "rules of the game").

[20] See, e.g., Model Code, DR 2-101(A) (prohibiting public communications containing fraudulent or similarly misleading claims); Model Rules, Rule 7.1 (same).

[21] See, e.g., Restatement (Second) of Agency §§13, 23, 393, 395 (1958) (stating generally that an agent has a duty not to compete or act adverse to his employer's interests).

[22] The court also relied upon its supervisory authority over practitioners as the basis for its "duty to provide an atmosphere conducive to proper attorney-client relationships, including those situations where, as here, associates assist other members of a firm in rendering legal services." *Adler, Barish,* 482 Pa. at 437, 393 A.2d at 1186.

[23] See Model Code, DR 2-103(A); see also supra §2.2.3.

[24] "No case on the list . . . was [the associates']. Rather, each case was an Adler Barish case on which [they] were working." *Adler, Barish,* 482 Pa. at 420, 393 A.2d at 1177.

[Their] contacts pose consequences more serious than mailing of
announcements in conformity with [the Model Code.] . . . [Their]
contacts make express their interest in Adler Barish clients' cases,
while announcements, at most, only suggest the same. Moreover,
[their] form letters and self-addressed envelopes, unlike announcements, provide [them] a means of benefitting from a clients'
[*sic*] immediate, perhaps ill-considered, response to the circumstances.[25]

In the court's view, the associates could inform clients of their
withdrawal by mailing them formal announcements, but they could
not transmit further information concerning the clients' rights
to change counsel or the manner in which the clients could effectuate a change. It was the clients' responsibility to determine that
contingent-fee contracts are terminable at will and to ascertain the
manner of causing a transfer of their files. Placing the burden of these
discoveries on the clients would undoubtedly redound to the benefit
of the clients' existing firm; the degree to which a result of clients'
retaining rather than changing their legal counsel is based on informed choices, however, is open to question.

Adler, Barish's reasoning with respect to the mailed communications also raises serious constitutional questions.[26] Relying
upon *Ohralik,* the court dismissed first amendment objections and
concluded that the associates' actions actually retarded informed
client choice.[27] The court found that the associates had engaged in a
type of raw solicitation that justified regulation in the name of client
welfare.[28] The dissent aptly illustrated the flaw in this reasoning:
"One need not be a legal scholar to see the distinction for First
Amendment purposes between the ambulance-chasing tactics used
by the lawyer in *Ohralik* and the written communications [in this
case]."[29] Later Supreme Court decisions support the dissent's position. In *R.M.J.,* the Supreme Court required the state to justify its
audience restrictions on the distribution of formal announcements

---

[25] Id. at 428 n.10, 393 A.2d at 1181 n.10.
[26] See supra §2.2.1.
[27] *Adler, Barish,* 482 Pa. at 425-427, 393 A.2d at 1180-1181.
[28] Id. at 428, 393 A.2d at 1181.
[29] Id. at 440, 393 A.2d at 1187 (Manderino, J., dissenting).

concerning the opening of a law firm,[30] and in *Shapero,* the Court eviscerated the Model Rules' attempt to prohibit direct mail solicitation.[31] Thus, particularly with respect to the mailings that the court found so offensive, the *Adler, Barish* court's easy dismissal of the associates' claims of constitutional protection may well reflect a different era's "rules of the game."

§3.1.4 Agency Principles

Because of constitutional considerations and because the *Adler, Barish* court was interpreting the Model Code rather than the more liberal and now more widely adopted Model Rules, the use of ethical standards as the basis for a claim of tortious interference with contractual relations may prove to be a temporary phenomenon. But *Adler, Barish* offered an alternative basis — the law of agency — for defining the rules of the game. This may prove a more enduring aspect of the opinion. The loyalty obligations of agents are discussed in the next section.

§3.2 The Loyalty Obligations of Agents

§3.2.1 Competition by Agents

Antisolicitation rules are most defensible when used to protect individuals from coercion, overreaching, or undue influence by lawyers.[1] Agency principles, on the other hand, address more directly the rights of competing lawyers currently or previously associated with a firm.

Associates, as employees, are agents of their firms. As such, they owe certain fiduciary responsibilities to their principals.[2] For exam-

---

[30] In re R.M.J., 455 U.S. 191 (1982); see also supra §2.2.1.
[31] Shapero v. Kentucky Bar Assn., 108 S. Ct. 1916 (1988).
§3.2 [1] See supra §2.2.
[2] See supra §2.4 n.15.

ple, an agent may not compete with the principal concerning the subject matter of the agency.[3] Restraints on competition, however, generally lapse with the termination of an agency relationship.[4] After termination, an agent may compete, but may not, in the words of the Restatement (Second) of Agency, "take advantage of a still subsisting confidential relation created during the prior agency relation."[5] On the basis of these general principles, the *Adler, Barish* court found that the associates breached their duties as agents:

> [The associates'] contacts were possible because Adler Barish partners trusted [them] with the high responsibility of developing its clients' cases. From this position of trust and responsibility, [they] were able to gain knowledge of the details, and status, of each case. . . . In the atmosphere surrounding [the associates'] departure, [their] contacts unduly suggested a course of action for Adler Barish clients and unfairly prejudiced Adler Barish. No public interest is served in condoning use of confidential information which has these effects. Clients too easily may suffer in the end.[6]

The court failed to note yet another provision of the Restatement relevant to the issue of post-termination competition. After the termination of an agency, the agent may not compete with the principal by using "trade secrets, written lists of names, or other similar confidential matters given to him only for the principal's use."[7] The Restatement adds, however, that the agent may use general information concerning the principal's method of business and any client names retained in memory.[8] The commentary offers the following guidance in drawing the line:

---

[3] See Restatement (Second) of Agency §393 (1958).
[4] See id. §396.
[5] Id. §396(d).
[6] Adler, Barish, Daniels, Levin & Creskoff v. Epstein, 482 Pa. 416, 435-436, 393 A.2d 1175, 1185 (1978), *cert. denied,* 442 U.S. 907 (1979).
[7] Restatement (Second) of Agency §396(b) (1958).
[8] Id.

[A] former agent cannot properly use [trade secrets] for his own purposes. On the other hand, during his agency, an agent frequently acquires information concerning the methods of his employer in doing business and becomes acquainted with his employer's customers and their desires. *Information of this sort is barred from use in competition with his employer only to the extent that, considering all the circumstances, it would be unfair to his former employer for the agent to use it.*[9]

The Restatement's general standard of unfairness to the employer is difficult to apply in the specific context of grabbing by lawyers. Is it unfair *to the firm* for associates to leave and, using information obtained while employed by the firm, compete for their former employer's business? If so, is it any more fair to allow competition while limiting the ability of departing associates to communicate with their former clients? Conversely, is it fair *to clients* to bar lawyers who are no longer associated with a firm from representing firm clients or, alternatively, to allow clients a free choice of lawyers while restricting information concerning how they may effectuate their preferences? Should a firm be able to effect through agency principles a restrictive covenant that violates professional ethics?[10] The conflict between the principle of client choice and an agent's duty of loyalty to a principal is clear.[11]

In light of the importance accorded client choice under ethical norms, considerations emphasizing fairness to the firm are not dis-

---

[9] Id. §396 comment b (emphasis added). The comment adds that an agent "is normally privileged to use, in competition with the principal, the names of customers retained in his memory as the result of his work for the principal." Id. In the law firm context, the memory test should not be applied rigidly, and there is little point in rewarding only those associates with the ability to memorize names and addresses of the clients for whom they have worked. Use of information, regardless of whether it was committed to memory, about clients not represented by the associates is another matter, as is removing files from the firm without the clients' consent.

[10] See supra §2.3.2.

[11] For an argument that knowledge about clients should be treated as confidential information, the use of which by a former employee would be improper, see Comment, Barefoot Shoemakers: An Uncompromising Approach to Policing the Morals of the Marketplace When Law Firms Split Up, 19 Ariz. St. L.J. 509, 540 (1987).

positive of the issues raised by post-withdrawal competition. To some extent, fairness concerns can be alleviated by compensation. When a firm loses contingent-fee clients to a lawyer not previously associated with the firm, it does not forfeit its right to compensation under quantum meruit principles for services performed prior to discharge.[12] Although a firm normally will prefer to carry a contingent-fee case to completion and receive the contractually based compensation rather than a quantum meruit recovery,[13] the increasing acceptance of compensation based on the value of services rendered prior to discharge accommodates the interests of both the firm and its former client. This accommodation may well be appropriate in the grabbing context.

§3.2.2 Pre-Withdrawal Competition

Although the ethical principles relating to the attorney-client relationship constrain a fairness inquiry concerning post-withdrawal competition by a former agent, pre-termination competition by firm members is another matter. The principle of client choice is not, or at least should not be, so overpowering that it shields all pre-termination competition by members of a firm. The *Adler, Barish* court's vague reference to the "atmosphere" surrounding the departure of the associates was a poor substitute for a more precise inquiry concerning whether they performed the actions before or after termination of employment. This timing inquiry is necessary, because leaving followed by grabbing is far less culpable than grabbing

---

[12] See supra §2.3.1.

[13] A professionals quantum meruit recovery normally will yield a smaller fee than recovery based on the contract. See Childres & Garamella, The Law of Restitution and the Reliance Interest in Contract, 64 N.W.U.L. Rev. 433, 451 (1969). Moreover, litigation involving fee collection is more likely in the case of quantum meruit than contractually based contingent fees, and ascertaining the value of services presents difficult evidentiary problems. Id. at 443. In addition, if quantum meruit recovery is conditioned on the occurrence of the contingency, inadequate representation by the grabbing attorney may convert an otherwise strong case into one yielding no compensation for any attorney. See supra §2.3.1.

followed by leaving.[14] In *Adler, Barish,* the associates did not solicit clients while in the firm's employ.[15] Although *Adler, Barish* suggests otherwise, agents may make, within limits, plans or arrangements in preparation for competition after the agency's termination.[16] The associates' most questionable pre-termination conduct was their arrangement of bank financing based on projected fees from prospective clients that they would grab from their former firm. This action might qualify as a breach of the associates' duty to their principal.[17] Even so, there is no other conduct discernible in *Adler, Barish*'s facts that is as clearly proscribed by the law of agency as the court suggested. A more detailed discussion of what is and is not acceptable conduct, both before and after termination of associate status, would have greatly benefited the court's goal of protecting the stability interests of law firms.

The essence of *Adler, Barish* is exemplified by an intriguing but undeveloped statement in the opinion. In describing the use of fee projections to secure a line of credit, the court commented: "No case on the list, however, was [the associates']. Rather, each case was an

---

[14] The references to "grabbing and leaving" in this book are not intended to suggest that the grabbing necessarily comes before the leaving.

[15] Adler, Barish, Daniels, Levin & Creskoff v. Epstein, 482 Pa. 416, 421, 393 A.2d 1175, 1177-1178 (1978), *cert. denied,* 442 U.S. 907 (1979); cf. Bray v. Squires, 702 S.W.2d 266, 270-271 (Tex. App. — Houston [1st Dist.] 1985, no writ) (holding that lawyers did not breach their fiduciary duty to their former firm because no solicitation activities occurred while they were still associates of the firm).

[16] The Restatement provides that:

Even before the termination of the agency, [the agent] . . . is entitled to make arrangements to compete, except that he cannot properly use confidential information peculiar to his employer's business and acquired therein. Thus, before the end of his employment, he can properly purchase a rival business and upon termination of employment immediately compete. He is not, however, entitled to solicit customers for such rival business before the end of his employment nor can he properly do other similar acts in direct competition with his employer's business.

Restatement (Second) of Agency §393 comment e (1958); see also Bray, 702 S.W.2d at 270 (stating that associates can make plans and preparations to compete with their firm without necessarily breaching their fiduciary duties).

[17] See Restatement (Second) of Agency §393 (1958).

Adler Barish case on which [they] were working."[18] Given such a premise, the court's conclusions are not surprising.[19]

§3.3 An Alternative Perspective: the Equal Opportunity to Compete for Clients

A 1989 Massachusetts decision distinguishes between the making of arrangements in anticipation of a withdrawal and more culpable conduct constituting a breach of fiduciary duties. In Meehan v.

---

[18] Adler, Barish, 482 Pa. at 420, 393 A.2d at 1177. The point was made even more dramatically in the concurrence to the intermediate appellate court's opinion:

> It is noble and daring to embark on a career of law by cutting the umbilical cord that ties one to an employment contract. But taking the heart and soul of the benefactor is immoral, illegal and repulsive. If they want their own firm, let them get their own clients.

Adler, Barish, Daniels, Levin & Creskoff v. Epstein, 252 Pa. Super. 553, 568, 382 A.2d 1226, 1233 (1977) (Spaeth, J., concurring), rev'd, 482 Pa. 416, 393 A.2d 1175 (1978), cert. denied, 442 U.S. 907 (1979).

[19] Other cases present divergent views on this issue. In Pratt, P.C. v. Blunt, 140 Ill. App. 3d 512, 515-516, 488 N.E.2d 1062, 1064 (1986), the solicitation activities by two former associates occurred only after their departure from a firm. The lawyers wrote clients whose matters they had previously handled, advising them (1) that the lawyers had formed a new firm, (2) that the clients were free to stay with the old or go with the new firm, and (3) that a decision to go with the new firm would require a letter to the old firm. They did not include either a form letter or an addressed, stamped envelope. Id. at 515, 488 N.E.2d at 1065. The lawyers engaged in some in-person contacts with clients, and one of the lawyers told a prospective client that he was still associated with the old firm. Id. Relying heavily upon Adler, Barish, the court concluded that the lawyers could be enjoined from any further solicitation of the firm's clients. Id. at 519-523, 488 N.E.2d at 1067-1070; cf. Saltzberg v. Fishman, 123 Ill. App. 3d 447, 454, 462 N.E.2d 901, 907 (1984) (holding that files taken by an associate were the property of his former firm). For a discussion of Pratt, see generally Robinson, Rights of Departing Attorneys to the Clients of Their Former Firm, 28 Law Off. Econ. & Mgmt. 321 (1988).

In Bray, 702 S.W.2d at 270-271, the court based its finding that departing associates competing with their old firm had not committed ethics violations in part on a showing that no solicitation activities took place while the lawyers were still associates of the firm.

Shaughnessy,[1] partners, prior to their departures, executed a lease for their new offices, prepared lists of clients they expected to take, and, with the help of the lists, secured financing. Describing these actions as permissible "in light of the attorneys' obligation to represent adequately any clients who might continue to retain them on their departure," the court found no breach of fiduciary duties in making such "logistical" arrangements in anticipation of a departure. It did find, however, the partners and an associate who left with them breached their fiduciary duties to the partnership by failing to give the partnership an "equal opportunity" to compete for clients. Although the case was decided largely on the basis of partnership law principles, the associate was held liable because his "fiduciary duties require this result."

Meehan is discussed more fully in the following chapter.[2]

§3.4 The Question of Status: Partners versus Associates

Adler, Barish involved grabbing and leaving by associates, but its holding might easily be extended to subject partners to the same rules of the game. If grabbing by associates involves solicitation, the same label should describe identical activities by partners.[1] Moreover, partners, like associates, are constrained by fiduciary standards.[2] If either fiduciary standards or ethical norms preclude associates from "soliciting" clients of firms for whom they have previously worked, similar restrictions may also apply to partners. Moreover, *Adler, Barish*'s unease with associates' grabbing of clients whom partners have "entrusted" to them may also extend to partners' grabbing of clients they entrust to each other.

---

§3.3 [1] 404 Mass. 419, 535 N.E.2d 1255 (1989).
[2] See infra §4.5.
§3.4 [1] Cf. In re Silverberg, 81 A.D.2d 640, 641, 438 N.Y.S.2d 143, 144 (1981) (holding that a partner's solicitation of clients for his own benefit before dissolution of the partnership was a breach of his fiduciary duty to his fellow partners and the partnership).
[2] See infra §4.3.2.

Arguably, partners are distinguishable from associates and therefore subject to different rules of the game. Associates are employees; partners, in theory, are co-owners. It is conceptually awkward to envision a partner stealing clients from himself. If, however, clients are "assets," no partner may assert a claim to the clients superior to that of the other partners.[3] Under this reasoning, it makes little difference whether the grabbing is by an associate or a partner. Both ranks would operate under the same rules of the game.[4]

The problem with an analysis emphasizing proprietary rights is that clients are not assets subject to possession or "bartering."[5] The "client of whom" question is problematical, and the answer should not turn on whether the grabbing attorney is an associate or a partner. The bias of the vocabulary of withdrawal suggests that the firm's rights are greater, but ethical standards offer mixed signals. Neither the Model Code nor the Model Rules resolve the relative rights of lawyers with respect to clients of their firms, although both emphasize lawyer-client rather than firm-client relationships.[6] In its

---

[3] See, e.g., Unif. Partnership Act §25, 6 U.L.A. 326 (1969).

[4] At least one court has adopted this position. See infra §4.4.2.2. But cf. C. Wolfram, Modern Legal Ethics §16.2.3, at 888 (1986) (suggesting that associates and partners who attempt to solicit their former firm's clients may be subject to different fiduciary obligations).

[5] See, e.g., ABA Comm. on Professional Ethics, Formal Op. 300 (1961) (striking down a restrictive covenant as improper because it represents an attempt to "barter in clients") in App. D.

[6] For example, the Model Rules begin with a mandate that the lawyer, rather than the firm, provide competent representation of a client. See Model Rules, Rule 1.1. The Model Rules also provide that partners must make reasonable efforts to assure that all lawyers within a firm conform to rules of professional conduct; otherwise, supervising lawyers may be responsible for another lawyer's violations. See id. Rule 5.1.

Rules 1.6 (confidentiality of information), 1.7 (general rule on conflict of interest), 1.8 (prohibited transactions), and 1.9 (conflict of interest involving a former client) are more specific and are directed to the lawyer rather than the firm. See id. Rules 1.6-1.9. Rule 1.10 provides for imputed disqualification of all lawyers within a firm in certain conflict situations but includes language emphasizing lawyer-client rather than firm-client relationships. See id. Rule 1.10 (c). This tension is reflected in the comment to the rule, which labors over the nature of a firm and observes: "The fiction that the law firm is the same as a single lawyer is no longer wholly realistic." See id. Rule 1.10 comment on lawyers

unqualified conclusion that clients belong to firms, the *Adler, Barish* court went too far.

---

moving between firms; see also id. Rule 1.16 (regulating the termination of representation and referencing the lawyer rather than the firm).

But an ABA committee held that a "client employs the legal services office as a firm and not a particular lawyer." ABA Comm. on Ethics and Professional Responsibility, Informal Op. 1428 (1979). The opinion dealt with what perhaps is best described as reverse grabbing, which occurs when neither the firm nor its withdrawing attorney wishes to continue representing a client. Both the Model Code and the Model Rules restrict the ability of lawyers to withdraw from representing clients. See Model Code, DR 2-110; Model Rules, Rule 1.16. Each refers to lawyers rather than their firms, raising the issue of whether the firm, a departing attorney, or both have continuing responsibilities concerning the representation of a client. The opinion concludes that the firm and the departing attorney share responsibility for withdrawal from employment and that the "instructions and wishes of the client should be considered." The opinion is interesting for two reasons. First, it offers one of the more unequivocal statements that clients employ firms rather than lawyers. Second, it fails to address, in light of the Model Code's restrictions on communications with clients following withdrawal, the process by which clients may make an informed choice. See Model Code, DR 2-102(A)(2). The conclusions of Informal Opinion 1428 are applicable to the withdrawal provisions of the Model Rules as well.

Chapter 4
LAW FIRMS AS PARTNERSHIPS

§4.1 In General

The preceding chapters largely have viewed grabbing and leaving from the perspective of ethical restrictions on the activities of attorneys. These ethical standards have diminished in importance as constraints on grabbing and leaving. A different set of norms, that arising from partnership law,[1] provides a more explicit source of

---

§4.1 [1] Most law firms are organized as partnerships. See Rogers, Has Your Firm Thought About Incorporating?, 50 Tex. B.J. 1194, 1194 (1987). An alternative form of organization is the professional corporation. See Chapter 5.

duties that may pass between lawyers as business associates. Partnership law and ethical norms have developed along quite independent lines, and there are numerous conflicts between the governing ethical standards for lawyers as professionals and the constraints on lawyers as business partners. This chapter examines the degree to which partnership law limits grabbing and leaving in ways that ethical standards do not.

§4.2 Dissolution: Its Meaning and Significance Under the Uniform Partnership Act

The vocabulary of partnership law is quite unlike that underlying legal ethics. Dissolution, for example, is a term of art under the Uniform Partnership Act (UPA)[1] and a pivotal concept governing the consequences of a partner's withdrawal. An appreciation of the consequences of dissolution requires an understanding of its meaning.[2]

§4.2.1 Dissolution and Partnerships Generally

The UPA defines dissolution of a partnership as "the change in the relation of the partners caused by any partner ceasing to be associated in the carrying on . . . of the business."[3] Accordingly, any time a partner leaves a law firm, the original partnership is

---

§4.2   [1] Unif. Partnership Act, 6 U.L.A. 1 (1969). Forty-nine states have adopted the UPA. 6 U.L.A. 1 (Supp. 1988).

[2] For an attempt to develop a framework for regulating grabbing and leaving independent of partnership and agency law, see Comment, Lateral Moves and the Quest for Clients: Tort Liability of Departing Attorneys for Taking Firm Clients, 75 Calif. L. Rev. 1809, 1831-1839 (1987).

[3] Unif. Partnership Act §29, 6 U.L.A. at 364. One commentator has observed that the definition is artless because it entangles cause with effect. See Ribstein, A Statutory Approach to Partner Dissociation, 65 Wash. U.L.Q. 357, 368 n.27 (1987).

dissolved. Dissolution may result from any one of a number of acts or conditions, including a partner's mere expression of a desire to dissolve.[4] Following dissolution, the partnership continues until it completes the winding up of partnership affairs.[5] Unless the dissolution was wrongful or the partners have agreed to the contrary, each partner has the power to compel a liquidation of partnership assets.[6]

For purposes of dissolution, the UPA largely eschews an entity view of partnerships in favor of an aggregate approach.[7] If the nondissolving partners continue the business after dissolution, they

---

[4] Section 31 of the UPA provides:

Dissolution is caused:
    (1) Without violation of the agreement between the partners,
        (a) By the termination of the definite term or particular undertaking specified in the agreement,
        (b) By the express will of any partner when no definite term or particular undertaking is specified,
        (c) By the express will of all the partners . . . ,
        (d) By the expulsion of any partner from the business bona fide in accordance with such a power conferred by the agreement between the partners;
    (2) In contravention of the agreement between the partners, where the circumstances do not permit a dissolution under any other provision of this section, by the express will of any partner at any time;
    (3) By any event which makes it unlawful for the business of the partnership to be carried on or for the members to carry it on in partnership;
    (4) By the death of any partner;
    (5) By the bankruptcy of any partner or the partnership;
    (6) By decree of court . . . under section 32.
Unif. Partnership Act §31, 6 U.L.A. at 376.

[5] Id. §30, 6 U.L.A. at 367.
[6] Id. §38(1), 6 U.L.A. at 456.
[7] Commentators have debated for years whether entity or aggregate theories should control. See, e.g., Crane, The Uniform Partnership Act: A Criticism, 28 Harv. L. Rev. 762, 766-768 (1915) (contending that the aggregate approach cannot be applied consistently); Jensen, Is a Partnership Under the Uniform Act an Aggregate or an Entity?, 16 Vand. L. Rev. 377, 386-387 (1963) (concluding that the UPA does not adopt either approach consistently); Lewis, The Uniform Partnership Act — A Reply to Mr. Crane's Criticism, 29 Harv. L. Rev. 158, 168-192 (1915) (defending the UPA's rejection of the entity theory); Lewis, The Uniform Partnership Act, 24 Yale L.J. 617, 639-641 (1915) (same).
    Some UPA provisions suggest entity status for a partnership. See, e.g., Unif. Partnership Act §8(3), 6 U.L.A. at 115 (allowing the partnership to acquire

do so through a new partnership.[8] Entity treatment of partnerships, on the other hand, would preserve the original partnership even in the case of a withdrawal. Providing greater entity treatment for partnerships has appealed to some[9] and might well represent a sensible reform of partnership law.[10] The UPA, however, presently

---

property in the partnership name); id. §9, 6 U.L.A. at 132 (stating that a partner is an agent of the partnership); id. §10(1), 6 U.L.A. at 155 (providing that a partner can convey title to real property in the partnership name). Others reflect an aggregate view. See, e.g., id. §6(1), 6 U.L.A. at 22 (defining a partnership as an "association" of persons); id. §15, 6 U.L.A. at 174 (providing for joint and several liability of partners); id. §25, 6 U.L.A. at 326 (providing that partnership property is owned by the partners as tenants in partnership).

   The definition of dissolution implies an aggregate approach. See id. §29, 6 U.L.A. at 364 ("The dissolution of a partnership is the change in the relation of the partners caused by any partner ceasing to be associated in the carrying on as distinguished from the winding up of the business."). The aggregate approach is more explicit in other dissolution provisions. See, e.g., id. §30, 6 U.L.A. at 456 (providing that partnership is terminated upon the completion of winding up); id. §41, 6 U.L.A. at 509 (referring to post-dissolution continuation of business through a new partnership as distinct from "the first or dissolved partnership").

   [8] See Unif. Partnership Act §41, 6 U.L.A. at 509.

   [9] See, e.g., Crane, The Uniform Partnership Act: A Criticism, 28 Harv. L. Rev. 762, 766-769 (1915) (arguing that "courts have been consciously or unconsciously tending toward the entity theory" because of the difficulty of consistently applying an aggregate approach); Jensen, Is a Partnership Under the Uniform Act an Aggregate or an Entity?, 16 Vand. L. Rev. 377, 382-383 (1963) (noting that some states allow partnerships to sue or be sued as an entity).

   [10] For larger firms, the problem lies in the fact that dissolution is, but need not be, a unitary concept. When one partner withdraws from a 300-person firm, the UPA requires treatment of the entire partnership as dissolved because of the "change in the relation" of partners effectuated by the departure. See Unif. Partnership Act §29, 6 U.L.A. at 364. Such treatment is unnecessary, and critics make this point indirectly when they chafe at the concept of such easy dissolution. A middle ground in the form of a bifurcated approach may represent a sensible reform of partnership law. This approach might treat withdrawal from a large firm as an act of dissolution only with respect to the relationship between the disassociating and the remaining partners; the dissolution of this relationship need not affect the relations of the nondissolving partners, and the original partnership may continue without dissolution with only a slight change in membership. Cf. Wilzig v. Sisselman, 182 N.J. Super. 519, 528, 442 A.2d 1021, 1026 (App. Div. 1982) (holding that agreement may require the surviving partners to carry on the business after a partner's death); Adams v. Jarvis, 23 Wis. 2d 453, 458, 127 N.W.2d 400, 403 (1964) (upholding agreement which provided that withdrawal results in dissolution only as to withdrawing partner). For a discussion of possible reforms of the UPA, see infra §4.7.

leaves little room for doubt that the partnership does not survive the withdrawal of one of its members.[11]

Even though they may not avoid dissolution after a withdrawal, partners may attempt through contract to accord their relationship

---

[11] California provides a notable and puzzling exception. California law corresponds to §31 of the UPA, except that California's version was amended in 1963 to provide an additional cause of dissolution:

> By withdrawal of a partner or admission of a new partner unless otherwise provided in an agreement in writing signed by all of the partners . . . before such withdrawal or admission . . . .
>   None of the provisions of any other section of this chapter shall prevent, or impair the effect or enforceability of, any agreement in writing that a partnership will not be dissolved [by the death, withdrawal, or admission of a partner].

Cal. Corp. Code §15031(7) (West 1977). Interestingly, this was California's second amendment of the UPA provisions on the causes of dissolution. An earlier 1961 amendment added an introductory phrase to the causes of dissolution allowing them to be altered by written agreement. See generally Selected 1960-61 California Legislation, 36 J. St. B. Cal. 643, 733-735 (1961) (discussing an amendment to California partnership law that allows partners to modify by written agreement the causes of dissolution). The 1963 amendments deleted this introductory phrase. Moreover, the California statute allows dissolution at the will of any partner, even in contravention of an agreement. See Cal. Corp. Code §15031(2).

All of this raises a question concerning the effect of the California variation. If a withdrawal is not a dissolution of the original partnership, then what is the status of the withdrawing partner, and how is this status different from that accorded by the UPA to a partner who withdraws under an agreement giving the other partners the right to continue the business? It is noteworthy that the California definition of "dissolution" as a "change in the relation of the partners caused by any partner ceasing to be associated in the carrying on . . . of the business" is the same as the UPA's. See Unif. Partnership Act §29, 6 U.L.A. at 364; Cal. Corp. Code §15029.

The effect of the California provision distinguishing withdrawal from dissolution is to establish entity status only for limited purposes. The withdrawing partner cannot demand liquidation, but partners may waive this right easily under the UPA through continuation agreements. Of greater significance is the effect of the California provision on contract rights that are terminable on dissolution. California's partnership act includes provisions for recording a "statement of partnership." See id. §15010.5. This permits purchasers of partnership property to rely upon partners identified in the statement, and withdrawal of a partner will not require the filing of a statement for a new partnership. Id.; see also id. §15035.5 (requiring publication of notice of dissolution). Similarly, because withdrawal is not a cause of dissolution, a partner's departure will not affect contracts between the partnership and third parties.

Arkansas takes a different and potentially broader approach. Its definition of "dissolution" excludes acts in contravention of the partnership agreement and

entity status and thus preserve the continuity of the partnership.[12] These efforts represent an understandable desire to stabilize what is otherwise a fragile relationship. Because according entity status to partnerships runs counter to the UPA's dissolution provisions, these agreements only permit partnerships to approach rather than actually achieve entity status.

Contract provisions conferring entity status typically take one of three forms. First, the partners may agree to permit the parties remaining after a withdrawal to continue the partnership. These agreements approximate entity treatment and achieve many of its desirable consequences.[13] In particular, the continuing partners avoid liquidation by purchasing the interest of the withdrawing partner, and creditors of the dissolved partnership become creditors of the new partnership.[14] Under these circumstances, the firm maintains the appearance of continuity and avoids the more disruptive effects that might otherwise accompany dissolution and liquidation. There are distinctions, however, between the approximation of entity status sought by continuation agreements and actual achievement of that goal. Even a technical dissolution, for example, may

---

denies a partner the power to dissolve by express will when that act is prohibited by agreement. See Ark. Stat. Ann. §§65-129, 65-131 (1947).

A number of states permit agreements to specify that death is not a cause of dissolution. See, e.g., Ala. Code §10-8-91(4) (1975); Cal. Corp. Code §15031 (4) (West 1977); Ga. Code Ann. §14-8-31(a)(5) (Supp. 1987); Iowa Code §544.31(4) (1987); Kan. Stat. Ann. §56-331(d) (1983); Miss. Code Ann. §79-12-61(4) (Supp. 1987); N.C. Gen. Stat. §59-61(4) (1982); Okla. Stat. tit. 54, §231(4) (1981); Tex. Rev. Civ. Stat. Ann. art. 6132(b), §31(4) (Vernon 1970).

[12] See generally A. Bromberg and L. Ribstein, Bromberg and Ribstein on Partnership §7.03 (1988).

[13] The liquidation right is subject to a contrary agreement among the partners. Unif. Partnership Act §38(1), 6 U.L.A. at 456; see also id. §41, 6 U.L.A. at 509 (referring to the continuation of the business without dissolution). See generally Bromberg, Partnership Dissolution — Causes, Consequences, and Cures, 43 Texas L. Rev. 631, 647-653 (1965) (discussing the choice between liquidation and continuation); Fuller, Partnership Agreements for Continuation of an Enterprise After the Death of a Partner, 50 Yale L.J. 202, 210-214 (1940) (discussing the advantages of continuation agreements); Note, Partnership Continuation Agreements, 72 Harv. L. Rev. 1302, 1304-1305 (1959) (examining survivorship in specific partnership property).

[14] See Unif. Partnership Act §41, 6 U.L.A. at 509.

terminate some contract rights of the old partnership.[15] More importantly, a continuation agreement between the partners of the firm cannot preclude the post-dissolution assertion of claims by third parties against a partner who has withdrawn.[16]

Second, partners may define by agreement a term or undertaking for their partnerships and, in so doing, achieve a measure of stability for their firms. Agreements specifying a partnership's term do not affect a partner's power to accomplish a premature dissolution, and the departure of a partner prior to the expiration of the term or undertaking still causes a dissolution of the partnership.[17] Such a premature dissolution is wrongful, however, and the non-breaching partners may avoid liquidation, continue the business, discount the account of the dissolving partner, and hold the dissolving partner liable for damages.[18]

Finally, partnership agreements among professionals often contain provisions that distinguish dissolution from withdrawal and recognize the former only upon the vote of a requisite number of partners.[19] These agreements typically specify that the departure of a single partner does not dissolve the firm or the partnership. As is discussed below,[20] agreements of this nature are common, in part because publications advising professionals routinely recommend treatment of withdrawal as an act distinct from dissolution.[21] A few

---

[15] See, e.g., Fairway Dev. Co. v. Title Ins. Co., 621 F. Supp. 120, 125 (N.D. Ohio 1985) (holding that a successor partnership involving one of three original partners had no standing to enforce title insurance contract). See generally Ribstein, supra note 151, at 370 (discussing effect of dissolution on executory contracts).

[16] See infra §4.6.

[17] See Unif. Partnership Act §31(2), 6 U.L.A. at 376.

[18] See id. §38(2)(b), 6 U.L.A. at 456. The partners who have not caused the dissolution wrongfully have the right to continue the partnership for the agreed term or undertaking if they indemnify the dissolving partner against all "present or future partnership liabilities." Id. They may also defer settlement of the account of the dissolving partner by securing its payment through a court-approved bond. Id. The account settlement may reflect damages caused by the premature dissolution and need not reflect elements of goodwill. Id.

[19] See 14 Am. Jur. Legal Forms 2d Partnership §194:62 (rev. 1982) (medical partnership agreement); id. §194:68 (accounting partnership agreement).

[20] See infra §4.2.2.

[21] For example, the Articles of Partnership for Law Firms, an important model for law firm partnership agreements, see infra §4.2.2, treats withdrawal differently from dissolution. Compare P. Carrington & W. Sutherland, Articles of Partnership for Law Firms 55-69 (1961) (providing for permanent withdrawal of a partner) with id. 96-98 (providing for dissolution and termination of the firm).

courts have enforced such provisions,[22] and at least one commentator contends that they are generally valid.[23] The support for such a conclusion is weak, however, and the inherent power of any partner

---

[22] See e.g., SRI Corp. v. First Natl. Bank, 75 Ill. App. 3d 350, 355, 393 N.E.2d 1287, 1291 (1979) (holding that if agreement provided for dissolution only by vote, change in membership did not result in dissolution); Bailey v. McCoy, 187 Neb. 618, 622–623, 193 N.W.2d 270, 273 (1971) (holding that "a partnership may continue, although it admits a partner or a partner retires."

[23] Professor Bromberg has commented:

> In fact, it is equally true that no dissolution occurs in a large partnership whose articles specify that there is no dissolution on death, retirement, incapacity, etc. Examples include accounting, law, and investment firms with dozens or hundreds of partners, and frequent changes in membership. There is no reason why legal theory should not accept this practical result, and it has done so. And there is no reason to limit it to larger firms.

A. Bromberg, Crane and Bromberg on Partnership §73 at 18 (1968) (citation omitted). The statement that legal theory accepts this "practical result" is supported only by a citation to the California partnership act, which modifies the UPA. Moreover, in an earlier work Professor Bromberg took a position that seems less certain. In describing statutes and decisions that permit partners to contract that death will not be a cause of dissolution, he commented:

> Plainly, such a result contradicts the general definition of dissolution since a partner does cease to be associated in the carrying on of the business. In the three states with statutes, the specific provision governs and impliedly amends the general definition. In the other states where the result is decisional, a reconciliation with the general definition has not been attempted. Three explanations are possible: (1) the courts may be thinking of the continuation of the business rather than of the partnership; (2) they may be oblivious of the general definition; or, (3) more justifiably, they may feel the general definition . . . is subject to modification by their agreement.

Bromberg, Partnership Dissolution — Causes, Consequences, and Cures. 43 Texas L. Rev. 631, 638 (1965) (footnote omitted). Of the three justifications, the most plausible is that the definition of dissolution is subject to modification by agreement. There are several problems, however, with this conclusion. First, the UPA is replete with provisions expressly subject to contrary agreement among the partners. See, e.g., Unif. Partnership Act §§18, 27, 37, 38, 40, 42, 43, 6 U.L.A. 213, 353, 444, 456, 468, 521, 543 (1969). If the UPA subjects the definition and causes of dissolution to the same bargaining process, it seems strange that the relevant sections contain no reference to modifications by agreement. Second, the related issue of whether partners can contract for indissoluble partnerships is settled against the enforceability of promises not to dissolve. See generally Hillman, Indissoluble Partnerships, 37 U. Fla. L. Rev. 691, 697-707 (1985) (outlining the reasons for the rule against indissolubility). Finally, if withdrawal is not a dissolution, the status of the departing partner is very unclear.

to dissolve a partnership, even in contravention of an agreement, is a central tenet of the partnership law of most jurisdictions.[24]

§4.2.2 Dissolution and Law Partnerships in Particular

Because the UPA does not accord separate treatment to professional associations,[25] the above principles apply to the dissolution of law partnerships. Accordingly, whenever a partner withdraws from a law firm, the partnership is dissolved.

Many law partnership agreements, however, ignore this seemingly straightforward principle of partnership law. For example, an important model partnership agreement for law practices, the Articles of Partnership,[26] refers to the "withdrawal" of a partner as an act

---

Nevertheless, a few cases support the contention that some partnerships may survive the withdrawal of one or more partners. In addition to the cases cited in the immediately preceding footnote, see Great Hawaiian Financial Corp. v. Aiu, 863 F.2d 617, 620 (9th Cir. 1988) (emphasis in original) ("[E]vidence that managing partners [of a real estate venture] withdrew from the partnership in 1981 indicates that the original partnership including those partners was dissolved as to *those partners*); Adams v. Jarvis, 23 Wis. 2d 453, 458, 127 N.W.2d 400, 403 (1964) (upholding a provision in a medical partnership agreement which provided that withdrawal results in dissolution only as to the withdrawing partners). Again, it is difficult to reconcile the reasoning of these cases with the unequivocal language of the statute.

[24] See Hillman, supra note 172, at 697-707; cf. D. Fessler, Alternatives to Incorporation for Persons in Quest of Profit 152 (2d ed. 1986) ("Make no mistake about it — a partnership cannot technically survive a partner's withdrawal . . . , but a drafting lawyer can serve a client's desire for stability by building in a considerable disincentive to any partner who might later contemplate a withdrawal."

[25] "Partnership" is defined as "an association of two or more persons to carry on as co-owners a business for profit." Unif. Partnership Act §6, 6 U.L.A. at 22. "Business" includes "every trade, occupation, or profession." Id. §2, 6 U.L.A. at 12.

[26] See Articles of Partnership, supra note 170. The model agreements were prepared for the American Bar Association's Standing Committee on Economics of Law Practice and were distributed without charge to members of the ABA. Id. at 3. The authors reviewed the partnership agreements of 124 law firms, id. at 13, and offered their own model partnership agreements for firms of 3 or fewer partners, id. at 15, and for firms of more than 4 partners, id. at 25. The agreement for the latter is the model discussed in this chapter. It is reprinted in 1 West's Legal Forms §10.47, at 408 (P. Lieberman 2d ed. 1981).

Ten years after the authors published the Articles of Partnership, they conducted a second study in anticipation of a revised edition. They concluded the revision was not necessary because most partnership agreements "were found to contain substantially the provisions recommended in the original forms." Id. at 431.

that does *not* cause dissolution of the partnership; under this agreement, only the vote of a substantial number of the partners can accomplish dissolution.[27] Other published form agreements follow a similar pattern.[28] It is likely that these models are influential and that many partnership agreements mirror their provisions.[29]

The inconsistency of contractual antidissolution provisions with partnership law raises an obvious question: why do many law partnerships operate under written agreements that attempt, ineffectually, to accord entity status to their firms by restricting the causes of dissolution? One explanation is that law partners do not know any better. The study of partnership law in law schools has suffered a steady decline during much of this century.[30] Many lawyers probably think of their firms not so much as partnerships but as being

---

[27] The Articles of Partnership define "permanent withdrawal" as a partner's "termination by his voluntary act of all his interest in the partnership." Articles of Partnership, supra note 170, at 30. This withdrawal merely entitles the partner to an account settlement. Id. at 55-59. The authors note that "[t]he more partners in a firm, the less likely it is that dissolution of the firm will be caused by a withdrawal notice." Id. at 56. Separate provisions in the Articles of Partnership specifically address "Termination and Liquidation of Firm," id. at 96-98, which requires a two-thirds vote, id. at 48. In commentary to the provisions dealing with termination, the authors reference "dissolution" rather than "termination." Id. at 98. These terms, however, are not interchangeable. See Unif. Partnership Act §30, 6 U.L.A. at 367.

[28] See, e.g., A. Bromberg, Crane and Bromberg on Partnership app. VI, at 610-612 (1968) (containing continuity provisions suitable for a professional firm, specifying that dissolution is not caused by a withdrawal but also providing that upon withdrawal an individual "shall immediately cease to be a partner"); Law Office Economics and Management Manual §2.0, art. f, at 11-12 (P. Hoffman ed. 1985) (providing that firm may decide by majority vote to dissolve after a partner withdraws).

[29] Authors Carrington and Sutherland offered the following caveat: "None of the forms and suggestions contained in this pamphlet are recommended by the authors." Articles of Partnership, supra note 170 at 5. They also disclaim any "attempt to pass upon the impact of the statutes" of individual states. Id. at 11.

At the time of the Articles of Partnership's publication in 1961, 41 states had adopted the UPA; the UPA has now been adopted in 49. See Unif. Partnership Act, 6 U.L.A. 1 (Supp. 1988). Although the authors may have urged law firms to tailor their agreements to state law, it is possible, indeed likely, that many existing agreements conform closely to the model. See supra note 175.

[30] See Hillman, Private Ordering Within Partnerships, 41 U. Miami L. Rev. 425, 425-432 (1987).

more like corporations, which have entity status and survive the withdrawal of a shareholder. As the size of a firm increases, the temptation to regard it as an entity may become irresistible. Law partners may also misunderstand the meaning of dissolution, which connotes destruction to a far greater degree than partnership law actually requires.[31]

Existing agreements may also reflect confusion of tax law with the substantive law of partnerships.[32] For tax purposes, termination, rather than dissolution, is the critically important event.[33] Moreover, termination under the tax laws is different from termination under the UPA,[34] and a partnership dissolved and terminated under the UPA might not be terminated for tax purposes.[35] Thus, the drafter of a partnership agreement may focus on the tax effects of changes in membership and fail to consider applicable principles of substantive partnership law.

A more plausible explanation for attempts to accord entity status to law firms is the desire of law partners to institutionalize their firms. Although this attitude may not always harmonize with partnership law, it may influence the ways partners view both their firms and their relationships with clients. All of this is harmless enough *if* partners recognize that the legal consequences of a withdrawal are the same as those of a dissolution followed by the continuation of the business by a new partnership. Most importantly,

---

[31] Cf. Webster's Third New International Dictionary of the English Language 657 (1981) (defining "dissolve" as "to cause to disperse or disappear . . . to cause the death of").

[32] For a discussion of the tax aspects of dissolution, see 3 A. Willis, J. Pennell & P. Postlewaite, Partnership Taxation §§131-133 (1988).

[33] See I.R.C. §708 (1982).

[34] Under the UPA, termination occurs at the end of the winding-up period following dissolution. See Unif. Partnership Act §30, 6 U.L.A. at 367. The Internal Revenue Code reflects a more restrictive view and provides that a partnership continues until it is terminated. I.R.C. §708(a) (1982). Termination occurs when the partnership ceases operations entirely or when, within a 12-month period, there is a sale or exchange of 50 percent or more of the total interest in partnership capital or profits. Id. §708(b)(1). Furthermore, if a partnership is divided into two or more partnerships, the code treats the resulting partnerships as continuations of the original partnership. Id. §708(b)(2)(B).

[35] This will often be the case when partnership agreements permit continuation of the business by nondissolving partners.

withdrawal does not discharge the departing partner from the partnership's existing liabilities or those that may arise in connection with the winding up of the partnership.[36] In the case of a law partnership, liabilities that seem trivial upon withdrawal may prove substantial over time.[37] If model agreements published for use by lawyers are any guide, many partnership agreements ignore the prospect of post-dissolution liabilities.[38]

Although agreements drafted along the lines of the Articles of Partnership do not achieve entity status for law firms, they do accomplish the purposes of more traditional continuation agreements. Generally, these agreements (1) preclude a liquidation of assets; (2) foster the impression of partnership continuity;[39] (3) establish a basis for both settling the account of a withdrawing partner and defining relative claims to income generated in the winding up of unfinished business;[40] and (4) provide, in some cases,

---

[36] Unif. Partnership Act §36, 6 U.L.A. at 436; see infra §4.6.

[37] See infra §4.6.

[38] Some continuation agreements include indemnification provisions protecting withdrawing partners. See A. Bromberg, Crane and Bromberg on Partnership §75 at 429 (1968). These may have the unintended effect of encouraging partners to jump ship while it is still floating and leave the remaining partners in a very disadvantageous position.

[39] A continuation agreement eliminates the right the withdrawing partner would otherwise have to compel a liquidation of the partnership's assets. See Unif. Partnership Act §38(1), 6 U.L.A. at 456. The more obvious assets of a law firm, such as the office equipment, leases, and the library, remain the property of the continuing partners. In most cases, the firm name is preserved, possibly along with the goodwill attached to it. All of this reinforces the impression of firm stability and continuity.

[40] Devising a policy for settling the accounts of withdrawing partners presents an intriguing planning problem, and partnership agreements vary widely on this issue. See P. Carrington and P. Sutherland, Articles of Partnership for Law Firms 59 (1961). More liberal withdrawal provisions may apply to retirement, death, or other situations in which the problem of postwithdrawal competition does not exist. Cf. Metaxas, Paying for a Partner's Departure, Natl. L.J., Feb. 17, 1986, at 1, col. 4; 8, col. 3 (quoting a partner's statement that if a partner leaves to go into competition, "we don't give him anything," but that a partner who leaves for a noncompetitive position will get some compensation, although less than that which would be paid upon retirement). Generous treatment of withdrawing partners may serve as an incentive for a partner to leave and, in the process, grab clients. Cf. id. (quoting a well-known management consultant who stated that "[t]here have been firms around who [in effect] pay . . . partners to take clients away. . . . The more lateral moves there are, the more adamant I am that they shouldn't pay people to do

guidelines for dividing a firm's clients.[41] The provisions concerning division of clients are, of course, subordinate to the freedom accorded clients to choose their lawyers. Although continuation agreements may obliquely attempt to restrict this freedom by including provisions concerning "custody" of client files, that custody changes at the direction of the clients.[42] Thus, the issues that lawyers might like to address most in continuation agreements — control of clients and departing partners' attempts to grab them — are inappropriate subjects for private ordering among partners.

§4.2.3 Fixed Term Law Partnerships: An Alternative to Restrictive Covenants?

Contrary to the assumptions of many lawyers, an agreement that a partnership continue until a majority of partners vote to dissolve does not establish a fixed term partnership.[43] Few, if any, law partnerships operate under a partnership agreement calling for a fixed term specified by a number of years. The unwillingness of lawyers to contract for fixed terms in their partnerships is curious,

---

this"). Harsh treatment, on the other hand, may discourage withdrawals, especially by those partners "that have passed their prime." This, in turn, may lead to acrimony and increase the possibility that more productive lawyers will grab clients and leave.

[41] For examples of possible guidelines, see Articles of Partnership, supra, at 58-59.

[42] See supra §2.3. With respect to matters that are not unfinished business of the partnership, one commentator has observed:

> Attempting to resolve the issue by referring to clients as "files" and debating which lawyer "owns," or to which lawyer a client "belongs" obscures and distorts the client-lawyer relationship. The compelling fact is that the client-lawyer relationship is personal; clients should accordingly have a free choice of counsel. The best way to accommodate interests that pull in sometimes conflicting directions is to permit clients to make their own choice. . . .

C. Wolfram, Modern Legal Ethics §16.2.3 at 888 (1986) (footnotes omitted).

[43] Cf. Meehan v. Shaughnessy, 404 Mass. 419, 433, 535 N.E.2d 1255, 1263 n.12 (1989) ("The partnership agreement, although providing that the firm 'shall continue indefinitely,' required that a partner who leaves to continue practicing elsewhere give three-months' advance notice. This, therefore, may not have been a purely 'at will' partnership which a partner has a right to dissolve at any time without triggering the remedies of [the UPA].").

for the establishment of a term for a business venture is a common device of business planning outside of the legal profession.[44]

The principal consequence of establishing a fixed term law partnership is that a partner wrongfully leaving the partnership prior to the expiration of the term is liable to the other partners for damages resulting from the premature withdrawal.[45] Typically, however, the nonbreaching partners are unable to recover their true economic losses following a premature withdrawal because of the reluctance of courts to award damages that are speculative in nature.[46] In the case of a law partnership, on the other hand, damages at least for the short term should be ascertainable when the withdrawing partner successfully grabs clients and shifts income from one firm to another.

To the extent that income is generated from the completion of business unfinished at the time of the withdrawal, the partnership from which the lawyer withdrew has a claim to the income. Classifying work of an ongoing, noncontingent-fee character as unfinished business of a law firm, however, is problematic.[47] In the case of a fixed term partnership, the characterization of work as "unfinished" is irrelevant, for the inquiry is directed to the damages suffered by the firm as a result of the premature and wrongful withdrawal of a partner.

Would the award of damages for the premature withdrawal from a fixed term law partnership conflict with the principle of client choice and, like covenants not to compete, compromise established norms of legal ethics emphasizing the importance of client choice?[48] There is something of a distinction. Damages from breach of a fixed term partnership are not contingent upon the successful grab of a client by the departing lawyer; if the firm loses the client as a result of the lawyer's departure, it suffers damage without regard to whether

---

[44] See generally A. Bromberg and L. Ribstein, Bromberg and Ribstein on Partnership §7.03 (1988); Hillman, The Dissatisfied Participant in the Solvent Business Venture: A Consideration of the Relative Permanence of Partnerships and Close Corporations, 67 Minn. L. Rev. 1, 9-33 (1982).

[45] See Unif. Partnership Act §38(2)(a).

[46] Gherman v. Colburn, 72 Cal. App. 3d 544, 561-565, 140 Cal. Rptr. 330, 341-343 (1977), offers one of the more complete discussions of damages arising from a wrongful dissolution. The partnership involved was not a law firm.

[47] See infra §4.4.3.

[48] See supra §2.3.1.

the lawyer continues to represent the client. Awarding damages from breach of a fixed term partnership agreement and enforcement of a restrictive covenant have the same result, however, in that both serve as disincentives to the continuing representation of a client by a lawyer changing firms. Each affects client choice, and the fate of one is likely to be shared by the other.

§4.3 Winding Up a Law Partnership

A partnership does not terminate upon dissolution, but instead enters the winding-up phase.[1] During this period, the partners complete the business of the partnership, liquidate the assets, settle the liabilities, and distribute any residual amounts among themselves.[2] Liabilities incurred in connection with winding up are the responsibilities of the original partners.[3] When the partnership continues its business and avoids liquidation, winding up and continuation occur simultaneously; the work of the original partnership is completed as the work of the new partnership continues.[4] Completion of the winding-up process terminates the original partnership.[5]

Winding up a law partnership may prove traumatic or smooth. In the case of firm destruction and disbandment, the process can be painful. Partners may disperse, grab clients, and attempt to salvage as much of their practices as possible.[6] A receiver may be appointed,

---

§4.3 [1] Unif. Partnership Act §30, 6 U.L.A. 367 (1969) (stating, "[o]n dissolution the partnership is not terminated, but continues until the winding up of partnership affairs is completed").

[2] See id. §40, 6 U.L.A. at 468 (providing rules for settling partners' accounts after dissolution).

[3] See id. §36, 6 U.L.A. at 463.

[4] See id. §41, 6 U.L.A. at 509.

[5] See id. §30, 6 U.L.A. at 367.

[6] See, e.g., Stille, The Fall of the House of Herrick, Natl. L.J., Feb. 24, 1986, at 6, col. 1 (describing the dissolution of a Boston law firm and the ability of partners to transfer their practices to new firms); Weingarten, Breaking Up: Requiem for a Heavyweight Law Firm, Natl. L.J., June 1, 1981, at 1, col. 2 (describing the breakup of a New York firm riddled with open dissension before the partners departed with their clients).

but a receiver of a disbanded partnership may face special difficulties in collecting the firm's accounts receivable.[7] Malpractice claims may arise if the firm's pre-dissolution decline made it more difficult for its attorneys to render services of a professional quality.[8] Liabilities may both increase in amount and accelerate in timing as the firm falls into default under such major obligations as its office leases and bank loans.[9] When the process is complete, the partners of the dissolved firm may discover one of the disadvantages of the partnership form of organization — their personal liability when the assets of the partnership are insufficient to satisfy claims.[10]

A more common and less dramatic occurrence is the creation of a successor partnership that will continue the business of the original firm.[11] This occurs when a partner "withdraws" under an agreement permitting continuation of the firm practice by the other partners.[12] Although the remaining partners might like to think otherwise, withdrawal does not eliminate the need to wind up the affairs of the original partnership. Winding up is an essential process, because a partner's withdrawal does not in and of itself terminate the obligations of the firm, its continuing members, or the departing partner.[13]

The winding up of a professional association such as a law firm often will differ markedly from the winding up of the typical busi-

---

[7] See Cox, A "Lifeboat" for Firms Going Under, Natl. L.J., Sept. 5, 1988, at 8, col. 1.

[8] Cf. Jensen, Now, the Unanswered Questions, Natl. L.J., Feb. 8, 1988, at 46, col. 2 (noting that an associate of a large dissolved law firm had filed suit alleging in part that the firm had engaged in unethical conduct to promote profit maximization immediately prior to the dissolution).

[9] See, e.g., Finley Kumble Sued by 4 Banks Over Loan Defaults, Wall St. J., Feb. 18, 1988, at 6, col. 4 (reporting on an $83 million law suit against a dissolved partnership).

[10] Liability is joint and several for tort and breach of trust claims, and joint for all other claims. See Unif. Partnership Act §§13-15, 6 U.L.A. 163, 173-174 (1969).

[11] A series of such actions may lead ultimately to the demise of the original "firm."

[12] See supra §4.2.

[13] Unif. Partnership Act §30, 6 U.L.A. at 367.

ness partnership.[14] Concluding the work of a law partnership may take years, particularly if the remaining partners maintain the appearance of a continuing firm. This is especially true with respect to litigation matters. Consider, for example, a firm retained to represent a plaintiff in a tort action. Several years may elapse before trial, and several more years may pass before the firm's client asserts any possible malpractice claims. Yet if the withdrawal of a partner forces dissolution shortly after the firm takes on the case, the work that the firm's attorneys must perform on the case after dissolution represents part of the winding up of the original partnership.[15]

Business partnerships normally wind up through the efforts of the partners operating within the governing framework of their partnership.[16] Although each partner is entitled to participate in winding up,[17] no partner is entitled to compensation for winding-up services.[18] These rules reflect an assumption that all partners will participate in winding up. Law partnerships, however, may vary substantially from this norm. When law partners withdraw, they leave the firm[19] in both a spiritual *and* physical sense. The departed

---

[14] For a further discussion of the differences, see Comment, Barefoot Shoe-makers: An Uncompromising Approach to Policing the Morals of the Marketplace When Law Firms Split Up, 19 Ariz. St. L.J. 509, 514-517 (1987); Winding Up Dissolved Law Partnerships: The No-Compensation Rule and Client Choice, 73 Calif. L. Rev. 1597, 1611-1615 (1985).

[15] See, e.g., Redman v. Walters, 88 Cal. App. 3d 448, 453, 152 Cal. Rptr. 42, 45 (1979) (illustrating that acceptance of a case shortly before dissolution may significantly prolong the life of a partnership).

[16] Dissolution terminates the authority of partners to act for the partnership except as may be necessary to wind up its affairs and complete unfinished business. See Unif. Partnership Act §33, 6 U.L.A. at 423-424.

[17] See id. §37, 6 U.L.A. at 423. A partner wrongfully causing a dissolution does not have the right to participate in winding up. Furthermore, a court may administer the winding-up process if cause is shown. Id.

[18] Id. §18(f), 6 U.L.A. at 213. Because burdens are not shared equally, an exception to the no-compensation rule exists for surviving partners who wind up a partnership dissolved by the death of a partner. See id.

[19] Many law partnership agreements require notice in advance of withdrawal. See Articles of Partnership, supra, at 55-56. One purpose of such a provision is to permit, loosely speaking, a winding-up period running from the data of notice to the date of withdrawal. For partnership law purposes, however, winding up commences on the date of dissolution. See Unif. Partnership Act §29 comment, 6 U.L.A. at 364-365.

partner has little contact with other partners, and the opportunity
for cross-supervision of work is minimal. Often, the partners divide
the client "files," and the withdrawing lawyer and the firm seemingly
go their separate ways.[20]

Two aspects of a law firm's winding up require special attention. The first is the allocation of income generated from the
winding-up process. The second is the relative responsibilities of
lawyers for liabilities arising after dissolution.

§4.4 Winding-Up Income

The critical premise underlying the UPA's winding-up rules is that a
partner's claim to income does not terminate upon the date of
dissolution. The partnership continues as originally composed until
it completes the winding-up process, and, absent a contrary agreement among the partners, all partners have an interest in income
from the completion of the partnership's unfinished business.[1] Although some partners may bear disproportionate burdens in winding up a firm's affairs, partnership law does not allocate them a
greater share of income for their efforts.[2] Despite dissolution, partnership law's emphasis on the viability of the partnership for pur-

---

[20] See Hazard, Ethical Considerations in Withdrawal, Expulsion, and Retirement, in Withdrawal, Retirement and Disputes: What You and Your Firm Need to
Know 32, 35 (E. Berger ed. 1986).

§4.4 [1] See Unif. Partnership Act §38, 6 U.L.A. at 456.

[2] See id. §18(f), 6 U.L.A. at 213. See generally Comment, Winding Up
Dissolved Law Partnerships: The No-Compensation Rule and Client Choice, 73
Calif. L. Rev. 1597, 1606-1610 (1985) (discussing the no-compensation rule in
the context of law partnerships). The compensation issue has been the subject of
much litigation. With rare exceptions, courts have applied the UPA's no-
compensation principle to professional partnerships. See, e.g., Jewel v. Boxer, 156
Cal. App. 3d 171, 177-180, 203 Cal. Rptr. 13, 17-19 (1984); Rosenfeld, Meyer &
Susman v. Cohen, 146 Cal. App. 3d 200, 216-220, 194 Cal. Rptr. 180, 189-192
(1983); Frates v. Nichols, 167 So. 2d 77, 80-81 (Fla. Dist. Ct. App. 1964). But see
Cofer v. Hearne, 459 S.W.2d 877, 880 (Tex. Civ. App. — Austin 1970, writ ref'd

poses of finishing up existing business may serve to restrain grabbing and leaving by some law partners.

§4.4.1 Legal Ethics and the Sharing of Post-dissolution Income

There is a certain tension between the sharing of winding-up income mandated by partnership law and the general proscription against fee splitting in the rules of legal ethics. Because anticipated fees may create powerful incentives for lawyers that are inconsistent with their clients' best interests, the codes of legal ethics sharply limit the ability of lawyers to split fees.[3] Lawyers within the same firm, of course, may share fees. For other lawyers, the factors of joint repre-

---

n.r.e.) ("We cannot bring ourselves to the voluntary acceptance of a rule which, in our opinion, is unconscionable and inequitable."); Comment, Winding Up, supra note 3, at 1619-1642 (evaluating alternatives to the no-compensation rule); Comment, Dissolution of a Law Partnership — Goodwill, Winding Up Profits, & Additional Compensation, 6 J. Legal Prof. 277, 284-291 (1981) [hereinafter Comment, Dissolution of a Law Partnership] (arguing that winding-up activities merit additional compensation).

Courts are divided on the issue of whether the allocation of winding-up income may be adjusted to reflect overhead expenses. See, e.g., *Jewel,* 156 Cal. App. 3d at 180-181, 203 Cal. Rptr. at 19-20 (allowing reimbursement of overhead expenses); Hawkesworth v. Ponzoli, 388 So. 2d 299, 301 (Fla. Dist. Ct. App. 1980) (denying reimbursement because of the rule against extra compensation).

Some public policy considerations, outlined in Jewel v. Boxer, support application of the no-compensation rule to law partnerships:

> The rule prevents partners from competing for the most remunerative cases during the life of the partnership in anticipation that they might retain those cases should the partnership dissolve. It also discourages former partners from scrambling to take physical possession of files and seeking personal gain by soliciting a firm's existing clients upon dissolution.

Jewel, 156 Cal. App. 3d at 179, 203 Cal. Rptr. at 18.

[3] See generally C. Wolfram, Modern Legal Ethics §9.2.4 at 510-512 (1986) (discussing fee-splitting rules under the Model Code, the Model Rules, and the Canons); Terry, Ethical Pitfalls and Malpractice Consequences of Law Firm Breakups, 61 Temp. L. Rev. 1055, 1082-1092 (1988). Most fee splitting involves the payment of referral fees. See, e.g., *Jewel,* 156 Cal. App. 3d at 175, 203 Cal. Rptr. at 16; Ellerby v. Spiezer, 138 Ill. App. 3d 77, 79, 485 N.E.2d 413, 415 (1985); Resnick v. Kaplan, 49 Md. App. 499, 502, 434 A.2d 582, 585 (1981); Smith v. Daub, 219 Neb. 698, 699, 365 N.W.2d 816, 818 (1985).

sentation, shared responsibilities, and client consent are important in determining whether fee splitting is permissible.[4]

Partnership law disregards such considerations and the disincentives to the optimal handling of winding-up business that may arise because of required income sharing. Adherence to the fiction of a continuing partnership during the winding-up period avoids a direct clash between partnership law and legal ethics. The fiction of the continuing partnership sanctifies what might otherwise be impermissible fee splitting, even though the files are divided and the lawyers are in separate firms.[5]

§4.4.2   Good Faith, Dissolution, and Winding Up

Ethical considerations aside, the principles underlying the UPA's dissolution and winding-up provisions are straightforward: any partner has the power to dissolve the existing relationship and cause the partnership to enter the winding-up process. Some courts, however, have read into the partner's obligations a duty to dissolve a partnership only in good faith. Subjecting a partner's *decision* to dissolve a partnership to a good faith standard renders the conse-

---

[4] See Model Code, DR 2-107(A) (permitting the sharing of fees with lawyers not in the same firm only if (1) the client consents after full disclosure, (2) the division of fees is proportionate to the services performed and the responsibility assumed by each lawyer, and (3) the total fees are not unreasonable); Model Rules, Rule 1.5(e) (permitting a division of fees by lawyers who are not in the same firm only if (1) the division is proportionate to services performed by the lawyers or, with the written consent of the client, each lawyer assumes joint responsibility, (2) the client is advised of the participation of all lawyers and does not object, and (3) the fees are reasonable). But cf. Model Code, DR 2-107(B) (permitting payments to a former partner or associate under a separation agreement).

[5] Cf. *Ellerby*, 138 Ill. App. 3d at 82, 485 N.E.2d at 416 (noting that it is proper for partners to share their fees because the partnership continues until its business is wound up). But cf. Champion v. Superior Court, 201 Cal. App.3d 777, 247 Cal. Rptr. 624, 627 (1988) ("An agreement to share fees in unfinished cases is not per se unconscionable. But the way in which this agreement shares the fees is unconscionable. A fee of this size, without any relationship to services rendered, must 'shock the conscience of lawyers of ordinary prudence practicing' in the community."); In re Silverberg, 75 A.D.2d 817, 427 N.Y.S.2d 817 (1980) (partnership agreement requiring a partner who left and took the client of another partner to remit 80 percent of the billings void as against public policy).

quences of dissolution uncertain and may thereby retard grabbing and leaving.

Partnerships may be either terminable at will or formed for a specified term or undertaking. Law partnerships are almost always the former,[6] and although the partnership agreement may attempt to control the consequences of a withdrawal, it cannot preclude withdrawal and bind partners to their firm. Consequently, partners are free to seek better opportunities. This would suggest that the relevance of good faith in the case of a law partnership is limited to a partner's compliance with the UPA's winding-up provisions. In winding-up activities, for example, the withdrawing partner is accountable to the other partners as a fiduciary,[7] and a misappropriation of partnership income is actionable. Post-dissolution income not attributable to winding up, on the other hand, is not income of the original partnership. The UPA thus reduces the principal problem to a relatively straightforward evaluation of whether income is attributable to the winding up of the original partnership.

§4.4.2.1 Good Faith Generally

Applying a good faith analysis not only to the dissolving partner's adherence to the rules of dissolution and winding up but also to the *decision* to dissolve adds unnecessary complications and uncertainties to partnership dissolutions. This development is exemplified by a string of California cases, the most recent of which involved a law partnership. Indeed, it is in the area of law firm dissolutions that the doctrine of good faith dissolution may have the most profound implications.

The source of the good faith doctrine is Page v. Page,[8] a

---

[6] See supra §4.2.3.

[7] Unif. Partnership Act §21(1), 6 U.L.A. 258 (1969).

[8] 55 Cal. 2d 192, 359 P.2d 41, 10 Cal. Rptr. 643 (1961). *Page* is also discussed in Hillman, The Dissatisfied Participant in the Solvent Business Venture: A Consideration of the Relative Permanence of Partnerships and Close Corporations, 67 Minn. L. Rev. 1, 26-35 (1982). For a more sympathetic reading of the opinion, see Comment, Barefoot Shoemakers: An Uncompromising Approach to Policing the Morals of the Marketplace When Law Firms Split Up, 19 Ariz. St. L.J. 509, 511-512 (1987).

frequently cited opinion of the California Supreme Court. In *Page*, one of two partners in a linen supply business sought a declaratory judgment concerning his right to dissolve the partnership after he realized that the venture's future success did not require the other partner's continued participation.[9] The lower court held that the partnership had been established for a fixed term and that a dissolution prior to the term's expiration would be wrongful.[10] The California Supreme Court overturned the lower court's finding of a fixed term for the partnership, concluding that the partnership was terminable at will.[11] The court added, however, that partnership law precludes bad faith dissolutions of even terminable-at-will partnerships:

> [P]laintiff has power to dissolve the [fixed-term] partnership by express notice to the defendant. If, however, it is proved that plaintiff acted in bad faith and violated his fiduciary duties by attempting to appropriate to his own use the new prosperity of the partnership without adequate compensation to his co-partner, the dissolution would be wrongful and the plaintiff would be liable . . . for violation of the implied agreement not to exclude defendant wrongfully from the partnership business opportunity.[12]

The problem with applying this approach to terminable-at-will partnerships is that it means either too much or nothing. *Page* means too much if it grants partners a life annuity funded by claims on all future income of other partners. It means nothing if it merely reaffirms that income generated during the winding-up period belongs to the partnership rather than to the partner who generates it. If there is a middle ground between these two extremes, the court did little to define it.

A second California Supreme Court decision affirmed the *Page* bad faith concerns without clarifying them. In Leff v. Gunter,[13] the

---

[9] *Page*, 55 Cal. 2d at 193, 359 P.2d at 42, 10 Cal. Rptr. at 644.
[10] Id.
[11] Id. at 194-196, 359 P.2d at 43-44, 10 Cal. Rptr. at 645.
[12] Id. at 197-198, 359 P.2d at 45, 10 Cal. Rptr. at 647.
[13] 33 Cal. 3d 508, 658 P.2d 740, 189 Cal. Rptr. 377 (1983).

parties formed a joint venture to bid on a construction project. Some of the participants subsequently withdrew from the venture and secretly submitted a bid on the project; they were eventually awarded the contract. These events prompted a suit by one of the original joint venturers alleging, in part, that the secret bidding represented unfair competition and a breach of fiduciary duties between the joint venture parties.[14] Citing *Page,* the California Supreme Court agreed:

> There is an obvious and essential unfairness in one partner's attempted exploitation of a partnership opportunity for his own personal benefit and to the resulting detriment of his copartners. . . . It is no less a violation of the trust imposed between partners to permit the personal exploitation of that partnership information and opportunity to the prejudice of one's former associates by the simple expedient of withdrawal from the partnership.[15]

This type of analysis has a certain breast-thumping quality. However satisfying it may be to moralize concerning partners' fiduciary duties, a vague application of such standards to partners' activities is neither realistic nor workable. Partnership law does not, and should not, preclude all attempts by a partner to pursue private advantage at the expense of other partners; such a rule would sharply limit or completely curtail partners' attempts to renegotiate terminable-at-will partnership agreements.[16] The premature termination of the partnership and the defendants' secret dealings *did*

---

[14] Id. at 513, 658 P.2d at 743, 189 Cal. Rptr. at 380.

[15] Id. at 514, 658 P.2d at 744, 189 Cal. Rptr. at 381.

[16] For a discussion of renegotiating existing partnership agreements, see Hillman, Private Ordering Within Partnerships, 41 U. Miami L. Rev. 425, 443-444 (1987). Professor Rosen has noted that:

> An important implication is that at-will contracts are not unilateral. Rather, they are inherently bilateral and have important partnership elements. For example, the arrival of a better offer for one party signals a need for negotiation and recontracting so that the previous terms can be modified (including possible abandonment of the relationship).

Rosen, Commentary: In Defense of the Contract at Will, 51 U. Chi. L. Rev. 983, 984 (1984).

constitute actionable wrongs in *Leff*,[17] but the court's reiteration of *Page's* fiduciary rhetoric greatly exaggerated the degree to which a standard of good faith can regulate partnership dissolutions.

§4.4.2.2 Good Faith and the Dissolution of Law Partnerships

Page and *Leff* have obvious implications for the dissolution of law firms, and it was only a matter of time before courts applied the cases in this context. In Rosenfeld, Meyer & Susman v. Cohen ("*RMS I*"),[18] a 19-partner law firm represented a plaintiff, Rectifier, in a major patent antitrust action. The firm (RMS) was to be compensated largely on a contingent-fee basis.[19] The heavy workload created by the case required the firm to rent additional space and increase its office staff. Two of the firm's senior partners, *C* and *R*, provided most of the services to the client. Over a five-year period, *C* and *R* spent more than 19 thousand hours on the case.[20]

After *C* and *R* concluded that the case would settle for at least 20 million dollars and, if tried, result in a judgment of 100 million dollars before trebling, they demanded a renegotiation of the partnership agreement to increase their share of income resulting from the antitrust litigation. When their attempts proved unsuccessful, *C* and *R* dissolved the partnership and formed a new firm. The departing attorneys retained the antitrust litigation under an agreement with Rectifier that reduced the contingent fee percentage, but, because they were now practicing alone, substantially increased the amount they would receive in fees. The case settled the following year for 33 million dollars.[21]

Drawing heavily from *Page* and *Leff*, the court concluded (1) that partners do not have the right to dissolve a terminable-at-will law partnership in bad faith and (2) that because the Rectifier litigation represented unfinished business of the original law firm,

---

[17] See Unif. Partnership Act §38(2)(b), 6 U.L.A. 456 (1969).

[18] 146 Cal. App. 3d 200, 194 Cal. Rptr. 180 (1983) [hereinafter *RMS I*].

[19] The client agreed to pay limited fees during the prosecution of the case, not to exceed one-third of the recovery. Id. at 209, 194 Cal. Rptr. at 185-186.

[20] Id. at 209, 194 Cal. Rptr. at 184. During this period, *C* and *R* received approximately $800,000 in income from the partnership. Id. at 209, 194 Cal. Rptr. at 185.

[21] Id. at 208-211, 194 Cal. Rptr. at 184-187.

the fees generated were attributable to the winding up of the firm.[22] As to good faith, the court recognized an

> established principle that even nonfiduciaries must exercise their rights in good faith, deal fairly with each other and refrain from injuring the right of another party to receive the benefits of an agreement or relationship. . . . Moreover, the law and motion department's ruling that as a matter of law a partner has the absolute right to dissolve a partnership at will without regard to breach of fiduciary consequences is contrary to the principle that a person may be estopped from exercising rights in bad faith.[23]

Three important implications follow from the court's good faith analysis: (1) existing clients represent income expectancies of

---

[22] The court gave additional impetus to the theory that grabbing and leaving may give rise to relief in tort for interference with contractual relations. See supra §3.1. The appellate court held that the trial department erred when it limited the firm's proof of interference to the communications by *C* and *R* to Rectifier that they were indispensable to the case and that the firm could not handle the matter adequately. *RMS I,* 146 Cal. App. 3d at 223, 194 Cal. Rptr. at 194. The court reasoned that the firm should have been permitted to prove interference in ways other than those specified by the trial department. Id. Moreover, the court reversed the ruling of the trial department and indicated that the firm could assert a cause of action based upon Rectifier's conspiracy to interfere with its own terminable-at-will contract with the firm. Id. at 227, 194 Cal. Rptr. at 197. The firm, however, ultimately did not prevail on its interference with contract claims.

[23] *RMS I,* 146 Cal. App. 3d at 215, 194 Cal. Rptr. at 188. Some commentators have applauded this reasoning with respect to good faith as consistent with general trends in modern contract law. See Feldman & Berkheiser, Dissolution: Good Faith, Bad Faith — Who Gets the Fee?, in Withdrawal, Retirement & Disputes: What You and Your Firm Need to Know 24, 28 (E. Berger ed. 1986). It is generally accepted that there is a duty of good faith and fair dealing in the performance and enforcement of contracts. See Restatement (Second) of Contracts §205 (1979). There is less acceptance, however, of the meaning of this duty as applied to the termination of at-will contracts. Some courts have found a good faith standard applicable to the discharge of employees and in obligations under insurance contracts, but a principal justification for these conclusions is that the parties possess inherently unequal bargaining power. See, e.g., Noble v. National Am. Life Ins. Co., 128 Ariz. 188, 189, 624 P.2d 866, 867 (1981) (recognizing an implied covenant of good faith in insurance contracts); Cleary v. American Airlines, Inc., 111 Cal. App. 3d 443, 453, 168 Cal. Rptr. 722, 727-728 (1980) (imposing a good faith standard on an employer when it discharges its employees). Similarly, the termination of automobile dealer franchises is subject to a good faith standard. See 15 U.S.C. §1222 (1982). To suggest, however, that *RMS I* is consistent with general trends in modern contract law is to exaggerate existing applications of a good faith standard to terminable-at-will relationships.

the partnership;[24] (2) it is improper to pursue private advantage vis-à-vis other partners by using the threat of withdrawal to renegotiate the division of income;[25] and (3) an actual withdrawal is not in good faith, and therefore open to challenge, if it results in the transfer of clients from the original firm to the firm of the withdrawing partner. What this doctrine adds to the more settled winding-up provisions of partnership law is unclear.[26]

If *RMS I* stood alone, the opinion might be dismissed as an eccentric but not unusual exaggeration of fiduciary principles.[27] Indeed, the subsequent litigation in the case illustrates the disparity between stating and applying rigid norms of conduct.[28] With the backdrop of *Page* and *Leff,* however, the principles enunciated in the decision create a cloud obscuring the ability of some partners to withdraw from firms and take clients with them. The dictum in *Page* that a "partner may not dissolve a partnership to gain the benefits of the business for himself, *unless he fully compensates his co-partner for his*

---

[24] The court described the maneuvers of C and R as leading to the "defeat [of] the reasonable expectations" of the other partners. *RMS I,* 146 Cal. App. 3d at 215, 194 Cal. Rptr. at 189. This is undoubtedly true, but would the expectations analysis extend to client matters not in progress at the time of dissolution?

[25] "In the instant case [the firm] sought to prove that [C and R] used their threat to resign and cause [the firm] a large loss as a weapon to attempt to change the partnership relationships at the expense of other . . . partners." Id. at 214, 194 Cal. Rptr. at 188.

[26] For a recent decision implicitly limiting *RMS I* by emphasizing the unfinished business, rather than good faith, analysis in the earlier opinion, see Fraser v. Bogucki, 203 Cal. App. 3d 604, 250 Cal. Rptr. 41, 45-46 (1988).

[27] See Hillman, Private Ordering Within Partnerships, 41 U. Miami L. Rev. 425, 454-471 (discussing the restraints on partnership renegotiation created by partners' fiduciary responsibilities). For an argument favoring strict application of fiduciary standards to lawyers in their dealings with each other, see Comment, Barefoot Shoemakers: An Uncompromising Approach to Policing the Morals of the Marketplace When Law Firms Split Up, 19 Ariz. St. L.J. 509, 541-542 (1987).

[28] The trial court had decided the issues on appeal in *RMS I* largely before trial, and the reversal was based upon conclusions that it had erroneously granted motions for partial summary judgment, judgment on the pleadings, and nonsuit. A cross-complaint by C and R had requested an accounting for certain unfinished business and damages for fraud based upon the concealment of profits. The RMS complaint and the C and R cross-complaint had been severed for separate trials, and the *RMS I* appeal involved only the former.

The C and R cross-complaint was tried while the appeal was pending, and it resulted in adjudications that C and R were entitled to share in winding-up income generated by RMS and that the firm's name partners were liable for fraud. Rosenfeld, Meyer & Susman v. Cohen, 191 Cal. App. 3d 1035, 1048, 237 Cal. Rptr. 14,

share of the prospective business opportunity[29] assumes immense significance if applied as a principle regulating the relationship between law partners.[30] By adding the gloss that fiduciary responsibilities, in the form of a good faith standard, restrain the decision to dissolve a terminable-at-will law partnership, the court in *RMS I* added to the mischief of *Page* and *Leff* in ways that it probably never imagined, invited litigation in connection with partnership dissolutions, and laid the foundation for chaotic development of dissolution principles as applied to professional associations.[31]

---

21 (1987) [hereinafter *RMS II*]. The firm and its name partners appealed that judgment, and *C* and *R* cross-appealed the lower court's allowance of deductions against gross winding-up proceeds and the denial of prejudgment interest. Id. at 1048, 1057, 237 Cal. Rptr. at 21, 27.

Not surprisingly, the parties presented a number of issues in the second appeal. The most relevant aspect of the appellate opinion for purposes of determining the constraints on grabbing and leaving is the court's holding that the trial judgment on the *C* and *R* cross-complaint would collaterally estop the firm from pursuing certain issues in its complaint. In short, the court upheld the application of the findings that *C* and *R* neither dissolved the firm in bad faith nor improperly interfered with the firm's contractual relationships. Id. at 1057-1063, 237 Cal. Rptr. at 27-30. The court correctly declined, however, to repudiate *RMS I*'s treatment of the Rectifier settlement as unfinished business of the firm. Id. at 1063, 237 Cal. Rptr. at 31.

[29] Page v. Page, 55 Cal. 2d 192, 197, 359 P.2d 41, 44, 10 Cal. Rptr. 643, 646 (1961) (emphasis added).

[30] The *RMS I* court undermined this dictum. See *RMS I*, 146 Cal. App. 3d at 220, 194 Cal. Rptr. at 192 (stating that although a partner may not seize business in existence at the time of dissolution, he "may take for his own account *new business* even when emanating from the dissolved partnership" (emphasis added)).

[31] Some commentators, however, ardently support the decisions: "Application of the good faith rule removes the financial incentives which might impel some lawyers to enter into a war with their firm, in the hope of winning the battle of the files." Feldman & Berkheiser, Dissolution: Good Faith, Bad Faith — Who Gets the Fee?, in Withdrawal, Retirement & Disputes: What You and Your Firm Need to Know 24, 29 (E. Berger ed. 1986); see also Comment, Barefoot Shoemakers: An Uncompromising Approach to Policing the Morals of the Marketplace When Law Firms Split Up, 19 Ariz. St. L.J. 509, 525 (1987) (applauding application of fiduciary principles as a standard higher than good faith); Comment, Winding Up Dissolved Law Partnerships: The No-Compensation Rule and Client Choice, 73 Calif. L. Rev. 1597, 1640 (1985) (supporting a good faith standard but arguing that the burden of proving bad faith should be on the nondissolving partners). It has been argued that the rule prevents client abuse and advances public policy. Feldman & Berkheiser, supra, at 28-29. But the client in *RMS I* was hardly abused. Indeed, Rectifier eventually negotiated a more favorable fee arrangement with *C* and *R*. *RMS I*, 146 Cal. App. 3d at 210, 194 Cal. Rptr. at 185.

§4.4.3 Pruning Clients

RMS I concerned the seemingly simple case of defining relative interests in a contingent fee. The court found a continuing partnership for purposes of allocating income from what it regarded as the firm's unfinished business.[32] Unlike the court's good faith analysis, this aspect of the opinion reflects a rather straightforward application of partnership law's winding-up principles.[33]

The UPA's winding-up principles place restraints on grabbing that may vary dramatically in effectiveness depending on the law practice involved. Consider, for example, a pattern common in the world of grabbing and leaving. The *XYZ* firm has grown steadily in size. Recognizing the need for a diverse practice, the firm allocates resources to the development of both a litigation and a business law practice. Partners *A* and *B* have specialized in providing general counseling services to corporations, and this element of the practice is proving more profitable to the firm than the litigation practice. *A* and *B* have excellent relationships with the corporate clients, so much so that they now decide to leave the partnership and establish their own firm. Not surprisingly, they do not regard fees for the services performed after their withdrawals as income from the winding up of the *XYZ* partnership.

Presumably, income generated by the *AB* partnership is not attributable to the "unfinished business" of *XYZ*. This case is arguably distinguishable from *RMS I,* because the representation of corporate clients has no clear point of termination and because *A* and *B* presumably are directly compensated by clients only for services performed after their withdrawal from the firm. Yet the purpose behind the withdrawal and establishment of a new firm may well be to avoid sharing with the original partners the very "new prosperity" *XYZ* worked so hard to create. In a real sense, *A* and *B* were free

---

[32] *RMS I,* 146 Cal. App. 3d at 219, 194 Cal. Rptr. at 191-192.

[33] Many state courts apply the same approach. See, e.g., Jewel v. Boxer, 156 Cal. App. 3d 171, 179-181, 203 Cal. Rptr. 13, 18-20 (1984) (involving mostly contingent fee cases); Ellerby v. Spiezer, 138 Ill. App. 3d 77, 81-82, 485 N.E.2d 413, 416-417 (1985) (involving contingent fees); Resnick v. Kaplan, 49 Md. App. 499, 507-509, 434 A.2d 582, 587-588 (1981) (same); Smith v. Daub, 219 Neb. 698, 703-705, 365 N.W.2d 816, 820-821 (1985) (same).

riders, and, in an even more real sense, good faith inquiries into their motivations for withdrawal are unlikely to provide a check on their grabbing.

All of this means that certain types of clients are more attractive targets of grabbing. Clients who offer discrete projects requiring substantial legal services over an extended period of time are less "valuable" to control than clients with business that departing partners might more easily label "new" at any point. Not only are the former less likely to offer repeat business for their lawyers, but also the need to share fees paid upon the completion of their projects lessens or eliminates the benefits of grabbing this type of client. On dissolution, partners may even attempt to shirk responsibility for substantial unfinished business matters because of the absence of an economic incentive to complete the cases.[34] Moreover, the required sharing of fees may serve as a disincentive to the optimal handling of winding-up business,[35] a problem that is aggravated when burdens are not shared equally.[36]

Even without regard to disparate treatment of various kinds of cases, there are problems in treating law firms, and perhaps many

---

[34] See Comment, Winding Up Dissolved Law Partnerships: The No-Compensation Rule and Client Choice, 73 Calif. L. Rev. 1597, 1599-1600 (1985) (noting that because of the no-compensation rule in partnership dissolution law, attorneys may be unwilling or unable to complete previous client representation).

[35] It is admittedly dangerous to generalize on this point. Some attorneys are motivated largely by economic reward. Others, however, regard pride of accomplishment as of equal or greater importance.

[36] Compare Fox v. Abrams, 163 Cal. App. 3d 610, 616, 210 Cal. Rptr. 260, 265 (1985) ("On balance, the allocation of fees according to each partner's interest in the former partnership should not work an undue hardship as to any partner where each partner completes work on the partnership's cases which are active upon its dissolution.") with Comment, Dissolution of a Law Partnership — Goodwill, Winding Up Profits, & Additional Compensation, 6 J. Legal Prof. 277, 290 (1981) ("Surely the effect of the no additional compensation rule is a decrease in the quality and amount of time and energy expended by attorneys for left over clients since they are certainly better compensated for their efforts on behalf of their new clientele."). See also Jewel, 156 Cal. App. 3d at 179-180, 203 Cal. Rptr. at 19 (commenting that attorneys may modify the no-compensation rule by including a provision on post-dissolution compensation of unfinished partnership business in their partnership agreements).

other service partnerships, like typical partnerships.[37] The UPA's winding-up provisions are premised on the assumption that all partners will cooperate in bringing the partnership's business to a close. This presumed cooperation justifies withholding compensation from partners for winding-up activities,[38] making all partners responsible for liabilities incurred in the course of winding up,[39] and giving each partner both the right and the duty to participate in winding up.[40] The partnership, in short, continues until all of its business is finished. Although the classic model of winding up may sometimes apply to law firms, more often the strained post-dissolution relations of law partners refute the idea that the winding up of a firm's unfinished business is a cooperative endeavor.

§4.5 Fiduciary Duties and the Process of Grabbing and Leaving: Meehan v. Shaughnessy

Meehan v. Shaughnessy,[1] a 1989 Massachusetts decision, offers the most comprehensive treatment to date of the issues raised by the

---

[37] Cf. Cook v. Brundidge, Fountain, Elliott & Churchill, 533 S.W.2d 751, 757 (Tex. 1976) ("There are, admittedly, compelling and unique considerations with respect to partners engaged in the practice of law. The fiducial obligations of a law partnership set it apart from commercial partnerships.").

One unfortunate byproduct of contests between lawyers fighting for clients is that the details of the relationship between a client and a lawyer may become the subject of public proceedings. See, e.g., Stacker & Ravich v. Simon, 411 N.W.2d 217, 221 (Minn. Ct. App. 1987) (containing details of a client's contract negotiated by an attorney). Citing an explosion of litigation over dissolutions that has reached "alarming proportions" and the disruptive effects on clients of fighting among lawyers, one report has recommended a voluntary arbitration procedure for resolving disputes among lawyers. See Committee on Arbitration and Alternative Dispute Resolution, Proposal for Association-Sponsored Arbitration of Disputes Among Lawyers, 42 Rec. A.B. City N.Y. 877, 878 (1987). Such programs are in place in a number of cities. See Pennsylvania Offers Program to Mediate Lawyers' Disputes, [4 Current Reports] Law. Man. on Prof. Conduct (ABA/BNA) 231, 231 (July 20, 1988).

[38] See Unif. Partnership Act §18(f), 6 U.L.A. 213 (1969).

[39] See id. §36, 6 U.L.A. at 436.

[40] See id. §37, 6 U.L.A. at 444.

§4.5 [1] 404 Mass. 419, 535 N.E.2d 1255 (1989).

grabbing and leaving activities of lawyers. The case is noteworthy both for the new perspective it offers and its emphasis on the importance of the manner in which withdrawing lawyers take clients from their firms.

§4.5.1 The Grab

The partnership agreement of the firm Parker, Coulter, Daley & White allowed withdrawing lawyers to take with them clients of the firm if they compensated the firm for its prior "service to and expenditures for" the clients.[2] The agreement also negated the usual sharing of income from the completion of unfinished business by providing, in essence, that departing partners were entitled to all post-withdrawal income generated from cases they took but had no claim to income from cases that remained with the firm.

Partners Meehan and Boyle decided in July to leave the firm. They did not inform their partners of this decision. For the next five months, they secretly made arrangements to launch their new firm. These arrangements included leasing office space, compiling lists of clients they expected to grab, securing financing, preparing on Parker Coulter stationery formal announcements to be mailed to clients, and discussing with certain associates and partners the possibility of joining their new firm. On three occasions, Meehan was asked by partners in the firm if rumors about his departure were true; each time, he denied he was leaving. In late November, Meehan and Boyle notified the partners that they and several other lawyers would be withdrawing. Although the partnership agreement called for a three-month notice of withdrawal, the parties agreed to shorten this period to 30 days.[3]

With the announcement of the Meehan group's departure, the

---

[2] The agreement permitted the taking of clients who came to the firm through the efforts of departing partners. The court, however, interpreted this to cover all clients who chose to have their cases removed from the firm. Id. at 431, 535 N.E.2d at 1262.

[3] Since Meehan and Boyle previously decided to give only 30 days notice, the adequacy of notice would have been at issue but for this agreement.

grab for clients began. The firm requested the departing lawyers to provide it with information on the cases they wished to take. Nearly three weeks passed before this information was provided. In the meantime, the Meehan group secured the consent of a large percentage of clients it intended to take from the firm. With the establishment of their new firm on January 1, Meehan and Boyle removed 142 of the 350 contingent fee cases pending at Parker Coulter. They also took with them a junior partner and three associates.

Parker Coulter declined to pay the departing partners amounts due under the withdrawal provisions of the partnership agreement.[4] Meehan and Boyle initiated a suit to recover these amounts and to obtain a declaration of the amounts owed Parker Coulter for the cases they removed. Parker Coulter counterclaimed that Meehan and Boyle had breached their fiduciary duties to the firm, breached the partnership agreement, and tortiously interfered with the firm's business and contractual relationships. The trial court denied Parker Coulter's claims for relief and ordered the firm to pay Meehan and Boyle amounts due them under the partnership agreement. It also ordered Meehan and Boyle to compensate the firm for time and expenses incurred on cases they removed. Parker Coulter appealed.

§4.5.2 The Issues in General

Three issues involving the fiduciary obligations of the withdrawing partners were addressed by the Massachusetts high court:

(1) Did the withdrawing lawyers improperly handle cases for their own benefit rather than Parker Coulter's?
(2) Did the withdrawing lawyers breach their fiduciary duties by secretly competing with the partnership?
(3) Did the withdrawing lawyers breach their fiduciary duties by unfairly obtaining the consent of clients and referring attorneys to withdraw cases from Parker Coulter?

---

[4] This included a return of their capital contribution and profits accrued to the date of withdrawal.

§4.5.3 Improper Handling of Cases

Using the "clearly erroneous" standard of review, the court upheld the trial court's finding that the withdrawing attorneys had not improperly handled cases for their benefit rather than that of the partnership: "We have reviewed the record, and conclude that the judge was warranted in determining that Meehan and Boyle handled cases no differently as a result of their decision to leave Parker, Coulter, and that they thus fulfilled their fiduciary duty in this respect."[5] The obvious inference of this statement is that withdrawing lawyers who defer settlements until after their departure or otherwise manipulate cases to their advantage will in so acting breach the fiduciary duties they owe their firm.

§4.5.4 Clandestine Competition with the Firm

The court also found no breach of fiduciary duty in the Meehan group's secret competition with the firm:

> Here, the judge found that Meehan and Boyle made certain logistical arrangements for the establishment of [their new firm]. These arrangements included executing a lease for an office, preparing lists of clients expected to leave Parker Coulter for [their new firm], and obtaining financing on the basis of these lists. We believe these logistical arrangements to establish a physical plant for the new firm were permissible [citation omitted], especially in light of the attorneys' obligation to represent adequately any clients who might continue to retain them on their departure from Parker Coulter.[6]

At first glance, this blending of fiduciary duties partners owe each other with the obligations they owe their clients may seem to do some violence to the "punctilio of an honor the most sensitive"[7]

---

[5] Id. at 435, 535 N.E.2d at 1264.

[6] Id.

[7] Meinhard v. Salmon, 249 N.Y. 458, 464, 164 N.E. 545, 546 (1928).

standard partners are expected to observe.[8] It is not, however, a carte blanche for those who grab and should be read in light of the court's conclusion, discussed below, that the withdrawing lawyers did breach their fiduciary duty to the partnership in denying Parker Coulter an opportunity to compete for the clients on equal terms.

§4.5.5 Jumping the Gun: Unfairly Securing the Consent of Clients

The court found the withdrawing partners breached their fiduciary duty to the partnership "by unfairly acquiring consent from clients to remove cases from Parker Coulter."[9] Before informing the partnership of their departure, the Meehan group met with one client to assess its interest in retaining their new firm, prepared (but did not send) announcements on Parker Coulter stationery of their new firm, and denied on three occasions rumors of their departure. They were thus "ready to move" the moment they informed the other partners.[10] Following that notice, they immediately notified their clients and obtained substitution consents from a majority before they provided the other partners with information they had requested on these same clients. Moreover, their communications to the clients gave the withdrawing lawyers a competitive advantage over the firm:

> By sending a one-sided announcement, on Parker Coulter letterhead, so soon after notice of their departure, Meehan and Boyle excluded their partners from effectively presenting their services as an alternative to those of Meehan and Boyle.[11]

Because of these "preemptive tactics" by the departing lawyers, the court remanded for a determination of which of the cases removed from the firm by the Meehan group were unfairly removed

---

[8] See generally Hillman, Private Ordering Within Partnerships, 41 U. Miami L. Rev. 425, 454-471 (1987) (discussing the limits of fiduciary principles in controlling the activities of partners).

[9] 404 Mass. at 436, 535 N.E.2d at 1264.

[10] Id.

[11] Id. at 434, 535 N.E.2d at 1265.

because client consent was improperly obtained.[12] Profits on these cases were to be shared by Meehan, Boyle, and Parker Coulter in ratios reflecting their respective ownership interests in the firm prior to the breakup.[13] Although the court did not require Meehan and Boyle to share with the firm profits on cases fairly removed,[14] they had the burden on remand of proving a client would have consented to removal had consent not been unfairly obtained. Factors relevant in this determination include: (1) the identity of the attorney who was responsible for attracting the client to the firm; (2) the identity of the attorney who managed the case at the firm; (3) the sophistication of the client and whether the client made the choice of counsel with full information; and (4) the reputations and skills of the removing attorneys.[15]

Finally, the court rejected the argument that its disposition reduces the incentive of Meehan and Boyle to use their best efforts in the cases in which profit sharing is required:

> We agree that punitive measures may infringe on a client's right to adequate representation, and to counsel of his or her choosing. . . . We believe, however, that the remedy we impose does not suffer from the . . . claimed defects. Under the constructive trust we impose, Meehan and Boyle will receive a share of the fruits of their efforts in the unfairly removed cases which is the same as that which they would have enjoyed at Parker Coulter. We note, moreover, that incentives other than profit motivate attorneys. These incentives include an attorney's ethical obligations to the client and the profession, and a concern for his or her reputation.[16]

---

[12] Id.

[13] The opinion indicated profit is to be determined by subtracting from fees reasonable overhead expenses, including actual costs but not profit margins. Id. at 446-447, 535 N.E.2d at 1270.

[14] The partnership agreement called for reimbursement of the firm for its time and expenses on removed cases, and the court did require Meehan and Boyle to reimburse the firm for 89.2 percent of its fair charges (time and expenses) on all cases they removed, fairly or unfairly.

[15] Id. at 443-444, 535 N.E.2d at 1268. The court required a junior partner and an associate who left with Meehan and Boyle to hold in constructive trust all profits from cases unfairly taken. Id. at 448, 535 N.E.2d at 1271.

[16] Id. at 447, 535 N.E.2d at 1271. The court dismissed Parker Coulter's claim of tortious interference with its relations with clients and employees because the damages sought under the claim were the same as those sought on the breach of fiduciary duty claim.

§4.5.6 The Significance of *Meehan*

Meehan attempts to level the playing field by preventing with-drawing partners from jumping the gun in their grab for clients. The opinion recognizes that a measure of order is required when firms break up to insure that client choice as to counsel is informed. By focusing on the *procedures* of grabbing and leaving rather than the motives underlying the *decision* itself, *Meehan* sidesteps the diffi-culties inherent in attempting to restrain partners in terminable at will partnerships from pursuing better opportunities.

Meehan has direct applicability to partnerships that eschew the UPA's winding up principles in favor of allocating post-withdrawal income to the firm or the departing lawyers, as the case may be, who win the favor of the client. In partnerships operating under these types of agreements, the timing of the grab is critical, and *Meehan's* emphasis on the importance of a level playing field is sensible. Timing considerations are less important for those partnerships in which income from the completion of unfinished business is shared. This raises the question of whether *Meehan* has applicability to partnerships that operate under the default mode of the UPA and enter a winding-up period following the withdrawal of a partner.

The opinion may be read narrowly or broadly. A narrow reading would highlight the withdrawal provisions of the Parker Coulter agreement that may be read to authorize grabbing and leaving if done fairly. A broader reading would note the court held liable an associate and junior partner who were not signatories to the agreement because "their fiduciary duties require this result."[17] Also significant is the court's failure to embrace the rhetoric and analysis of the California line of cases emphasizing the motives of those who depart and its focus instead upon the process of withdrawal.[18] Moreover, *Meehan's* rejection of a sweeping application of fiduciary principles that would negate the ability of partners to secretly plan and make "logistical" pre-departure arrangements is not limited to partnerships operating under the type of agreement utilized by

---

[17] Id. at 448, 535 N.E.2d at 1271.
[18] See supra §4.4.2.

Parker Coulter. And the court spoke broadly in justifying its place-ment of the burden of proof to show cases were not taken unfairly:

> [R]equiring these partners to disprove causation will encourage part-ners in the future to disclose seasonably and fully any plans to remove cases. This disclosure will allow the partnership and the departing partner an equal opportunity to present to clients the option of continuing with the partnership or retaining the departing partner individually.[19]

Although the Meehan group could hardly be said to have prevailed in this litigation, the opinion for the most part is a victory for those who grab and leave rather than their firms. Consider points in *Meehan* unfavorable to Parker, Coulter and other firms faced with lawyers who grab: (1) partners secretly may make plans and arrange-ments to withdraw;[20] (2) the firm could not use the breach of fiduciary duty as a basis for withholding from departing partners their capital contributions and profits accrued to the date of with-drawal;[21] (3) the firm could not reduce or eliminate the withdraw-ing partners' compensation during the period of their breach be-cause the value of their services was equal to their compensation;[22] and (4) partners may not by contract limit the rights of departing partners to grab only those clients they brought to the firm.[23] More-over, the court declined to address Parker Coulter's claim that Mee-han and Boyle impermissibly competed with the firm by inducing its employees to join their new firm; it refused to address the issue because Parker Coulter could not identify specific losses from the claimed breach.

Meehan is something of a victory for mobile lawyers rather than their firms, but certain facts emphasized in the opinion may provide a basis for distinguishing the case from other grabbing and leaving controversies. At several points, the court expressed high regard for

---

[19] Id. at 442, 535 N.E.2d at 1267. Along this line, the court sensibly suggested joint rather than unilateral notifications of clients. Id. n.16.

[20] See id. at 435-436, 535 N.E.2d at 1264.

[21] See id. at 539, 535 N.E.2d at 1266.

[22] See id. at 440, 535 N.E.2d at 1266-1267.

[23] Id. at 431, 535 N.E.2d at 1262.

Meehan and Boyle,[24] and it was careful to point out that they did not manipulate the settlement timing for their cases and throughout the period prior to their withdrawal "worked as hard, and were as productive as they had always been." The factual posture of other cases may be less favorable to those who grab and leave.

§4.5.7 Some Troubling Aspects of *Meehan*

Although the court noted that Meehan thrice denied rumors he was leaving, it used his misrepresentations as support for its conclusion that client consent was unfairly secured, not as part of its analysis of whether arrangements for a departure may be done in secrecy. This raises the issue of whether misrepresentations would be permissible absent a planned and executed preemptive strike in obtaining the consent of clients. Given the UPA's command that "[p]artners shall render on demand true and full information of all things affecting the partnership to any partner,"[25] it should take a more serious threat to client interests than was apparent in *Meehan* to justify misrepresentations to one's law partners.

Misrepresentations aside, *Meehan*'s denial of an affirmative disclosure obligation on the part of the withdrawing partners is sensible in light of the facts of the case and the issues that were contested. The partnership agreement included a notice provision, compliance with which was not at issue. Early disclosure would either have prolonged the period of turmoil or forced an abrupt departure by the Meehan

---

[24] For example, it noted that Meehan and Boyle had developed "outstanding reputations as trial lawyers." Id. at 423, 535 N.E.2d at 1257. It also seemed reluctant to employ certain labels in describing their activities:

> We repeatedly, later in the opinion, refer to "preemptive conduct" of Meehan and Boyle, as well as their "breach of duty." Undoubtedly, these are accurate descriptions, but we do not wish to leave the impression that [they] were unfair in the totality of their conduct in departing from the firm. For instance, we recount early in this opinion that Meehan and Boyle left undisturbed with their partners, and made no attempt to claim, a very large amount of business which Meehan had attracted to Parker Coulter. [Id. n.5.]

[25] Unif. Partnership Act §20. See generally A. Bromberg and L. Ribstein, Bromberg and Ribstein on Partnership §6.06 (1988).

group, possibly to the prejudice of their clients. In light of the court's requirements restricting preemptive grabbing, the benefits to be derived by mandating disclosure are not at all clear.

This may not be the case, however, when a firm suffers more than a loss of clients as a result of the departure of a group of lawyers. Law firms make and implement business plans. They hire employees, open branch offices, lease office space, purchase office equipment, and make other commitments of resources based upon information available at the time. A subsequent departure by a group of partners, clients in tow, may in retrospect render those actions ill advised. If partners secretly planning a withdrawal know that decisions of a material nature are being made by the partnership in reliance upon their continued membership in the firm, the imposition of an affirmative disclosure obligation is appropriate.

Finally, requiring the former partners to share fees on cases unfairly removed from the firm is a remedy that flows naturally from the court's finding of a breach of fiduciary duty. It is also, however, a remedy of potentially great harshness, for Meehan and Boyle were limited to only 10.8 percent of the profits derived from the completion of cases unfairly removed. Since the firm was not required to share any of its post-withdrawal income with departed partners, Meehan and Boyle were left with a one-sided sharing of income yielding an economic disincentive as to cases in which income was shared and an economic incentive as to all other cases.[26] It may well be true that ethical obligations and considerations of reputation motivate some lawyers to excel even when economic rewards will not be realized. But concerns over similar disincentives have prompted the regulation of fee splitting among lawyers[27] and have led to the voiding of agreements placing economic disincentives on post-withdrawal competition.[28]

---

[26] Although the court noted the former partners' incentives with respect to the unfairly removed cases remained the same as when they were at Parker, Coulter, it ignored the fact that requiring them to share income on some of their current cases creates a relative disincentive when those cases are compared to cases in which income sharing is not required.

[27] See supra §4.4.1.

[28] See supra §2.3.3.

§4.6 *Winding Up and Malpractice Liabilities*

§4.6.1 In General

Just as dissolution does not terminate a partner's claim to income, neither does it discharge a partner from liabilities incurred by the partnership.[1] Partnership agreements typically provide some method for settling a withdrawing partner's account and defining or terminating multiple claims to post-withdrawal income.[2] These agreements, however, address only half of the picture, and the rights of third parties are not subject to such summary disposition. Post-dissolution liabilities may arise at various times during the winding-up period, even long after a withdrawal, and may take several forms. In the context of grabbing and leaving, malpractice claims may prove the most vexing of these liabilities.[3]

Lawyers are obviously responsible for their own malpractice. Vicarious liability for the malpractice of other partners, on the other hand, is a product of partnership law rather than of the norms of legal ethics.[4] At least in theory, partners in ongoing firms may protect themselves from vicarious malpractice liability by maintaining adequate insurance and establishing internal controls to monitor instances of malfeasance or nonfeasance.[5] Malpractice arising during

---

§4.6   [1] A partnership continues until the winding up is completed. Id. §30, 6 U.L.A. at 367. Dissolution does not, of itself, discharge the "existing liability" of any partner. Id. §36(1), 6 U.L.A. at 436. A discharge of liability may be accomplished by agreement, express or implied, among the partner, the creditor, and the person continuing the business, id. §36(2), 6 U.L.A. at 436, or, if liabilities are assumed, by the consent of the creditor to a material alteration in the timing or nature of payment of the liabilities, id. §36(3), 6 U.L.A. at 436. Generally, dissolution terminates the authority of partners to act for the partnership, see id. §33, 6 U.L.A. at 423, but each partner has the power to bind the others by "any act appropriate" for completing partnership business, id. §35, 6 U.L.A. at 429.

[2] Cf. P. Carrington & W. Sutherland, Articles of Partnership for Law Firms 56-62 (1961) (suggesting several provisions for settling withdrawing partners' accounts).

[3] Although an aggrieved client may base a malpractice action either on contract or tort, the latter has proven more important. See C. Wolfram, Modern Legal Ethics §5.6.2, at 209 (1986).

[4] See generally R. Mallen & V. Levit, Legal Malpractice §33 (2d ed. 1981) (discussing partnership liability for malpractice claims).

[5] See id. §§12-13.

the winding up of a law partnership may prove more problematic. Because the responsibility for the winding up of a given case is not normally shared, both the firm and the withdrawing partner may feel that responsibility follows the file and decline to supervise the work of the other.[6] When the work is in the winding-up stage, however, this reasoning is dangerously ill conceived.

Most law partners are probably unaware of the possibility of post-dissolution liabilities arising from malpractice claims. The withdrawal provisions of the Articles of Partnership,[7] for example, are largely silent on liabilities, and an essay in a recently published work of the American Bar Association cheerfully advises withdrawing law partners on their post-dissolution responsibilities to clients:

> Typically the various clients will have been served more or less specifically by particular lawyers in the firm, and those relationships usually will continue as regards clients served by lawyers remaining in the firm. In the absence of any indications to the contrary, an exiting lawyer can assume the need to be concerned only for "his" or "her" clients, that is, assume that the remaining lawyers will take care of the clients they served. Furthermore, the remaining lawyers ordinarily can assume that the exiting lawyer will protect the interests of the clients that are taken from the firm.[8]

This assumption ignores the possibility of vicarious liability arising long after the partner's withdrawal. The case of Redman v. Walters[9] aptly illustrates the problem. The firm of MacDonald, Brunsell & Walters agreed to represent a client in a litigation matter. One year later a name partner, Walters, withdrew from the firm and

---

[6] The right to participate in winding up is assured to each partner who has not wrongfully dissolved the partnership. See Unif. Partnership Act §37, 6 U.L.A. at 444. Applying this principle to law firms, however, may infringe on the right of the client to select a lawyer.

[7] See P. Carrington & W. Sutherland, Articles of Partnership for Law Firms 55-69 (1961).

[8] Hazard, Ethical Considerations in Withdrawal, Expulsion, and Retirement, in Withdrawal, Retirement and Disputes: What You and Your Firm Need to Know 32, 35 (E. Berger ed. 1986).

[9] 88 Cal. App. 3d 448, 152 Cal. Rptr. 42 (1979).

commenced practice elsewhere. Walters had never met the client and was unaware of the nature of the action.[10] Following the dissolution, the firm of MacDonald & Brunsell continued representation of the client, and MacDonald, Brunsell & Caton eventually became, without formal substitution, the client's attorneys of record. Four years after Walters' withdrawal and the original firm's dissolution, the court dismissed the client's lawsuit for failure to bring it to trial within five years. The client then sued both Walters and MacDonald, Brunsell & Caton for malpractice.[11]

Finding that the client had neither expressly nor impliedly consented to release Walters from his obligations as a partner, a California appellate court reversed the trial court's grant of summary judgment dismissing the plaintiff's action against Walters.[12] Thus, four years after he left the firm, Walters had to respond to a malpractice action concerning a client he never met and a case of which he knew nothing. Although it is likely that Walters settled his account at the time of his withdrawal and that he had no economic interest in the case carried forward by the firm, these facts are irrelevant to the issue of malpractice liability arising during the winding-up period. However unsettling it may be to lawyers who move between firms, this result conforms to the winding-up principles of partnership law.[13]

Redman should surprise no one, and it may well prove a landmark case in the development of firm-dissolution law. It was only a matter of time before the clash would become apparent between traditional ethical standards discouraging or prohibiting communications to clients by withdrawing partners and the pressures of vicarious liability arising under partnership law. The California State Bar responded to *Redman* with an ethics opinion that contrasts sharply with more conservative and traditional approaches to the

---

[10] Id. at 451, 152 Cal. Rptr. at 43-44.

[11] Id. at 451, 152 Cal. Rptr. at 44.

[12] Id. at 454-456, 152 Cal. Rptr. at 45-46.

[13] A more debatable aspect of the opinion is the court's conclusion that the client had not implicitly agreed to discharge Walters from responsibility. See Redman, 88 Cal. App. 3d at 454-455, 152 Cal. Rptr. at 45-46. The message, however, is clear: any doubts concerning whether a client has consented to relieve an attorney from winding-up responsibilities will be resolved against the attorney.

conflict between legal ethics and partnership law.[14] Concluding that both the firm and the withdrawing partner *must* notify clients of a withdrawal or dissolution,[15] the opinion provides rather specific guidelines for communications and conduct involved in the grabbing process.[16]

---

[14] See Standing Comm. on Professional Responsibility and Conduct of the State Bar of California, Formal Op. 1985-86, reprinted in Law. Man. on Prof. Conduct (ABA/BNA) 901:1601 (Apr. 27, 1988) [hereinafter Cal. Op. 1985-86].

[15] As early as 1863, courts recognized that a client should be notified of the withdrawal of a partner whose identity was relevant to an earlier decision to retain the firm. In Smyth v. Harvie, 31 Ill. 62 (1863), the client retained a firm of two partners to collect a debt. The partners dissolved the firm, and one of them, Harvie, continued the practice. Id. at 66. After the dissolution, Harvie, received money for the client's account but never paid it over to the client. Id. The court held the withdrawing partner, Tuley, responsible for Harvie's misdeeds:

> For aught we know, the fact that Tuley was a partner, may have been the inducement to confide the business to the care of the firm.
>
> Even if a dissolution of the partnership could have released the members from liability for a failure to complete the business, it could only have been after notice of the dissolution. In the absence of such notice, plaintiffs had no option in determining whether they would continue the cause in the hands of the member who took charge of the business of the firm, or would place it in the hands of another attorney. [Id. at 67.]

[16] The full opinion states:

Both the law firm and the attorneys involved in a dissolution or withdrawal of a partnership must provide the clients with fair and adequate notice of the change in order to permit them the opportunity to make an informed choice of counsel. All of the attorneys involved have a fiduciary duty to the clients affected and must act in their clients' best interests. The lawyers must give timely and accurate notice to the clients and deliver to them all papers and property. The attorneys involved must be careful that the notice of dissolution they send to the client does not contain false, misleading or deceptive advertising. Where practical, the attorneys should provide joint notice which identifies the withdrawing attorneys, identifies the field in which the withdrawing attorneys will be practicing law, gives their addresses and telephone numbers, provides information as to whether the former firm will continue to handle similar legal matters, and tells who will be handling ongoing matters during the transition. The client should also be advised of his right to select the former firm, the withdrawing attorneys, or new counsel to handle his future legal matters, as well as of his right to obtain all of his files and property. A lawyer from the dissolving firm may not attempt to influence the client's choice of counsel by communicating with clients in person, by telephone or through agents. However, if the client makes direct inquiries concerning his rights, the lawyer has an obligation to truthfully and accurately answer the questions in the best interests of the client.

Redman cannot be dismissed as an aberration unique to California, for it expresses a principle that is an underpinning of partnership law. Nor does *Redman* stand alone. A more recent decision applying Pennsylvania law reaches a similar conclusion. In Palomba v. Barish,[17] the asserted malpractice occurred long after an attorney's withdrawal from a firm.[18] In denying the attorney's motion for summary judgment, the court noted that the withdrawal from the firm two years prior to the alleged malpractice "is of little moment to whether or not [the attorney] can be held liable for the malpractice of his former partners."[19] Even denial of access to client files did not, in the *Palomba* court's view, release the attorney from his responsibilities to firm clients and his "duty" to notify clients of his withdrawal.[20] To make the nature of the withdrawing partner's responsibilities even clearer, the court added: "Moreover, the very fact that [another partner] was permitted to wind up affairs for the former partnership *may in itself be a reckless act.*"[21]

In light of increasing lawyer mobility, cases like *Redman* and *Palomba* charge grabbing and leaving activities with a good deal of risk for both the firm and the grabbing partner. Successful grabs by a withdrawing lawyer do not relieve former partners of the risk of malpractice liability arising in the winding up of grabbed cases. Moreover, the lawyer who leaves without grabbing remains at risk for the malpractice of the firm and its members for an extended period of time, even though the departing lawyer may have neither knowledge of the cases nor the ability to control the manner in

---

Cal. Op. 1985-86, supra note 269. See also 404 Mass. 419, 535 N.E.2d 1267 n.16 (1989) (suggesting joint notification).

[17] 626 F. Supp. 722 (E.D. Pa. 1985).

[18] The attorney alleged he had been expelled from the firm and denied access to client files. Id. at 726.

[19] Id. at 725.

[20] Id. at 726. It is interesting to note that the firm involved in *Palomba* was Adler, Barish. See supra §3.1. The court commented that "the matter before the Supreme Court in [*Adler, Barish*] is sufficiently distinguishable from the dilemma facing defendant Daniels; thus, the holding's prohibition [against client communication other than by means of formal announcements] would not affect Daniel's duties to notify clients of his former firm." *Palomba,* 626 F. Supp. at 726. Some things come full circle.

[21] Id. (emphasis added).

which they are handled. Under these circumstances, the lawyer who assumes that former partners will take care of the cases does so at peril.

§4.6.2 Insuring the Risks

One obvious way of dealing with the risks posed by such cases as *Redman* and *Palomba* is through insurance.[22] The degree to which insurance covers lawyers for vicarious liability arising from post-dissolution malpractice, however, is open to question. Insurers typically offer malpractice coverage on a claims-made basis, which provides insurance only for claims asserted during the life of the policy.[23] To facilitate a firm's change in insurance carriers, these policies may cover acts occurring prior to the policy period if the firm asserts the claim during the policy's term.[24] Nevertheless, it is unclear whether such coverage extends to new members of a firm who may suffer vicarious liability for the winding-up malpractice of other lawyers who, for all practical purposes, are in another firm.[25]

---

[22] For discussions of malpractice policy coverage, see generally 2 R. Long, The Law of Liability Insurance §§12.01-.04 (1987); R. Mallen & J. Smith, Legal Malpractice §§28.1-28.25 (1989).

[23] See 2 R. Long, The Law of Liability Insurance §12.02, at 12-3 (1987).

[24] Id.

[25] The issue of coverage is primarily a matter of policy interpretation, and coverage will vary from carrier to carrier. A review of several policies illustrates the problem.

A specimen claims-made policy issued by the Lawyer's Mutual Insurance Company provides coverage for the "insured," which is defined to include (1) the firm named in the policy, (2) lawyers working for the firm as of the effective date of the policy, and (3) lawyers who later join the firm *if* the carrier is notified within thirty days of the date they commenced employment or became partners. See Lawyers' Mut. Ins. Co., Claims-Made Policy, form 1, art. 1.9 (specimen 1987). As to the latter two categories, however, the policy only covers acts on behalf of the firm or a predecessor firm. Id. art. 1.9(b)-(d). Moreover, claims made against a "business enterprise" not named in the policy declarations in which an insured is a partner are excluded from coverage. Id. art. 3.6. Although the policy is far from clear, the inference is that a lawyer is not insured against vicarious liability for his or her acts in another firm.

The Home Insurance Companies' policy excludes coverage for any claim made against a "business enterprise not named in the Declarations . . . in which the Insured is a partner or employee." The Home Ins. Cos., Professional Liability

Unless the lawyer changing firms individually purchases either prior-acts coverage under the new firm's policy or tail coverage under the old firm's policy,[26] he or she may be uninsured against winding-up malpractice by former partners. If, as casual empiricism suggests, most lawyers are unaware of the problem of post-dissolution vicarious liability, it is also unlikely they are taking steps to insure against the risks.[27]

§4.6.3 Forcing Client Choice

Although *Redman* and *Palomba* highlight the dangers of post-dissolution liabilities, they also suggest a method by which lawyers may reduce the risks. Both cases suggest that client consent will

---

Insurance Policy: Lawyers, §C, pt. I(b). Similarly, the policy used by the American Home Assurance Company and the National Union Fire Insurance Company does not cover "any claim arising out of any insured's activities as an officer or director of any . . . company or business other than that of the Named Insured." American Home Assurance Co. & Natl. Union Fire Ins. Co. of Pittsburg, Pa., Lawyers Professional Liability Policy, Exclusions, pt. (f) (1985).

A policy used by the Los Angeles County Bar Association covers any "error or omission in Professional Services." Los Angeles County Bar Assn., Lawyers Professional Insurance, cl. I-A-1. It then defines such services in a way to exclude services "outside the conduct" of the insured firm's business unless the "services are undertaken with the prior written knowledge and consent" of the insured firm. Id. cl. II-K-2. Whether this would cover vicarious liability for the acts of "former" partners is unclear.

Even if a policy's language arguably restricts coverage, a carrier may choose to interpret the terms more liberally. In Stevens v. Lawyers Mut. Liab. Ins. Co., 789 F.2d 1056 (4th Cir. 1986), Nimocks, a partner in the firm of Nimocks & Taylor, defended Stevens in a criminal prosecution. Stevens' conviction was later overturned on ineffective assistance of counsel grounds. In the meantime, the Nimocks & Taylor firm had disbanded, and Taylor had joined a new firm. Stevens filed a malpractice action against Nimocks and the defunct partnership. The claim against Nimocks was discharged in bankruptcy, and Stevens sought a declaratory judgment that the policy of Taylor's new firm covered any liability he may have because of the malpractice action. Id. at 1058. Initially, the insurer vigorously denied coverage, and the district court accepted this position. Id. The appellate court, however, inferred that the policy covered the claim. But it did not rule on this point because the insurer reversed its position at the appellate level and conceded coverage. Id. at 1060.

[26] See 2 R. Long, The Law of Liability Insurance §12.02, at 12-4 (1987).

[27] In *Redman,* Walters represented himself. See Redman v. Walters, 88 Cal. App. 3d 448, 450, 152 Cal. Rptr. 42, 43 (1979). This suggests that he was not insured against the claim asserted.

convert what might otherwise be winding-up activities, for purposes of malpractice liability, into new business for the party gaining control of the client.[28] There is little reason for extending vicarious liability to the lawyer or law firm "losing" the client when conditions of joint representation do not exist. The reasoning that would release either the firm or the departing lawyer from duties to former clients should also apply to claims to income based on winding-up activities. When client choice is informed, unequivocal, and intended to relieve a lawyer from what would otherwise be winding-up responsibilities, it is anomalous to conclude that winding up continues for purposes of allocating income.[29] Most reported post-dissolution income disputes concern contingent-fee cases, and a quantum meruit recovery for the value of services rendered prior to dissolution will represent adequate, although perhaps not optimal, compensation for firms subjected to grabbing and leaving.[30]

Converting cases from the status of winding-up business to that of new business may also benefit clients. Even allowing for a measure of recovery based upon the value of services prior to dissolution, the compensation of the firm or the attorney handling the matter as new business may exceed that which would have been awarded under winding-up treatment. To the degree that an additional incentive is present, that incentive may improve the quality of representation without imposing additional costs on the client.

Client choice is the method by which an extended winding-up period may be shortened, and notice often will be the means by

---

[28] Palomba v. Barish, 626 F. Supp. 722, 726 (E.D. Pa. 1985); *Redman,* 88 Cal. App. 3d at 455, 152 Cal. Rptr. at 46.

[29] Some courts have rejected the idea that client choice, affirmatively expressed, affects the relative claims of partners to income, usually on the rationale that it is of no concern to clients how lawyers divide their fees. See, e.g., Jewel v. Boxer, 156 Cal. App. 3d 171, 178, 203 Cal. Rptr. 13, 17 (1984) ("Once the client's fee is paid to an attorney, it is of no concern to the client how that fee is allocated among the attorney and his or her former partners."); Ellerby v. Spiezer, 138 Ill. App. 3d 77, 81, 485 N.E.2d 413, 416 (1985) (holding that the right of a client to choose counsel "is distinct from and does not conflict with the rights and duties of the partners between themselves with respect to profits from the unfinished partnership business"). By concluding that the partnership continues during the winding-up phase, these opinions are able to elude ethics restrictions on fee splitting when lawyers are not members of the same firm. See supra §4.4.1.

[30] See supra §2.3.1.

which the choice is prompted.[31] For this purpose, notice means something more than the traditional withdrawal announcement contemplated by the Model Code.[32] Notice should advise the client of the withdrawal of a lawyer, indicate whether the firm and the lawyer have reached a tentative understanding concerning continuing responsibility for the client's matters, and inform the client of the right to select as his counsel the firm, the withdrawing lawyer, or any other lawyer or firm.[33] For years, standards of legal ethics operated to inhibit the exercise of free choice by restricting the ability of a withdrawing lawyer to communicate with clients. These barriers are now falling, and at least under more enlightened court decisions[34] and the Model Rules,[35] notification designed to facilitate client choice is both permissible and reasonable. The lesson of *Redman* and *Palomba* is that partnership law provides strong incentives to utilize the withdrawal of a partner as a means of forcing a choice on the part of the client and abbreviating what might otherwise be an extended period for winding up the business of the law partnership.[36]

---

[31] Of course, this will not affect winding up as it pertains to other third-party claims.

[32] See supra §2.2.3.

[33] Cf. Standing Comm. on Professional Responsibility and Conduct of the State Bar of California, Formal Op. 1985-86, reprinted in Law. Man. on Prof. Conduct (ABA/BNA) 901:1601 (Apr. 27, 1988) (setting out requirements for notice of dissolution or partner's withdrawal).

[34] See, e.g., Vollgraff v. Block, 117 Misc. 2d 489, 493, 458 N.Y.S.2d 437, 440 (Sup. Ct. 1982) (holding that the fiduciary relationship between a law firm and its clients required that clients receive notification of dissolution of a three-person firm).

[35] See supra §2.2.4.

[36] *Redman* and *Palomba* present issues of reverse grabbing, which arise when either the firm or the withdrawing lawyer wishes to terminate responsibility for the affairs of a client. Absent consent by the client, the partners may be powerless to modify their winding-up obligations to a client. *Redman* suggested, however, that consent need not be express: "Among the partnership affairs . . . to be 'wound up' was the performance of its agreement with Redman, or that party's consent, express or implied, or perhaps by estoppel, to nonrepresentation by the outgoing partner. . . ." Redman v. Walters, 88 Cal. App. 3d 448, 453, 152 Cal. Rptr. 42, 45 (1979). This is a sensible approach. In a similar context, the UPA provides that a partner is discharged from existing liability upon dissolution by agreement with a creditor and that the "agreement may be inferred from the course of dealing between the creditor having knowledge of the dissolution and the person or partnership continuing the business." Unif. Partnership Act §36(2), 6 U.L.A. 436 (1969).

§4.7 Possible Reform

Recent years have seen several proposals for reform of the UPA,[1] and the National Conference of Commissioners has authorized a

---

For larger firms, routine notification of clients upon the withdrawal of a partner may prove difficult. It is one thing for clients to receive information concerning the withdrawal of a partner who has previously performed services for the clients; this is the standard use of notice to promote grabbing. It is quite another to routinely notify all clients of the firm whenever any partner withdraws. When a partner withdraws from a firm of 300 partners, for example, notifying all clients of the firm (even those who never knew of the existence of the withdrawing partner) may prove an expensive and excessive response to the threat of vicarious winding-up liability illustrated by *Redman,* particularly if it is likely the firm will maintain adequate malpractice insurance and the risk of vicarious liability is minimal.

§4.7 [1] A report prepared by a subcommittee of the American Bar Association's Section on Corporation, Banking, and Business Law offers a series of recommendations for revisions in the Uniform Partnership Act. See U.P.A. Revision Subcomm. of the ABA Comm. on Partnerships and Unincorporated Business Orgs., Should the Uniform Partnership Act be Revised?, (1986) reprinted in 43 Bus. Law. 121, 124 (1987). Among other things, the report advocates greater entity treatment for partnerships, and it recommends enforcement of partnership agreements providing that a withdrawal is not a dissolution. Id. at 125.

One commentator has criticized the UPA's dissolution provisions and advocated that withdrawal of a partner should not automatically cause the dissolution of the partnership. See Ribstein, A Statutory Approach to Partnership Dissociation, 65 Wash.U.L.Q. 357, 368 (1987). He argues:

> [I]f the business continues, dissolution should not have a drastic effect on liability. In fact, it does not because the continuing partnership is liable for any debts it incurs without regard to §35. Therefore, the principal effect of dissolution where the partnership business continues is merely to cut off the liability and the power to bind of a withdrawn partner or estate. Accomplishing this result by destroying the partnership entity is like removing a door from a building by demolishing the building and then rebuilding it without the door. A partner's authority obviously can be terminated as effectively under the U.P.A. without the costs resulting from dissolution of the partnership entity.

Id. at 370. In his proposed revisions to the statute, Professor Ribstein defines circumstances under which a partner may "dissociate" without causing a dissolution of the partnership. Id. at 417-420. His proposals provide that a partner who ceases to be a partner "shall not be personally liable as a partner for any partnership debt incurred, and shall not have the power to bind the partnership" unless the other party to the transaction either (1) was a creditor at the time of the event, or had extended credit within the previous two years, and had no knowledge of the "dissociation," or (2) had known of the change in status of the individual as a

revision of the act. A preliminary reading of a revised act occurred in August of 1989, and a further reading is scheduled for the following summer.[2]

It is quite possible the Commissioners will approve revisions according a greater degree of entity status to the partnership. But unless the revisions abandon all features of the aggregate approach, including the joint liability of partners, most of the issues concerning post-withdrawal claims to income and vicarious liability discussed in this chapter will continue to be important to law partnerships. For example, a new partnership act may provide that withdrawal under specified conditions does not constitute a technical dissolution. This is the approach presently followed in California.[3] But if the withdrawing partner has any continuing liability for the acts of co-partners or debts of the partnership, some process for finishing the business on which there is shared liability must exist. Under present law, this undertaking is called "winding up," an essential process unless an entity is made solely responsible for liabilities. Although a

---

partner but could not be charged with the knowledge of the event because notice of the "dissociation" had not been published. Id. at 422. This, Professor Ribstein recognizes, reaches the same general result as the current law. Id.; see Unif. Partnership Act §35, 6 U.L.A. 429 (1969). Although Professor Ribstein would permit a partnership to survive the withdrawal of the partner, his proposals seemingly do not eliminate the threat of liability for pre-withdrawal claims or claims arising from the completion of business undertaken prior to the withdrawal.

One response is to require an indemnification of the former partner by the continuing partners. Professor Ribstein's proposals include provisions requiring a buyout of the withdrawing partner's interest together with an indemnification "by the partnership against all liabilities for which the partner is held liable by reasons of having been a partner in the partnership." Ribstein, supra, at 420-421. There are some problems, however, with this proposal. Claims may be unknown at the time of the buyout, but arise later if the former partner's interest was valued without knowledge of these liabilities, and if the individual is indemnified later by the continuing partners, the account valuation may prove too generous to the withdrawn partner. Moreover, if a partnership is in a state of decline, indemnification will provide an incentive for partners to "bail out" of the partnership early and demand indemnification for liabilities that are not fully reflected in the valuation of the partner's interest, but which are later asserted against the partnership.

[2] For the views of the project's reporter, see Weidner, A Perspective to Reconsider Partnership Law, 16 Fla. St. U.L. Rev. 1 (1988).

[3] See supra §4.2.1.

revised law may both change the terminology of "dissolution" and "winding up" provisions and provide that the original partnership continues following a partner's "withdrawal," it will not likely permit a partner to shed all liabilities through the simple expedient of leaving the partnership.

Chapter 5
THE RELEVANCE
OF INCORPORATION

§5.1 The Birth of the Professional Corporation

In the past, corporations were barred from practicing the so-called learned professions, including law. A number of reasons were advanced in support of the restriction: (1) a corporation is not eligible for a license to practice the profession; (2) the relationship between a professional and a client is personal in nature, and a corporation cannot have the personal qualifications necessary to sustain the relationship; (3) a professional employed by a corporation would have conflicting duties to the employer and the client; (4) a corporation would be beyond the reach of professional discipline; and (5) a corporate entity would shield the professional from liability for malpractice.[1]

The negation of the corporate option denied professionals associated in practice significant tax advantages, the most important of which was the opportunity to establish pension plans offering greater benefits than those available to partnerships. In the early 1960s, pressure to permit professionals to incorporate their practices began to develop. In response, state legislatures enacted statutes enabling professionals to form what have been called "professional corporations" or "professional associations."[2] By legislation and judicial rule-making, lawyers now have the option of incorporating their practices.[3]

---

§5.1   [1] See Jones, The Professional Corporation, 27 Fordham L. Rev. 353, 354–355 (1958).

[2] Most statutes and court rules speak of a "professional corporation" or a "professional service corporation." A few states use the label "professional association." The term "association" has varied meanings. For example, the UPA defines a partnership as an "association of two or more persons to carry on as co-owners a business for profit." Unif. Partnership Act §6. In that context, the term is used to mean nothing more than a coming together. For federal income tax purposes, the definition of a corporation includes "associations." See IRC §7701(a)(3). Needless to say, the term "association" should be viewed and used with caution. In the present context, a "professional association" may be either identical to a professional corporation or a form of organization that does not require incorporation but has significant attributes of a corporation.

[3] A 1961 ethics opinion of the American Bar Association's Committee on Professional Ethics concluded attorneys may practice through corporate firms if certain safeguards are met: (1) the lawyer remains personally responsible to the client for services rendered; (2) restrictions on liability of other lawyers in the firm must be made apparent to the client; (3) none of the stockholders may be non-lawyers; (4) there must be no sharing of profits with employees who are not lawyers; and (4) only lawyers may participate in the management of the firm. See ABA Comm. of Professional Ethics, Formal Opinion 303 (1961). See also Model Rules, Conduct Rule 5.1 (requiring a partner or shareholder of a law firm to make reasonable efforts to ensure that the firm has measures in effect to assure that all lawyers in the firm conform to the rules of professional conduct, but adding that a lawyer is responsible for another lawyer's violation of these rules only if the lawyer orders or ratifies the conduct or has direct supervisory authority over the other lawyer, knows of the conduct, and fails to take remedial action).

The dramatic tax advantages accorded professionals opting for the corporate form of organization no longer exist, and most law firms operate under the partnership form of organization. Many, however, are incorporated. This raises the question of whether the incorporation of a law firm changes in any meaningful way the relative rights and obligations of its members if the firm breaks up.

Viewed *solely* from the perspective of corporate law, the presence of an incorporated entity alters the relative rights of its owners in the event of a breakup. Continuity of life means the corporation, unlike the partnership, survives the departure of an owner, whose withdrawal in and of itself does not cause a technical dissolution of the firm. With the purchase of his or her shares, the shareholder's interest in the corporation is terminated. And an entity that survives the withdrawal of its owners might plausibly assert a "possessory" right to clients superior to that of any of its shareholders.

This, however, is only the corporate law perspective. A more comprehensive picture requires a consideration of the degree to which associated lawyers' obligations to each other (the partnership law perspective) and their clients (the legal ethics perspective) modify the "corporate" character of the incorporated law firm.

§5.2 The Professional Law Corporation as a Partnership: Fox v. Abrams

An important 1985 case indicates that partnership rather than corporate law will control the relative rights of attorneys to fees following the breakup of a professional law corporation. In Fox v. Abrams,[1] the dispute concerned the rights of lawyers previously associated in a professional corporation to fees generated from cases in process at the time of the resignations. A buy-sell agreement permitted withdrawing shareholders to share in profits for a period of time following their withdrawals but did not require expressly the former shareholders to share with the firm their post-withdrawal

---

§5.2 [1] 163 Cal. App. 3d 610, 210 Cal. Rptr. 260 (1985).

income. The court refused to interpret the agreement as requiring nonreciprocal profit sharing. In so ruling, it relied heavily on Jewel v. Boxer,[2] which earlier had reached the unsurprising conclusions that law partners share fees for completion of unfinished business in the same ratio that they divided income prior to a dissolution and that no partner is entitled to additional income for completion of the cases. *Fox* applied the same principles to the professional corporation:

> Applying the reasoning of *Jewel* is fair to both sides and prevents the lawyers from scrambling for the work in process as the law firm breaks up. Respondents' reasoning leads to a one-sided result, based upon an arbitrary characterization of themselves as "departing" and appellant as "remaining," left holding the bag to pay compensation to the departed members. The law should simply recognize that the lawyers once practiced together and are now practicing separately on the same cases as before, and no good purpose is served by characterizing one entity as the members who left and the other entity as the members who remained.
>
> Jewel v. Boxer is also based in part upon fiduciary obligations of law partners. It is well-known that the primary purpose of the laws permitting professionals to incorporate was to allow them to take advantage of various tax benefits available to corporate employers and employees. There is no reason to hold that when lawyers decide to practice together in corporate form rather than partnership, they are relieved of fiduciary obligations toward each other with respect to the corporation's business.[3]

Fox's reasoning is seductive and does reflect the widely held view that professional corporations exist largely for tax reasons.[4] It is

---

[2] 156 Cal. App. 3d 171, 203 Cal. Rptr. 13 (1984).

[3] *Fox*, 163 Cal. App. 3d at 616, 617, 210 Cal. Rptr. at 265. See also Kreutzer v. Wallace, 342 So. 2d 981 (Fla. App. 1977) (applying partnership law principles to the winding up of a dissolved professional corporation).

[4] See, e.g., In re Florida Bar, 133 So. 2d 554, 556 (1961) ("We construe the legislation . . . as a frank and forthright effort to adapt certain business and professional relationships to the requirements of the Internal Revenue Service in order that the members of such businesses or professions may be placed on an equal footing with other taxpayers."); In re Rhode Island Bar Assoc., 263 A.2d 692, 695 (1970) ("The professional service corporation law in this state was enacted for the purpose of enabling members of the covered professions, not previously allowed to incorporate, to form corporations, thus putting such members on an equal footing with other taxpayers.").

also consistent with contemporary thought that closely held businesses resemble more closely partnerships than corporations and should be liberated from the more rigid and technical application of corporate formalities. To a considerable extent, the law applicable to close corporations has been reformed to allow participants in "intimate" business ventures to structure their relationships by agreement, thus allowing the closely held corporation to more closely resemble a partnership. If *Fox* had been written on a clean slate, the opinion would offer a sensible framework for resolving a wide variety of disputes developing from the breakup of law firms.

And therein lies the difficulty. Although the professional corporation may be a product of tax planning, it is a distinct association under state law and possesses many of the attributes of a corporation. These include, to one degree or another, continuity of life, free transferability of interests, centralization of management, and limited liability. In assuming the incorporated status of a law firm is relevant only for tax purposes, *Fox* disregarded the myriad of state law provisions sharply distinguishing professional corporations from partnerships, including limitations on the liability of withdrawing shareholders and requirements that those who leave an incorporated firm must promptly terminate their interests in that firm. As the following sections discuss more fully, *Fox*'s rather romantic notion that shareholders of an incorporated law firm are "partners" except for tax purposes simply does not comport with the corporate characteristics assigned their firms by state law.[5]

§5.3 Limitations on Liability

A withdrawing shareholder will carry from the law firm no risk of liability for tort or contract claims against the firm *unless* the same

---

[5]Cf. Jones v. Teilborg, 151 Ariz. 240, 727 P.2d 18 (Ariz. App. 1986) (Although an agreement entitled withdrawing shareholders to their accounts receivable, and the law corporation would be liable in the event of nonpayment, remaining shareholders were not individually liable for these amounts because the withdrawing shareholders were "estopped" from denying the existence of the corporation: "The appellees cannot take advantage of the corporate entity when convenient, and disregard it when inconvenient.").

liability existed when the lawyer was in the firm. Accordingly, the possibility of liability in the breakup setting will turn on whether the professional law corporation, like the business corporation, successfully limits the liability of owners for claims against the firm or other members of the firm. This is an issue of some controversy.[1] It is also one on which states vary widely, and the degree to which any such liability exists is determined by a curious and sometimes contradictory mix of legal ethics and principles of corporate law grounded in statutes.

By court rule, statute, or a combination of both, every state permits lawyers to incorporate their practices. The rules and statutes make available to professionals the benefits of the corporate form of organization for the business aspects of their practices at the same time that they preserve the traditional obligations owed by professionals[2] to their clients. Thus, the lawyer-shareholder remains liable for his or her own professional misconduct, and the status of a firm as a corporation does not alter the relationship between the lawyer and the client.[3] As to the business aspects of the firms, the statutes

---

§5.3 [1] See generally C. Wolfram, Modern Legal Ethics §5.5.6 at 237 (1986); Pass, Professional Corporations and Attorney-Shareholders: The Decline of Limited Liability, 11 J. Corp. L. (1986); Grippando, Don't Take it Personally — Limited Liability for Attorney Shareholders Under Florida's Professional Service Corporation Act, 15 Fla. St. U. L. Rev. 279 (1987); Kalish, Lawyer Liability and Incorporation of the Law Firm: A Compromise Model Providing Lawyer-Owners with Limited Liability and Imposing Broad Vicarious Liability on Some Lawyer-Employees, 29 Ariz. L. Rev. 563 (1987).

[2] Court rules, of course, are directed only at attorneys.

[3] See, e.g., Fla. Stat. Ann. §621.07 (West Supp. 1989) ("Nothing contained in this act shall be interpreted to abolish, repeal, modify, restrict, or limit the law now in effect in this state applicable to the professional relationship and liabilities between the person furnishing the professional services and the person receiving such professional service and to the standards for professional conduct. . . . "); Ohio Rev. Code Ann. §1785.04 (1985) ("[The professional corporation provisions] do not modify any law applicable to the relationship between a person furnishing professional service and a person receiving such service, including liability arising out of such professional service."); Tenn. Code Ann. §48-3-407 (Michie 1988) ("[N]othing contained in this part shall change the law or existing standards applicable to the relationship between the person furnishing a professional service and the person receiving such service including, but not by way of limitation, the rules of privileged communication and the contract, tort and other legal liabilities and professional relationships between such persons."). See also Model Prof. Corp. Supp. §34(a) (1984) ("Each individual who renders professional services as an

invariably incorporate by reference all provisions of the state's business corporations law not inconsistent with the professional corporation statute.[4] Beyond this, there are significant variations. With the caveat that generalizations are chancy and the language of the specific state statute should be consulted, the following represent the

---

employee of a . . . professional corporation is liable for a negligent or wrongful act or omission in which he personally participates to the same extent as if he rendered the services as a sole practitioner.").

[4] See, e.g., Ariz. Rev. Stat. Ann. §10-904 (West 1977) ("Professional corporations shall be governed by the laws applicable to other Arizona private corporations organized for profit except insofar as such laws shall be limited or enlarged by or contrary to the provisions of this chapter."); Cal. Corp. Code Ann. §13403 (Deering's 1989) ("The provisions of the General Corporation Law shall apply to professional corporations, except where such provisions are in conflict with the provisions of this part."); Del. Code Ann. tit. 8, §618 (Michie 1983) ("This title shall be applicable to a corporation organized pursuant to this chapter, except to the extent that any of the provisions of this chapter are interpreted to be in conflict with the provisions of this title, and in such event the provisions and sections of this chapter shall take precedence with respect to a corporation organized pursuant to this chapter."); Mich. Stat. Ann. §21.315(13) (Callaghan 1983) (The corporation act "shall be applicable to a corporation organized pursuant to this act except to the extent that any of the provisions of this act are interpreted to be in conflict with the provisions of this act."); N.Y. Bus. Corp. Law §1513 (McKinney 1986) ("This chapter . . . shall be applicable to a professional service corporation except to the extent that the provisions thereof conflict with this article."); Okla. Stat. Ann. tit. 18, §804 ("The Oklahoma General Corporation Act shall be applicable to professional corporations . . . except where inconsistent with the letter and purpose of this act."); S.C. Code Ann. §33-19-102 (Law. Co-op. 1988) ("Chapters 1 through 17 apply to professional corporations . . . to the extent not inconsistent with the provisions of this chapter."); Wis. Stat. Ann. §180.99(3) (West Supp. 1988) ("Other provisions of this chapter shall be applicable to such corporations, including their organization, and they shall enjoy the powers and privileges and be subject to the duties, restrictions and liabilities of other stock corporations, excepting as such powers may be limited or enlarged by this section. . . . If any provision of this section conflicts with any other provision of this chapter, or with other provisions of the statutes, this section shall control."). See also Model Prof. Corp. Supp. §2 (1984) ("The [Model] Business Corporation Act applies to professional corporations . . . to the extent not inconsistent with the provisions of this Supplement.").

Some states expressly reject application of partnership law to professional associations. See, e.g., Ga. Code Ann. §84-4318 (1985). Nevada permits both professional corporations and professional associations. Provisions of the business corporations act apply to professional corporations unless inconsistent with the chapter on professional corporations. See Nev. Rev. Stat. §89.030 (1985). Although corporate law is not made expressly applicable, the statute indicates that the UPA does not apply to professional associations. Id. §89.200.

main approaches to the issue of joint and several liability of share-holders.

- Lawyers are responsible only for their own acts, errors, or omissions.[5]
- Lawyers are responsible for their acts, errors, and omissions as well as those of individuals under their direct supervision and control.[6]
- All shareholders arc jointly and severally liable for claims arising from the rendition of professional services.[7]
- All shareholders are jointly and severally liable for claims arising from the rendition of professional services unless the firm maintains professional liability insurance in specified amounts.[8]
- Lawyer-shareholders are required to personally guarantee the payment of errors and omissions claims against their firms up to specified amounts.[9]

A number of states expressly relieve shareholders of liability for debts of their firm not arising from the performance of professional

---

[5] See, e.g., Alaska Stat. §10.45.140 (1985); Ky. Rev. Stat. Ann. §274.055 (Michie 1988).

[6] See, e.g., Conn. Gen. Stat. Ann. §33-182(e) (West 1987); D.C. Code Ann. §29-611 (Michie 1981); Fla. Stat. Ann. §621.07 (West Supp. 1989); Mich. Stat. Ann. §21.315(6) (Callaghan 1983); Minn. Stat. Ann. §319A.10 (West 1989) (no person is personally liable in tort for any act not personally participated in); N.Y. Bus. Corp. Law §1505 (McKinney 1986); N.J. Rev. Stat. Ann. §14A:17-8 (West 1988) (rules of the New Jersey Supreme Court, however, require law corporations to obtain professional liability insurance in specified amounts); Me. Rev. Stat. Ann. tit. 13, §708 (West 1981) (joint and several liability for shareholders participating in a professional capacity in rendering services).

[7] See, e.g., Ariz. Rev. Stat. Ann. §10-905 (West 1977); Del. Sup. Ct. Rules, Rule 67(h) (Michie 1988); Haw. Sup. Ct. Rules, Rule 6(g)(1); Ill. Sup. Ct. Rules, Rule 721(d); Ind. Rules for Admission to the Bar and the Disc. of Attor., Rule 27(c); Or. Rev. Stat. Ann. §58.185 (Butterworth 1988); Wis. Stat. Ann. §180.99(8) (West Supp. 1988). See also Nelson v. Patrick, 326 S.E.2d 45, 50 (N.C. Ct. App. 1985) ("As a partner in defendant professional corporation, defendant Flournoy could be held jointly and severally liable for any negligence of his partner. . . .").

[8] See, e.g., Colo. Rules of Civil Proc., Rule 265G; S.D. Codified Laws Ann. §47-13A-2(7) (1983).

[9] See Law Corp. Rules of the St. Bar of Cal., Rule IVB (1986).

services for client,[10] although this is implicit in the statutes of others calling for the application of business corporation laws to the extent consistent with the professional corporation statutes. Ohio is a notable and, as will be seen shortly,[11] feisty exception. A sweeping rule of its supreme court provides:

> The participation of an individual as a shareholder of a legal professional association shall be on condition that such individual shall, and by such participation does, guarantee the financial responsibility of the association for its breach of any duty, whether or not arising from the attorney-client relationship.[12]

Ohio notwithstanding, the incorporation of a law practice in virtually any state alters the degree to which "partners" are individually responsible for claims against their firms and colleagues, at least when those claims are not based upon malpractice or other wrongful conduct.[13] In the large number of states that do not provide for joint and several liability as to these claims, the alteration is significant.[14]

§5.4 *Judicial Invalidation of Statutory Limitations on Liability*

As noted, most states have statutes permitting professionals to incorporate; many states have supreme court rules covering the same

---

[10] See, e.g., Ky. Rev. Stat. Ann. §274.055 (Michie Supp. 1988); Or. Rev. Stat. Ann. §58.185 (Butterworth 1988); Wis. Stat. Ann. §180.99(8) (West 1988).

[11] See infra §5.4

[12] Sup. Ct. Rules for the Gov. of the Bar of Ohio, Rule III(4).

[13] Some exculpatory provisions give rise to interpretive difficulties. The Georgia statute, for example, relieves shareholders from liability (other than that arising from the rendition of professional services) "unless the member or shareholder has personally participated in the transaction for which the debt or claim is made out or out of which it arises." Ga. Code Ann. §84-4307 (1985). The meaning of "personally participated" is unclear, particularly as applied to business transactions.

For a discussion of shareholders' nonmalpractice liability, see 50 ALR4th 1276.

[14] Claims arising from business debts may be substantial. Cf. Jensen, An Offer the Lawyers Just Couldn't Refuse, Natl. L.J., May 29, 1989, at 8, col. 1.

subject; and some states have both. Traditionally, the judiciaries of
the states have borne primary responsibility for regulating the legal
profession and attempting to ensure that lawyers perform their
services with a modicum of professional responsibility. The notion
that courts are vested with the "inherent power" to set the standards
of the profession and oversee the administration of justice[1] has been
the basis for judicial invalidation of a number of statutes affecting
the courts and the bar.[2] Because in many states enabling a law firm to
incorporate eliminates the joint and several liability of a firm mem-

---

§5.4 [1] See, e.g., In re Florida Bar, 133 So. 2d 554, 555 (1961) (noting in
connection with its approval of professional corporation rules that "the responsibility which the Constitution imposes upon us to supervise admissions to the practice
of law and the discipline of those admitted, necessarily requires an examination by
this Court into any proposal that directly affects these two constitutional functions"). Sometimes, a court's view of its inherent power is made explicit in its own
rules. Rule 39 of the Nevada Supreme Court, for example, provides:

> Inherent Powers of Courts. Attorneys being court officers and essential
> aids in the administration of justice, the government of the legal profession is
> a judicial function. . . . The supreme court rules set forth in this Part III are
> the exclusive rules for the governing of the legal profession in Nevada.

See also In re Rhode Island Bar Assoc., 263 A.2d 692, 695 (R.I. 1970) ("It must be
assumed . . . that in enacting the professional service corporation law, the General
Assembly . . . recognized in inherent and exclusive power of this court to license
attorneys at law, to admit them to practice, and to control the practice of law
generally.").

  [2] See, e.g., Board of Commissioners of Ala. State Bar v. Baxley, 295 Ala. 100,
324 So. 2d 256 (1975) (striking down a statute limiting the reexamination rights of
bar applicants); Idaho State Bar Assn. v. Idaho Pub. Utilities Commn., 102 Idaho
672, 637 P.2d 1168 (1961) (striking down a statute permitting nonlawyers to
represent clients before administrative agencies); Archer v. Ogden, 600 P.2d 1223
(Okl. 1979) (striking down a statute establishing residency requirements for attorneys). See generally C. Wolfram, Modern Legal Ethics §2.2.3 (1988); Dowling,
The Inherent Power of the Judiciary, 21 A.B.A.J. 635 (1935); Note, The Inherent
Power of the Judiciary to Regulate the Practice of Law, 60 Minn. L. Rev. 783
(1976).

  Some courts are reluctant to exercise inherent power:

> [T]he radical form of the negative inherent powers doctrine is followed by a
> large number, perhaps a majority, of American jurisdictions. Some courts are
> more restrained. They assert the less jealous doctrine that the courts will share
> the power to regulate lawyers with other branches of government so long as
> this poses no threat to the continued vitality of the judicial branch.

C. Wolfram, supra. §2.2.3 at 27.

ber for claims against the firm,[3] there is a potential for conflict between legislatures limiting the liability of professionals who incorporate and judiciaries intent on using the threat of economic sanctions as a means of prompting lawyers to ensure that all members of their firms provide services in a professional manner.[4] In some states, any potential for conflict is avoided by statutory provisions expressly authorizing the judiciary to develop guidelines applicable to attorneys who incorporate their practices.[5] Most statutes, however, are silent on this point, and a few authorize only those judicial guidelines that are not inconsistent with the statute.[6]

§5.4.1 The Assertion of Inherent Power to Expand Lawyer Liability

One of the more candid and assertive expressions of inherent power with respect to attorney misconduct was articulated by the Georgia Supreme Court in First Bank & Trust Co. v. Zagoria.[7] The

---

[3] Under partnership law, partners are jointly and severally liable for the wrongful conduct of a partner and jointly liable for all other debts and obligations of the partnership. See Unif. Partnership Act §§13-15. See generally A. Bromberg and L. Ribstein, Bromberg and Ribstein on Partnership §4.07 (1988).

[4] Hawaii provides a good example of the preemption of legislative liability standards by tougher judicial guidelines. The Hawaii statute on professional corporations provides for the joint and several liability of shareholders with respect to professional services provided by employees acting within the scope of their employment or with apparent authority. The liability is eliminated if the corporation secures insurance in amounts specified by the appropriate licensing authority. See Haw. Rev. Stat. §415A-11 (Supp 1988). The Hawaii Supreme Court, however, set forth its own financial responsibility standards: (1) the incorporation of a law firm does not limit the liability of shareholders, officers, and directors of the firm, and (2) the shareholders, officers, and directors have the same liability as partners for claims arising out of the performance of professional services. See Haw. Sup. Ct. Rules, Rule 6(g)(1). The court also declined to set any minimum amount of security, noting "[t]his court will not permit the posting of limited security as an alternative to the unlimited liability" imposed by the rule. Id. Rule 6(g)(2).

[5] See, e.g., Ill. Stat. Ann. ch. 32, §415-16 (West 1988) ("[T]he provisions of this Act shall be applicable to attorneys at law only to the extent and under such terms and conditions as the Supreme Court of Illinois shall determine to be necessary and appropriate.").

[6] See N.Y. Bus. Corp. Law §1515 (McKinney 1986); Or. Rev. Stat. Ann. §58.365(3) (Butterworth 1988).

[7] 250 Ga. 844, 302 S.E.2d 674 (1983).

Georgia statute provides that, except for the performance of professional services by the shareholder, a shareholder of a professional corporation is not personally liable "for the debts of, or claims against, the professional association unless such member had personally participated in the transaction for which the debt or claim is made or out of which it arises."[8] Reasoning that the statute accords shareholders in a professional corporation the same privileges and immunities as shareholders in a business corporation and that a shareholder is not liable for the acts of another shareholder, the intermediate appellate court exonerated a shareholder in a professional law corporation from liability for the nonpayment of checks written on the firm's escrow account by another shareholder.[9] The Georgia Supreme Court reversed:

> We do not view this case as one in which we need to interpret the statute providing for the creation and operation of professional corporations. We rather view this case as one that calls for the exercise of this court's authority to regulate the practice of law. . . .
>
> The diligence of this court has been directed toward the assurance that the law practice will be a professional service and not simply a commercial enterprise. The primary distinction is that a profession is a calling which demands adherence to the public interest as the foremost obligation of the practitioner. . . .
>
> By enacting the professional corporation statute, the legislature performed a useful and constitutional act. . . . The shareholders of a professional corporation have the same insulation from liability as shareholders of other corporations with respect to obligations of a purely business and nonprofessional nature. However, the influence of the statute upon the professional corporation cannot extend to the regulation of the law practice so as to impose a limitation of liability

---

[8] Ga. Code Ann. §84-4307 (Harrison 1985). See also id. §84-4318 (Harrison 1985) ("A professional association organized pursuant to this chapter shall be governed generally by all laws governing or applying to corporations, where applicable, and not in conflict with this chapter; and no such association shall be held or deemed to be a partnership nor shall such association be governed by laws relating to partnerships.").

[9] See Zagoria v. Dubose Enterprises, Inc., 163 Ga. App. 880, 296 S.E.2d 353 (1982), *rev'd sub nom.* First Bank & Trust Co. v. Zagoria, 250 Ga. 844, 302 S.E.2d 674 (1983).

for acts of malpractice or obligations incurred because of a breach of a duty to a client.

The professional nature of the law practice and its obligations to the public interest require that each lawyer be civilly responsible for his professional acts. . . . It is inappropriate for the lawyer to play hide-and-seek in the shadows of the corporate veil and thus escape the responsibilities of professionalism. . . .

We hold that when a lawyer holds himself out as a member of a law firm the lawyer will be liable not only for his own professional misdeeds but also for those of the other members of the firm. We make no distinction between partnerships and professional corporations in this respect. We cannot allow a corporate veil to hang from the cornices of professional corporations which engage in the law practice.[10]

Similar reasoning on inherent judicial power was advanced by the Ohio Supreme Court in a case involving contract claims against a law firm. In South High Development, Ltd. v. Weiner, Lippe & Cromley,[11] a property owner sought to hold the shareholders personally liable for their law corporation's breach of an office lease. Although the Ohio constitution includes a guarantee of limited liability for shareholders, the court distinguished professional from business corporations on the ground that shareholders of the former are more active in their firms and "closer" to management than

---

[10] 302 S.E.2d at 675-676. The court also rejected the argument that Ethical Consideration 6-6, which allows a stockholder in a law corporation to limit his or her liability for the malpractice of associates "to the extent permitted by law," is self-executing: "We find nothing in the record of this case to indicate that any contract or arrangement for limitation of liability was ever entered into by [the attorney] and the clients of his professional corporation." Id. at 676.

Zagoria's rejection of statutory limitations of liability for professional misconduct means that shareholders in states with judiciaries that are activists on matters affecting the legal profession cannot rely on statutes that directly limit their liability. The case is unusual in that courts retaining control over liability issues typically enunciate their position in rules rather than reported opinions addressing actual controversies. See Grippando, Don't Take it Personally — Limited Liability for Attorney Shareholders Under Florida's Professional Service Corporation Act, 15 Fla. St. U.L. Rev. 279, 313 (1987).

[11] 4 Ohio St. 3d 1, 445 N.E.2d 1106 (1983).

shareholders of the latter.[12] On the basis of this distinction, the court justified and enforced its rule requiring lawyers to "guarantee the financial responsibilities" of their professional corporations.[13]

§5.4.2 The Softer View: Reconciling Inherent Power with Statutory Provisions Concerning Liability

In contrast to *Zagoria* and *South High Development* are decisions that resolve possible conflicts between legal ethics and statutory or constitutional provisions affecting liability in a more conciliatory manner.

In We're Associates v. Cohen, Stracher & Bloom,[14] a professional law corporation breached a lease and the landlord sought to hold the shareholders of the corporation liable. The New York Business Corporation Law provides that a shareholder of a professional service corporation is liable for his own negligence or misconduct as well as that of persons under his direct supervision and control, but it is silent on the question of liability for business debts of the firm.[15] Rejecting the reasoning of *South High Development,* the New York Court of Appeals concluded the statute carved only a limited exception to the principal of limited liability and, absent an abuse of the corporate form or the presence of personal guarantees, shareholders of professional corporations cannot be held personally liable for the business debts of their firms. The court added that

---

[12] "The shareholders of the professional corporation will have direct contact with the running of the corporation, so limited liability is not necessary for them." 445 N.E.2d at 1108. This analysis is criticized, correctly, in Paas, Professional Corporations and Attorney-Shareholders: The Decline of Limited Liability, 11 J. Corp. L. 371, 388 (1986).

[13] For the text of the rule, see supra §5.3. See also Street v. Sugermen, 202 So. 2d 749, 751 (Fla. 1967) (permitting a creditor of attorneys to levy upon their stock in a law corporation and commenting that the "privilege of incorporation was most definitely not created or extended in order that those availing themselves of the benefits could be cloaked with an immunity inimical to legal order and public interest").

[14] 65 N.Y.2d 148, 480 N.E.2d 357, 490 N.Y.S.2d 743 (1985).

[15] See N.Y. Bus. Corp. Law §1505 (McKinney 1986).

nothing in the New York Code of Professional Responsibility suggests the imposition of personal liability in this type of case.[16]

On the malpractice front, a recent decision of a Utah intermediate appellate court reached a similar conclusion. In Stewart v. Coffman,[17] the court held that a shareholder of a law corporation is not liable for the acts or omissions of another shareholder. The court reasoned that although the Utah Constitution authorized the supreme court to "govern the practice of law," legislation affecting the joint and several liability of lawyers for malpractice does not impermissibly tread on judicial terrain because regulation by the court is directed toward discipline rather than civil toward liability. The Utah Supreme Court granted *certiorari* on *Stewart,* but the case was settled before disposition by the court.

§5.4.3 An Evaluation

Stewart is sensible in its emphasis on the disciplinary function of legal ethics. At least in the area of negligence (as opposed to breach of fiduciary duty or fraud), legal ethics, although often cited in opinions, have not provided an independent basis for a significant number of civil awards.[18] Along this line, the preamble to the Model Rules of Professional Conduct rejects use of the rules as a basis for civil liability.[19]

A broader issue is whether making attorneys liable for the misdeeds of their "partners," as in *Zagoria,* or personally responsible

---

[16] Interestingly, the New York statute defers to judicial regulation "except to the extent in conflict herewith." N.Y. Bus. Corp. Law §1515 (McKinney 1986).

[17] 748 P.2d 579 (Utah App. 1988).

[18] See generally R. Mallen and J. Smith, Legal Malpractice §1.9 (1989).

[19] See Model Rules, Scope ("The Rules are designed to provide guidance to lawyers and to provide a structure for regulating conduct through disciplinary agencies. They are not designed to be a basis for civil liability."). Cf. Model Code, Preliminary Statement ("The Model Code . . . does [not] undertake to define standards of civil liability of lawyers for professional conduct."). For an argument that the Model Rules will nevertheless prove important in civil litigation, see Hoover, The Model Rules of Professional Conduct and Lawyer Malpractice Actions: The Gap Between Code and Common Law Narrows, 22 New Eng. L. Rev. 595 (1988).

for all claims against their firms, as in *South High Development,* is an appropriate exercise of supervisory power over the legal profession in light of contrary statutory limitations on liability. Although few would deny that separation of power considerations do give rise to inherent judicial power to invalidate legislation impeding the ability of the judiciary to oversee the administration of justice, the power is not limitless. In defining the boundaries of the power, the focus is appropriately placed on statutes materially interfering with the adjudicatory process:

> In American democratic theory, popularly elected legislatures are the primary source of lawmaking, whether judges enjoy their secondary lawmaking role or not. Legislatures are specifically the constitutionally preferred source of initiatives for altering the modes of regulating occupations such as the legal profession. [T]he judiciary should insist upon its own conceptions of how to regulate the legal profession only in instances in which yielding to another branch would directly and substantially impair the ability of the courts to adjudicate cases and conduct other business necessarily and properly before them.[20]

It is difficult to see in either *Zagoria* or *South High Development* the kind of threat to the adjudicatory process that would justify disregard of duly enacted statutes or constitutional provisions. In only the most tangential way do bounced checks and a broken office lease affect the judiciary's capacity to oversee the administration of justice. Had the courts been faced with legislation exculpating attorneys from liability for their own malpractice, the assertion of inherent judicial power would have been defensible, indeed necessary. That, however, was not the case in either *Zagoria* or *South High Development.*

---

[20] C. Wolfram, Modern Legal Ethics §2.2.3 at 31 (1988). See also Note, The Inherent Power of the Judiciary to Regulate the Practice of Law, 60 Minn. L. Rev. 783, 795-804 (1976) (suggesting an analysis focusing on interference with the adjudicatory process).

§5.5 *Joint and Several Liability in the Breakup Setting*

Because a significant number of jurisdictions make a shareholder jointly and severally liable for the acts, errors, or omissions of others in the firm, a question arises as to when the joint and several liability of an attorney who withdraws from a professional corporation ends. Unfortunately, the statutes provide little guidance on this important question.

§5.5.1   The Inapplicability of Winding Up Principles

If the breakup of a law corporation is governed by a partnership law model, the withdrawal of a shareholder would cause the shareholder to cease to be associated in the carrying on of the business. The shareholder would, however, be associated with the other shareholders in the winding up of unfinished business. During this winding-up period, matters in which the withdrawing shareholder and the remaining shareholders have a joint interest would be brought to a close. Absent a contrary agreement, income on these cases would be divided on the basis of pre-withdrawal ratios, and the "partners" would have joint and several liability for malpractice in the winding up of the cases.[1] Fox v. Abrams[2] treated a professional law corporation as a partnership for purposes of the right to share income from the completion of unfinished business. The logical extension of an approach that keeps the partnership alive, for sharing of income purposes, until unfinished business is completed would be to employ partnership law liability principles as well.

Applying winding up principles to the incorporated law firm, however, seems inconsistent with a number of statutes and rules requiring an abrupt termination of the relationship between lawyers and the firms they are leaving. The push to separate comes in a

---

§5.5   [1] A few malpractice claims are based upon breach of contract, in which case the liability of partners would be joint but not several. See Unif. Partnership Act §15.

[2] See supra §5.2.

variety of forms, including mandates for prompt transfer of shares to the corporation or other eligible shareholders following a with-drawal,[3] restrictions on ownership of stock in more than one profes-sional corporation,[4] requirements that shareholders must be active employees of the corporation,[5] denials of voting rights following resignation and without regard to record ownership of shares,[6] and provisions, applicable in the absence of an agreement to the contrary, calling for the valuation of a withdrawing shareholder's interest on the basis of book value as of the month *preceding* the withdrawal.[7] Statutes commanding a prompt termination of interest seemingly defy the extended relationship that partnership law's winding up provisions entail.

---

[3] See, e.g., Ariz. Rev. Stat. Ann. §10-909(D) (West 1977) (shares must be transferred within ninety days); Del. Code Ann. tit. 8, §611 (Michie 1983) (shares must be transferred forthwith); Ky. Rev. Stat. Ann. §274.095 (Michie 1988); Neb. Sup. Ct. Rules on Prof. Service Corporations, Rule I(D) (shares must be trans-ferred forthwith); R.I. Sup. Ct. Rules, Rule 41(g) (nine months).

[4] See, e.g., Alaska Stat. §10.45.060 (1985); Law Corp. Rules of the St. Bar. of Cal., Rule IVC (1986) (shareholder cannot practice law for another corporation); Vt. Stat. Ann. tit. 11, §806 (Equity 1984). This obviously renders intra-firm movement difficult unless shares are surrendered immediately upon departure from a firm. A number of states either expressly permit ownership of stock in more than one professional corporation or have dropped earlier restrictions on this subject. See, e.g., Fla. Stat. Ann. §621.06 (West 1977). Delaware and Illinois dropped restrictions they once had on the ownership of stock in more than one professional corporation, and a proposal by the state bar to eliminate California's restriction is under review by the supreme court.

[5] See, e.g., Ind. Rules for Admission to Bar and the Discipline of Attorneys, Rules 27(e) and (f); Mass. Sup. Jud. Ct. Rules, Rule 3:06; Neb. Sup. Ct. Rules on Professional Service Corp., Rule I(C); R.I. Gen. Laws §7-5.1-5 (Michie 1985) (an ineligible shareholder includes one who withdraws from active employment in the corporation). But see, e.g., D.C. Code Ann. §29-608 (Michie 1981) ("Nothing in this chapter shall require a shareholder . . . to have a present or future employment relationship with the corporation or actively to participate in any capacity in the production of income of, or performance of professional service by, such corpora-tion."); Md. Corps. & Assns. Code Ann. §5-106 (Michie 1985).

[6] See, e.g., Ariz. Rev. Stat. Ann. §10-909(D) (West 1977).

[7] See, e.g., Ala. Code §10-10-14 (Michie 1980) (book value determined by independent certified public accountant employed by the corporation for this purpose); Del. Code Ann. tit. 8, §613 (Michie 1983) (book value as determined by an independent certified public accountant employed by the corporation for this purpose); D.C. Code Ann. §29-617 (1981) (book value determined by use of generally accepted accounting principles, consistent with the method of accounting utilized by the corporation for federal income tax purposes).

Most state statutes on professional corporations do not include specific provisions mandating a quick termination of interest. Virtually every state statute, however, calls for the treatment of a professional corporation as a business corporation to the extent not inconsistent with the provisions of the professional corporation statute. The concept of completing unfinished business during a winding-up period is antithetical to the corporate model calling for a termination of shareholder status upon the surrender of shares. But this straightforward application of corporate law rather than partnership law can be neither the answer nor the rationalization, because under those statutes that provide for joint and several liability, the simple act of withdrawal may not in and of itself eliminate the risk of liabilities later asserted.

§5.2 Post-Withdrawal Liabilities Undetected at the Time of Withdrawal

The acts or omissions giving rise to liability may have occurred prior to the withdrawal but be undetected at that time. For example, the liability arising from a negligently drafted contract may not be apparent for some time after the legal services were provided.[8] In the case of the latent liability, the argument that withdrawal extinguishes any accountability a shareholder may have is fanciful. This conclusion is dictated not by partnership law's winding-up provisions, but rather by the direct and, in some states, joint and several liability of shareholders in professional corporations, a feature that distinguishes these shareholders from those of business corporations.

§5.5.3 Post-Withdrawal Liabilities Arising Subsequent to Withdrawal

More problematic are claims that develop in connection with work in process at the time of a shareholder's departure. By virtue of withdrawing, is the shareholder relieved of liability for the malprac-

---

[8] On the related issue of when statutes of limitations begin to run, see R. Mallen and J. Smith, Legal Malpractice §§18.9-18.18 (1989).

tice of former colleagues in completing the work in process? Generally, the statutes establishing joint and several liability imply an affirmative response by coupling liability with shareholder status, thereby suggesting that one who is no longer a shareholder has no joint and several liability.[9] Although this result may defeat the expectations of the client who retains a firm because of the reputation of one or more of its lawyers who subsequently leave the firm, it does comport with the reality that shareholders who withdraw from professional law corporations lack the capacity to monitor and, for this reason, should not be vicariously liable for malpractice occurring after their withdrawals.[10]

---

[9] Delaware is a good example: "Each *shareholder* shall be jointly and severally liable for damages proximately caused by an attorney employed by the corporation to a person for whom professional services are being rendered for any negligent or wrongful act or omission to the same extent as if the negligent or wrongful act or omission had been committed by the shareholder." Del. Sup. Ct. Rules, Rule 67(h) (emphasis added). Apparently, the court was not thinking of the problem presently discussed when it offered the following the commentary on the rule:

> Liability imposed upon lawyers practicing in professional service corporations with respect to acts or omissions committed in the course of delivering professional services should be the same as that applicable to lawyers practicing in any other form. Shareholders who stand to benefit financially through the corporate entity will be liable for professional derelictions as if the corporation were a law partnership and they were partners in it.

The Hawaiian position is similar, although the rule is somewhat more ambiguous. The supreme court rejected legislative restrictions on liability and provided that "the financial responsibility of [attorneys] is not limited by reason of being shareholders. . . ." This could be read to apply to a former shareholder as well. In the same sentence, however, the rule goes on to provide:

> [T]he liability of shareholders . . . for [malpractice] arising out of the performance of professional services by the corporation *while they are shareholders* . . . is joint and several to the same extent as if the shareholders . . . were general partners. . . .

Haw. Sup. Ct. Rules, Rule 6(g)(1) (emphasis added). See also Mass. Sup. Jud. Ct. Rules, Rule 3.06(e)(3)(b) ("All the individuals who are shareholders of the corporation *at the time of any negligent or wrongful act* [are jointly and severally liable within defined limits].") (emphasis added); Or. Rev. Stat. Ann. §58.185(2) (Butterworth 1988) ("A *shareholder* [may be held] . . . jointly and severally liable with all of the other shareholders. . . .") (emphasis added).

[10] Cf. Vinall, D.D.S., P.C. v. Hoffman, 133 Ariz. 322, 651 P.2d 850 (1982) (requiring the buyout of a dentist's interest in a professional corporation because, among other reasons, he might remain liable for the actions of those still practicing in the corporation if he remained a shareholder after resigning employment).

§5.5.4 Determining the Date of Withdrawal

There remains the problem of determining the point at which a lawyer "withdraws" from a professional corporation and thereby eliminates the risk of liability for subsequent malpractice. The possibilities are numerous. Withdrawal might occur on the date the lawyer physically departs the offices of the firm, the effective date of the lawyer's resignation, the date the lawyer loses all economic interest in the corporation, the date of any agreement concerning the valuation and sale of the lawyer's shares, the date on which the shares are transferred, or the date on which payment for shares is made.

Statutory provisions defining shareholder status in business corporations are a starting point for determining the date of withdrawal. In most states, status as a shareholder in a business corporation is determined by record ownership of shares.[11] By agreement or by statute, however, the economic and voting rights of a shareholder in a professional corporation may be eliminated at the point of resignation even if some time will pass before the shares are transferred to the corporation or other eligible shareholders. If that is the case, the importance of record dates of ownership is diminished, and the withdrawal should be deemed to have occurred when the withdrawing lawyer lost the rights and privileges normally accorded shareholders in the corporation.

§5.6 The California Conundrum

Rules adopted by the California state bar and approved by the state supreme court require shareholders to file with the state bar written

---

[11] See, e.g., Model Business Corp. Act §1.40(22) (1984). But cf. Hamlin, Segers & Mouton, P.A. v. Mouton, 382 So. 2d 752 (Fla. Dist. Ct. App. (1980) (affirming a circuit court order determining that a shareholder "effectively tendered his stock in the professional association, so obligated the association to buy his stock on terms stated by the 'buy and sell agreement' . . . , and thus became a general creditor of the corporation having rights superior to other shareholders in the subsequent litigation").

agreements jointly and severally guaranteeing payment by the corporation of claims based on errors and omissions.[1] The guarantees must be in an amount equal to at least $50 thousand for each claim and $100 thousand for all claims in the year. These figures are multiplied by the number of lawyers in the firm, subject to maximum guarantee limits of $500 thousand for each claim and $5 million for all claims in a year.[2]

A shareholder withdrawing from a California professional corporation is well advised promptly to cancel a previously issued guarantee.[3] The effect of that cancellation, however, is unclear. Presumably, the guarantee would remain in force with respect to malpractice that had occurred but was undetected at the time of the withdrawal. Moreover, it is unclear whether cancellation of a guarantee will serve to foreclose claims against the guarantee for subsequent malpractice by the firm in the completion of work in process at the time of the lawyer's departure. Unlike state statutes and court rules establishing joint and several liability for malpractice occurring while the lawyer is a shareholder, the California rules call for "a written agreement executed by each of the shareholders, jointly and severally guaranteeing payment by the corporation of all claims established against it by its clients for errors or omissions arising out of the practice of law by the corporation. . . ."[4] An aggrieved client might plausibly argue a lawyer's guarantee in effect at the time the client came to the firm continues in force until the work for which the firm was retained is completed.

Additional problems arise under the California rules. Since a lawyer who is not actively employed by the corporation is ineligible to be a shareholder, the withdrawing shareholder must quickly transfer his or her shares. The rules call for a transfer within ninety days, which may prove impossible if the breakup is bitter and the parties are unable to agree on the terms of the transfer. Moreover,

---

§5.6   [1] See Law Corp. Rules of the St. Bar of Cal., Rule IV(B).

[2] The rules are silent, as is the statute, on whether the guarantees constitute the limit of the shareholders' liability for claims against the firm.

[3] The state bar takes the position that a shareholder's guarantee cannot be cancelled while he or she is still the owner of record of the shares.

[4] Law Corp. Rules of the St. Bar of Cal., Rule IV(B)(1)(c).

intra-firm movements by lawyers are complicated considerably by a ban on the lawyers owning stock in more than one professional corporation or, under the state bar's interpretation of the rules, being a partner in one law firm and a shareholder in another.[5] The California Supreme Court is now considering a proposal by the state bar that this latter prohibition be eliminated.

§5.7 Terminating a Withdrawing Shareholder's Interest in a Law Corporation

§5.7.1 Buyout Agreements

Ideally, lawyers will anticipate the future withdrawals of members of their firms and develop written and specific agreements providing for the purchase of a withdrawing shareholder's interest by the corporation or other shareholders. In practice, however, lawyers more often devote their drafting and planning skills to the affairs of their clients rather than to their own. Agreements that do exist frequently were structured without awareness that the method of valuing a withdrawing shareholder's interest will bear on that shareholder's ability to grab and leave. Generous provisions valuing stock on the basis of a firm's receivables and work in process, for example, may encourage withdrawals, while paying a shareholder only the value of his or her paid-in capital and earnings to the date of withdrawal may have the reverse effect.[1]

Similarly, lawyers often fail to recognize that the choice of accounting techniques may tilt the balance in favor of the firm or the withdrawing shareholder. Cash versus accrual accounting, adjusted versus unadjusted book value, federal income tax accounting principles versus GAAP, bad debt reserves versus unadjusted receivables

---

[5] The state bar has interpreted the rules to prohibit status as a partner in one firm and a shareholder in another.

§5.7 [1] For an excellent discussion of this point, see B. Hildebrandt and J. Kaufman, The Successful Law Firm: New Approaches to Structure and Management 127-146 (1988).

are among the accounting choices that may measurably affect the value accorded a withdrawing shareholder's interest in a firm. Again, to the extent valuation techniques increase the price to be paid a withdrawing shareholder, that shareholder's grabbing and leaving activities are subsidized by the firm.

Frequently, buyout agreements reduce payments in the event that a withdrawing partner competes with the firm.[2] As has been discussed, such provisions may be unenforceable if they impede the ability of clients to retain the lawyers of their choice.[3]

§5.7.2 Buyouts Mandated by Law

By statute or court rule, a few states require the buyout of a withdrawing lawyer's interest in a professional corporation. Although the mandate is clear, the provisions requiring buyouts are generally incomplete and leave much room for disagreement. Some states require the inclusion of provisions concerning the purchase or redemption of a withdrawing shareholder's interest in the incorporation documents or private agreements.[4] Others provide for valuation on the basis of "book value,"[5] a vague accounting concept that, at least in the eyes of the withdrawing lawyer, may understate the

---

[2] See, e.g., id. at 140 (1988) (recommending this approach).

[3] See supra §2.3.

[4] See, e.g., Ariz. Rev. Stat. Ann. §10-909 (West 1977) (articles of incorporation or bylaws shall provide method of computing value); Ky. Rev. Stat. Ann. §274.095 (Michie 1988) (articles, by laws or private agreements must provide for the purchase or redemption of a withdrawing shareholders interest); Neb. Sup. Ct. Rules on Prof. Service Corporations, Rule I(D) (articles of incorporation must include provisions requiring withdrawing shareholder to dispose of shares "forthwith").

[5] See, e.g., Ala. Code §10-10-14 (Michie 1980) (book value determined by independent certified public accountant employed by the corporation for this purpose); Del. Code Ann. tit. 8 §613 (Michie 1983) (book value as determined by an independent certified public accountant employed by the corporation for this purpose); D.C. Code Ann. §29-617 (Michie 1981) (book value determined by use of generally accepted accounting principles, consistent with the method of accounting utilized by the corporation for federal income tax purposes).

true worth of a firm whose principal product is services.[6] Unfortunately, only a small number of states provide precise guidelines on value and appraisal procedures to resolve disputes.[7]

§5.7.3 Termination of a Shareholder's Interest through Application of Partnership Law Dissolution Principles

Fox v. Abrams held that, in the absence of an agreement to the contrary, the withdrawal of a shareholder from a law corporation initiates a winding-up period in which income from the work in process at the time of withdrawal is shared in the ratios that applied prior to the withdrawal.[8] *Fox* thus keeps the "partnership" alive, at least for purposes of determining rights to post-withdrawal income. Although this treatment may comport with the expectations of many lawyers, it ignores the degree to which legislation and judicial rulemaking have accorded professional corporations significant corporate attributes. Virtually every statute declares that the state's business corporation law applies to professional corporations unless that result would be inconsistent with the provisions of the professional corporation law. Some states expressly reject the application of partnership law to professional corporations. Others require a prompt termination of a withdrawing shareholder's interest. *Fox*'s suggestion that the relevance of incorporating a law practice is limited to tax considerations ignores the significant degree to which professional corporations have significant corporate attributes.

§5.7.4 Buyouts by Judicial Decree

Although professional corporation statutes typically include provisions for the purchase or redemption of the interest of a de-

---

[6] Cf. S.C. Code Ann. §33-19-250 (Law. Co-op. 1988) (mandating a buyout on the basis of "fair value").

[7] See, e.g., R.I. Sup. Ct. Rules, Rule 41(g)(4); S.C. Code Ann. §33-19-250 (Law. Co-op. (1988).

[8] See supra §5.2.

ceased or disqualified shareholder,[9] most fail to specify a right or an obligation on the part of a withdrawing shareholder to dispose of shares held. A Wisconsin decision implied that such a right may exist. In Melby v. O'Melia,[10] a shareholder withdrew from a law corporation and sought liquidation of his interest in the corporation, a partnership law remedy. In denying the requested remedy, the court held that corporate law standards governed the dissolution of professional corporations. Although those standards did not afford the shareholder the right to demand a redemption or purchase of his shares, the court added, in dictum, that ethical considerations *may* require such a remedy when the corporation is a law corporation, adding that it would "specifically address this issue . . . when it comes before us."[11]

An elaboration on the nature of ethical concerns that would require a purchase or redemption was offered in Vinall, D.D.S., P.C. v. Hoffman.[12] In requiring a dental corporation to redeem the shares of a withdrawing shareholder, the Arizona Supreme Court observed:

> Ethical considerations require the result we reach today. Principle 1-(I) of the *Principles of Ethics and Code of Professional Conduct* of the American Dental Association provides that "Dentists shall not accept or tender 'rebates' or 'split fees.' . . . ." In Arizona, a professional corporation cannot do what the person licensed to practice cannot do. . . . If the corporation paid a dividend to Dr. Hoffman when he did not work there it could be subject to sanctions for splitting a fee on work not performed.[13]

Vinall was interpreting a state statute requiring a repurchase upon the "retirement" of a shareholder, which the court read to mean retirement from a firm rather than the profession. For this reason, it

---

[9] See, e.g., Model Professional Corp. Supp. §23 (1984). A large number of states having such provisions, however, define a disqualified person as one who is legally disqualified from owning shares in a professional corporation. Mere withdrawal will not normally disqualify an individual from holding shares.

[10] 93 Wis. 2d 51, 286 N.W.2d 373 (Wis. Ct. App. 1979).

[11] *Melby,* 286 N.W.2d at 375.

[12] 133 Ariz. 322, 651 P.2d 850 (1982).

[13] *Vinall,* 651 P.2d at 852.

is distinguishable from a case in which the statute is silent on the subject of repurchases, although language in the opinion concerning the *requirements* of ethical considerations might be the basis for mandatory buyouts even in the absence of statutory provisions.

A Florida case, however, held that ethical considerations do not necessitate mandatory redemptions or purchases. In *Corlett, Killian, Hardeman, McIntosh and Levi, P.A. v. Merritt,*[14] the court recognized that the absence of an agreement or statutory requirements calling for a buyout may leave shareholders who withdraw from law corporations in the unfortunate position of owning unmarketable stock. It concluded, however, the solution lies in intelligent planning by lawyers rather than court intervention: "Where an employee who purchases such shares for valuable consideration either lacks the foresight or the bargaining power to insist upon a redemption agreement in the event of his resignation, it is not incumbent upon the courts to protect him from his own improvidence or lack of strength."[15] Nor did the court share *Vinall*'s concern over ethical considerations:

> The appellees urge that the considerations moving the Arizona court to construe its ambiguous legislation as requiring redemption upon withdrawal of a professional and those engendering the Wisconsin court's dicta should persuade us to engraft judicially a redemption requirement upon Florida's professional service corporation act. They add to the parade of horribles that protracted litigation between partners of a law firm undermines the legal system and erodes public confidence in the profession; withdrawing shareholders would have an ongoing right of access to the corporation's books and records, which arguably could make them privy to certain client confidences; and a professional service corporation is specifically prohibited from engaging in the practice of law, except through its officers, agents and/or employees. In our view, none of these ethical dilemmas . . . are so compelling as to warrant a court-imposed redemption obligation on the part of the corporation.[16]

---

[14] 478 So. 2d 828 (Fla. Dist. Ct. App. 1985).

[15] *Corlett,* 478 So. 2d at 834.

[16] Id. at 834. The court added that any right of access to books and records would not extend to client files, and the requirement that a corporation practice law only through its officers, directors, and shareholders raises no ethics concerns because under Florida law an attorney may be a shareholder in more than one professional corporation.

Corlett's doubts concerning the seriousness of the ethics concerns raised in *Vinall* are generally well founded. The ethics problems, however, are not trivial. It is not enough to note, as *Corlett* did, that a shareholder's access to books and records does not extend to client files, for many of the financial records of a law firm contain information on the identity of clients and services performed for them by the firm. Similarly, the fee splitting issue raised by *Vinall* could prove troublesome,[17] although the fact that the income of law corporations is generally distributed in the form of salaries reduces the chance a passive shareholder will share in the income.[18] In a given case, these ethics considerations might pose serious problems. As a general proposition, however, the ethics problems seem more theoretical than real, and *Corlett* is correct in declining to find in these factors a sufficient reason to order a buyout.

But if legal ethics provide an insufficient foundation to support a court-ordered redemption, does it follow that the withdrawing shareholder in a law corporation should be placed in exactly the same position as the disgruntled minority shareholder in a business corporation? One possible distinction is that an "investment" in a professional corporation is integrally related to the attorney's employment by the corporation. Admittedly, professional corporations are not investment media for passive investors. But the same is true of many close corporations where stock ownership is important principally for the employment opportunities it provides.[19] In the absence of more compelling ethics concerns, the case for putting attorney-shareholders on a better footing than shareholders in closely held business corporations is not strong.[20]

---

[17] See infra §5.8. This is assuming that a shareholder who is not an active employee of the firm would not be considered a member of the firm.

[18] *Vinall* itself recognized "professional corporations rarely, unless they have accumulated large capital surpluses, declare dividends. Instead they dispose of most of the profits as salary." 651 P.2d at 852.

[19] See F. O'Neal & R. Thompson, O'Neal's Close Corporations §1.07, at 1-25 (1987) ("Employment by the corporation is often the shareholder's principal source of income. As a matter of fact, providing for employment may have been the principal reason why the shareholder participated in organizing the corporation.").

[20] Much has been written on the problem of the illiquidity of a shareholder's interests in a closely held corporation. See, e.g., Haynsworth, The Effectiveness of Involuntary Dissolution Suits as a Remedy for Close Corporation Dissension, 35 Clev. St. L. Rev. 25 (1987); Hetherington & Dooley, Illiquidity and Exploitation: A Proposed Statutory Solution to the Remaining Close Corporation Problem, 63

Moreover, what distinguishes attorneys from other professionals? The plight of attorneys who withdraw from their law corporations is not significantly different from that of other professionals who withdraw from their corporations. Accordingly, if a buyout right exists for shareholders of law corporations, it should exist for shareholders of all professional corporations. Such a result, however, does at least some violence to the typical statutory mandate that the provisions of the business corporation act apply to professional corporations unless inconsistent with the professional corporations statute. If attorneys and other professionals are to be rescued from their lapses in planning when shareholders in business corporations are not, it should be accomplished through statutory reform rather than ad hoc judicial determinations.

Of course, in jurisdictions where the statutes are silent as to the disposition of shares, lawyer-shareholders without buyout agreements may face serious problems. Attorneys, however, are at least as well equipped to anticipate and plan around the problem as shareholders in business corporations. The difficulties that arise from

---

Va. L. Rev. 1 (1977); Hillman, The Dissatisfied Participant in the Solvent Business Venture: A Consideration of the Relative Permanence of Partnerships and Close Corporations, 67 Minn. L. Rev. 1 (1982); Thompson, Corporate Dissolution and Shareholders' Reasonable Expectations, 66 Wash. U.L.Q. 193 (1988).

All state business corporation statutes provide for involuntary dissolution under certain circumstances. Most are patterned after the Model Business Corporation Act, which permits involuntary dissolution upon a showing of deadlock, waste or misapplication of corporate assets, or fraudulent, illegal, or oppressive conduct. See Model Business Corp. Act §14.30 (1984). In recent years, a number of courts have found the denial of a shareholder's reasonable expectations to be "oppressive" conduct. See, e.g., Haynsworth, supra, at 37-39; Hillman, supra, at 49-55; Thompson, supra at 211, 238. Some of the statutes authorize relief other than dissolution, including mandated buyouts, and a number of courts have held the trial judge has inherent power to order any legal or equitable relief. See Haynsworth, supra, at 41. Thus, in jurisdictions where courts have expansive views of "oppression" and forms of available relief, shareholders who have withdrawn from law corporations may appropriately have available a remedy in the form of a court ordered buyout. Cf., e.g., Gimpel v. Bolstein, 125 Misc. 2d 45, 477 N.Y.S.2d 1014, 1022 (1984) (refusing to order the dissolution of a closely held corporation but requiring the majority shareholders either to commence payment of dividends or to purchase the interest of a passive shareholder).

See also Cafcas v. DeHaan & Richter, P.C., 699 F. Supp. 679 (N.D. Ill. 1988) (fiduciary principles apply to close corporations because they resemble partnerships; no effort to distinguish law corporation from other close corporations).

poor planning or weak bargaining positions are not unique to the legal profession.

The case for court-ordered buyouts is much stronger in jurisdictions with statutes that require the prompt termination of a withdrawing shareholder's interest.[21] Such statutes reflect a legislative determination to move away from the application of normal corporate law principles when a shareholder withdraws from a professional corporation. Although the statutes may be silent on how the disposition of shares is to be accomplished, a buyout by judicial decree is an appropriate of means of giving effect to the legislative intent.[22]

§5.8 Fee Splitting

Many agreements covering withdrawal provide for some form of fee sharing arrangement giving the firm a percentage of fees on cases taken by a withdrawing lawyer and giving the lawyer a percentage of fees collected on work in process at the time of the withdrawal. We have seen that if the firm is organized as a partnership, the fiction of partnership that continues until unfinished business is completed salvages what might otherwise be unethical fee splitting.[1] But if a firm is incorporated and a withdrawing lawyer's interest is purchased or redeemed, the result might be different unless, under the reasoning of Fox v. Abrams,[2] the corporate status of the firm is disregarded and the relationship between the withdrawing lawyers and other members of the firm is treated as one of partnership.

---

[21] See infra §5.5.1

[22] An alternative would be to require dissolution of the corporation if a purchase or redemption does not occur. Cf. Ky. Rev. Stat. §274.095 (Michie 1988) (The corporate charter will be cancelled if the articles of incorporation provide for a purchase or redemption and a buyout does not occur within one year of a shareholder's withdrawal.).

§5.8 [1] See supra §4.4.1.

[2] See supra §5.2.

Chapter 6
CONCLUSION

This book has examined the law and ethics of grabbing and leaving by law partners,[1] an activity that has led to the destabilization of many law firms.[2] It has focused on the disparate areas of partnership law, corporate law, agency law, tort law, and legal ethics, none of which alone yields an adequate picture of the degree to which grabbing and leaving is subject to regulation. When considered together, the law regulating the relations of business partners and the rules applicable to the conduct of lawyers as professionals yield standards that are conflicting, fluid, and, to a considerable extent, ignored by many lawyers in their quest for better opportunities.

The courts or the profession could easily retard or even terminate grabbing and leaving and thereby promote the stability of firms

---

[1] For a discussion of the relevance of incorporation, see Chapter 5.

[2] The actual effects of grabbing and leaving on law firms remain unclear. Most of the reported litigation involving grabbing and leaving has involved smaller firms, which receive little attention in the legal tabloids. The extensive reporting of the movements of partners and entire departments from larger law firms may leave an exaggerated impression of turmoil within, and damage to, law firms. It is nevertheless likely that many firms, large and small, have suffered at the hands of partners who grab and leave. Conversely, many other firms have prospered from the rapid development of their practices through the lateral hiring of partners.

vulnerable to such activities. Reversing the ban on restrictive covenants, or permitting firms to enter into long-term contracts binding
clients to their firms, would sharply restrict the abilities both of
partners to grab and leave and of clients to choose their lawyers.
Whether such a "reform" is desirable is another question.

That some lawyers prosper from grabbing while others suffer is
likely evidence of market forces at work. A significant factor underlying the growth of grabbing and leaving is the inability of many firms
to develop a method of compensation acceptable to their more
mobile partners. Because there is now a market for lawyers who can
carry a substantial "portfolio" of clients to another firm,[3] these
lawyers have something to auction. Viewed from this perspective,
the solution to the problem of grabbing may lie more in the modification of business practices, particularly those pertaining to compensation, than in law reform.[4]

A laissez faire approach to the machinations of law partners is
not without its drawbacks, however. One of the more important
problems is that a hands off attitude fails to address the interests and
values advanced in a more stable environment for law firms. An
atmosphere conducive to grabbing encourages the hoarding of clients by lawyers within the same firm. At least a modicum of cooperation is required to maximize the value of a firm to both its lawyers
and clients. Furthermore, firms need some sense of confidence concerning the client base in order, as businesses, to engage in long-
term planning and commitments in such areas as the hiring and
promotion of associates and support staff, the purchase of equipment, the expansion of office space, the opening of branch offices,
and the assumption of debt.

One consequence of a system that provides incentives to those
who successfully hoard clients is that lawyers less able to attract,
retain, and move clients will suffer. Partners sometimes become

---

[3] See supra §1.1.

[4] For a thoughtful discussion of why a sharing system of dividing income may
permit a large firm to develop firm-specific (and nonmovable) capital and thereby
become more attractive to its members than alternative firms, see Gilson &
Mnookin, Sharing Among the Human Capitalists: An Economic Inquiry into the
Corporate Law Firm and How Partners Split Profits, 37 Stan. L. Rev. 313,
353-371 (1985).

"rainmakers" because they are indeed excellent lawyers. In other cases, however, success in controlling clients derives less from the partner's lawyering skills than from marketing acumen, political notoriety, club memberships, or family connections. All of this raises the question of whether the legal regime underlying firm practice should promote greater incentives for rainmaking rather than alternative methods of defining professional success. If so, those firm members who are excellent lawyers but less gifted in the fine art of rainmaking will be the losers.

It may be that another kind of market — a market for stable law firms — already exists and may develop further over time.[5] A firm savaged by grabbing will have comparatively greater difficulty than more stable firms in maintaining the type of reputation and working environment that facilitates both the attraction and retention of clients and the recruitment of lawyers to do the work generated by rainmakers. Those firms presently enjoying relative stability of membership are well positioned to capture gains in an environment of instability. Whether and how firms currently crippled by partner turnover can enter that market, and the effect of such a trend on small and medium-sized firms, are open questions.[6]

An alternative approach to the laissez faire mentality would be to modify clients' freedom to change lawyers. An environment that encourages grabbing rests upon clients' freedom to change lawyers or firms at will. This principle of client choice is neither constitutionally mandated nor an undisputed tenet of natural law. When a client's discharge of a lawyer or firm pertains to the very reason that the principle of client choice is applied on such an absolute basis — dissatisfaction with the lawyer's work, lack of trust, or related concerns — the interests of the discharged party are properly subor-

---

[5] See, e.g., McMahon, Old Fashioned — And Proud of It, Natl. L.J., Feb. 1, 1988, at 1, col. 1 (describing the positive reactions of partners within a firm that employs a lockstep compensation system).

[6] See Gilson & Mnookin, Sharing Among the Human Capitalists: An Economic Inquiry into the Corporate Law Firm and How Partners Split Profits, 37 Stan. L. Rev. 313, 386-389 (1985) (speculating on the future of law firms and predicting that many large law firms, notwithstanding increased competitive pressures, will remain relatively stable and retain seniority-based compensation systems).

dinated.[7] At the other extreme, when the client is sophisticated and the choice is based on more expedient considerations,[8] the case for discharge at will becomes less compelling.

In any event, the law and ethics of grabbing and leaving remain a contradictory and perplexing set of principles sorely in need of reconciliation. That will not occur as long as the functioning of lawyers as business associates is viewed as distinct from their status as professionals.

---

[7] See supra §2.3.2.

[8] Perhaps the grabbing lawyer originally inherited the client from another partner, and the client's choice to follow the lawyer to a new firm is based upon the pragmatic consideration that the lawyer, by virtue of work while a partner at the firm, simply knows the business of the client better than any lawyer remaining at the firm.

Appendix A
THE UNIFORM PARTNERSHIP ACT (1914)*

Commissioners' Prefatory Note

---

* This act has been printed through the permission of the National Conference of Commissioners on Uniform State Laws, and copies of the act may be ordered at a cost of $5.00 each at 676 North St. Clair St., Suite 1700, Chicago, Illinois 60611.

Commissioners' Prefatory Note

The subject of a uniform law on partnership was taken up by the Conference of Commissioners on Uniform State Laws in 1902, and the Committee on Commercial Law was instructed to employ an expert and prepare a draft to be submitted to the next annual Conference. (See Am. Bar Assn. Report for 1902, p. 477.) At the meeting in 1903 the committee reported that it had secured the services of James Barr Ames, Dean of the Law School of Harvard University, as expert to draft the act. (See Am. Bar Assn. Report for 1903, p. 501.)

In 1905 the Committee on Commercial Law reported progress on this subject, and a resolution was passed by the Conference, directing that a draft be prepared upon the mercantile theory. (See Am. Bar Assn. Reports, 1905, pp. 731-738.) And in 1906 the committee reported that it had in its hands a draft of an act on this subject, which draft was recommitted to the committee for revision and amendment, with directions to report to the next Conference for discussion and action. (See Report, C.U.S.L., 1906, p. 40.)

In 1907 the matter was brought before the Conference and postponed until the 1908 meeting. (See Report, C.U.S.L., 1907, p. 93.) In 1908 the matter was discussed by the Conference. (See Am. Bar Assn. Reports, 1908, pp. 983, 1048.) And in 1909 the Second Tentative Draft of the Partnership Act was introduced and discussed. (See p. 1081 of Am. Bar Assn. Reports for 1909.)

In 1910 the committee reported that on account of the death of Dean Ames no progress had been made, but that Dr. Wm. Draper Lewis, then Dean and now Professor of Law at the Law School of the University of Pennsylvania, and Mr. James B. Lichtenberger, of the Philadelphia Bar, had prepared a draft of a partnership act on the so-called entity idea, with the aid of the various drafts and notes of Dean Ames, and that they had also submitted a draft of a proposed uniform act, embodying the theory that a partnership is an aggregate of individuals associated in business, which is that at present accepted in nearly all the states of the Union. (See Report C.U.S.L., 1910, p. 142.) Dean Lewis expressed his belief that with certain modifications the aggregate or common law theory should be adopted. A resolution was passed by the Conference that any action that might have theretofore been adopted by it, tending to limit the Committee on Commercial Law in its consideration of the partnership law to what is known as the entity theory, be rescinded and that the committee be allowed and directed to consider the subject of partnership at large as though no such resolution had been adopted by the Conference. (See p. 52.)

In the fall of 1910 the committee invited to a Conference, held in Philadelphia, all the teachers of, and writers on, partnerships, besides several other lawyers known to have made a special study of the subject. There was a large attendance. For two days the members of the committee and their guests discussed the theory on which the proposed act should be drawn. At the conclusion of the discussion the experts present recommended that the act be drawn on the aggregate or common law theory, with the modification that the partners be treated as owners of partnership property holding by a special tenancy which should be called tenancy in partnership. (See section 25 of the act recommended.) Accordingly, at the meeting of the Conference in the summer of 1911, the committee reported that, after hearing the discussion of experts, it had voted that Dean Lewis be requested to prepare a draft of a partnership act on the so-called common law theory. (See Report, C.U.S.L., 1911, p. 149.)

The committee reported another draft of the act to the Conference at its session in 1912, drawn on the aggregate or common law theory, with the modification referred to. At this session the Conference spent several days in the discussion of the act, again referring it to the Committee on Commercial Law for their further consideration. (See Report, C.U.S.L., 1912, p. 67.)

The Committee on Commercial Law held a meeting in New York on March 29, 1913, and took up the draft of the act referred back to it by the Conference, and after careful consideration of the amendments suggested by the Conference, prepared their seventh draft, which was, at their annual session in the summer of 1913, submitted to the Conference. The Conference again spent several days in discussing the act and again referred it to the Committee on Commercial Law, this time mainly for protection in form.

The Committee on Commercial Law assembled in the City of New York, September 21, 1914, and had before them a new draft of the act, which had been carefully prepared by Dr. Wm. Draper Lewis with valuable suggestions submitted by Charles E. Shepard, Esq., one of the commissioners from the State of Washington, and others interested in the subject. The committee reported the Eighth Draft to the Conference which, on October 14, 1914, passed a resolution recommending the act for adoption to the legislatures of all the States.

Uniformity of the law of partnerships is constantly becoming more important, as the number of firms increases which not only carry on business in more than one state, but have among the members residents of different states.

It is however, proper here to emphasize the fact that there are other reasons, in addition to the advantages which will result from uniformity, for the adoption of the act now issued by the Commissioners. There is probably no other subject connected with our business law in which a greater number of instances can be found where, in matters of almost daily occurrence, the law is uncertain. This uncertainty is due, not only to conflict between the decisions of different states, but more to the general lack of consistency in legal theory. In several of the sections, but especially in those which relate to the rights of the partner and his separate creditors in partnership property, and to the rights of firm creditors where the personnel of the partnership has been changed without liquidation of partnership affairs, there exists an almost hopeless confusion of theory and practice, making the actual administration of the law difficult and often inequitable.

Another difficulty of the present partnership law is the scarcity of authority on matters of considerable importance in the daily conduct and in the winding up of partnership affairs. In any one state it is often impossible to find an authority on a matter of comparatively frequent occurrence, while not infrequently an exhaustive research of the reports of the decisions of all the states and the federal courts fails to reveal a single authority throwing light on the question. The existence of a statute stating in detail the rights of the partners inter se during the carrying on of the partnership business, and on the winding up of partnership affairs, will be a real practical advantage of moment to the business world.

The notes which are printed in connection with this edition of the Act were prepared by Dr. Wm. Draper Lewis, the draftsman. They are designed to point out the few changes in the law which the adoption of the act will effect, and the many confusions and uncertainties which it will end. [Notes not reprinted here.]

Walter George Smith

Part I. Preliminary Provisions

§1 Name of Act

This act may be cited as Uniform Partnership Act.

§2 Definition of Terms

In this act, "Court" includes every court and judge having jurisdiction in the case.

"Business" includes every trade, occupation, or profession.

"Person" includes individuals, partnerships, corporations, and other associations.

"Bankrupt" includes bankrupt under the Federal Bankruptcy Act or insolvent under any state insolvent act.

"Conveyance" includes every assignment, lease, mortgage, or encumbrance.

"Real property" includes land and any interest or estate in land.

§3 Interpretation of Knowledge and Notice

(1) A person has "knowledge" of a fact within the meaning of this act not only when he has actual knowledge thereof, but also when he has knowledge of such other facts as in the circumstances shows bad faith.

(2) A person has "notice" of a fact within the meaning of this act when the person who claims the benefit of the notice:

(a) States the fact to such person, or

(b) Delivers through the mail, or by other means of communication, a written statement of the fact to such person or to a proper person at his place of business or residence.

§4 Rules of Construction

(1) The rule that statutes in derogation of the common law are to be strictly construed shall have no application to this act.

(2) The law of estoppel shall apply under this act.

(3) The law of agency shall apply under this act.

(4) This act shall be so interpreted and construed as to effect its general purpose to make uniform the law of those states which enact it.

(5) This act shall not be construed so as to impair the obligations of any contract existing when the act goes into effect, nor to affect any action or proceedings begun or right accrued before this act takes effect.

§5 Rules for Cases Not Provided for in This Act

In any case not provided for in this act the rules of law and equity, including the law merchant, shall govern.

Part II. Nature of a Partnership

§6 Partnership Defined

(1) A partnership is an association of two or more persons to carry on as co-owners a business for profit.

(2) But any association formed under any other statute of this state, or any statute adopted by authority, other than the authority of this state, is not a partnership under this act, unless such association would have been a partnership in this state prior to the adoption of this act; but this act shall apply to limited partnerships except in so far as the statutes relating to such partnerships are inconsistent herewith.

§7 Rules for Determining the Existence of a Partnership

In determining whether a partnership exists, these rules shall apply:

(1) Except as provided by section 16 persons who are not partners as to each other are not partners as to third persons.

(2) Joint tenancy, tenancy in common, tenancy by the entireties, joint property, common property, or part ownership does not of itself establish a partnership, whether such co-owners do or do not share any profits made by the use of the property.

(3) The sharing of gross returns does not of itself establish a partnership, whether or not the persons sharing them have a joint or common right or interest in any property from which the returns are derived.

(4) The receipt by a person of a share of the profits of a business is prima facie evidence that he is a partner in the business, but no such inference shall be drawn if such profits were received in payment:

(a) As a debt by installments or otherwise,

(b) As wages of an employee or rent to a landlord,

(c) As an annuity to a widow or representative of a deceased partner,

(d) As interest on a loan, though the amount of payment vary with the profits of the business,

(e) As the consideration for the sale of the good-will of a business or other property by installments or otherwise.

§8 Partnership Property

(1) All property originally brought into the partnership stock or subsequently acquired by purchase or otherwise, on account of the partnership, is partnership property.

(2) Unless the contrary intention appears, property acquired with partnership funds is partnership property.

(3) Any estate in real property may be acquired in the partnership name. Title so acquired can be conveyed only in the partnership name.

(4) A conveyance to a partnership in the partnership name, though without words of inheritance, passes the entire estate of the grantor unless a contrary intent appears.

Part III. Relations of Partners to Persons Dealing with the Partnership

§9 Partner Agent of Partnership as to Partnership Business

(1) Every partner is an agent of the partnership for the purpose of its business, and the act of every partner, including the execution in the partnership name of any instrument, for apparently carrying on in the usual way the business of the partnership of which he is a member binds the partnership, unless the partner so acting has in fact no authority to act for the partnership in the particular matter, and the person with whom he is dealing has knowledge of the fact that he has no such authority.

(2) An act of a partner which is not apparently for the carrying on of the business of the partnership in the usual way does not bind the partnership unless authorized by the other partners.

(3) Unless authorized by the other partners or unless they have abandoned the business, one or more but less than all the partners have no authority to:

(a) Assign the partnership property in trust for creditors or on the assignee's promise to pay the debts of the partnership,

(b) Dispose of the good-will of the business,

(c) Do any other act which would make it impossible to carry on the ordinary business of a partnership,

(d) Confess a judgment,

(e) Submit a partnership claim or liability to arbitration or reference.

(4) No act of a partner in contravention of a restriction on authority shall bind the partnership to persons having knowledge of the restriction.

§10 Conveyance of Real Property of the Partnership

(1) Where title to real property is in the partnership name, any partner may convey title to such property by a conveyance executed in the partnership name; but the partnership may recover such property unless the partner's act binds the partnership under the provisions of paragraph (1) of section 9, or unless such property has been conveyed by the grantee or a person claiming through such grantee to a holder for value without knowledge that the partner, in making the conveyance, has exceeded his authority.

(2) Where title to real property is in the name of the partnership, a conveyance executed by a partner, in his own name, passes the equitable interest of the partnership, provided the act is one within the authority of the partner under the provisions of paragraph (1) of section 9.

(3) Where title to real property is in the name of one or more but not all the partners, and the record does not disclose the right of the partnership, the partners in whose name the title stands may convey title to such property, but the partnership may recover such property if the partners' act does not bind the partnership under the provisions of paragraph (1) of section 9, unless the purchaser or his assignee, is a holder for value, without knowledge.

(4) Where the title to real property is in the name of one or more or all the partners, or in a third person in trust for the partner-

ship, a conveyance executed by a partner in the partnership name, or in his own name, passes the equitable interest of the partnership, provided the act is one within the authority of the partner under the provisions of paragraph (1) of section 9.

(5) Where the title to real property is in the names of all the partners a conveyance executed by all the partners passes all their rights in such property.

§11 Partnership Bound by Admission of Partner

An admission or representation made by any partner concerning partnership affairs within the scope of his authority as conferred by this act is evidence against the partnership.

§12 Partnership Charged with Knowledge of or Notice to Partner

Notice to any partner of any matter relating to partnership affairs, and the knowledge of the partner acting in the particular matter, acquired while a partner or then present to his mind, and the knowledge of any other partner who reasonably could and should have communicated it to the acting partner, operate as notice to or knowledge of the partnership, except in the case of a fraud on the partnership committed by or with the consent of that partner.

§13 Partnership Bound by Partner's Wrongful Act

Where, by any wrongful act or omission of any partner acting in the ordinary course of the business of the partnership or with the authority of his co-partners, loss or injury is caused to any person, not being a partner in the partnership, or any penalty is incurred, the partnership is liable therefor to the same extent as the partner so acting or omitting to act.

§14 Partnership Bound by Partner's Breach of Trust

The partnership is bound to make good the loss:

(a) Where one partner acting within the scope of his apparent authority receives money or property of a third person and misapplies it; and

(b) Where the partnership in the course of its business receives money or property of a third person and the money or property so received is misapplied by any partner while it is in the custody of the partnership.

§15 Nature of Partner's Liability

All partners are liable

(a) Jointly and severally for everything chargeable to the partnership under sections 13 and 14.

(b) Jointly for all other debts and obligations of the partnership; but any partner may enter into a separate obligation to perform a partnership contract.

§16 Partner by Estoppel

(1) When a person, by words spoken or written or by conduct, represents himself, or consents to another representing him to any one, as a partner in an existing partnership or with one or more persons not actual partners, he is liable to any such person to whom such representation has been made, who has, on the faith of such representation, given credit to the actual or apparent partnership, and if he has made such representation or consented to its being made in a public manner he is liable to such person, whether the representation has or has not been made or communicated to such person so giving credit by or with the knowledge of the apparent partner making the representation or consenting to its being made.

(a) When a partnership liability results, he is liable as though he were an actual member of the partnership.

(b) When no partnership liability results, he is liable jointly with the other persons, if any, so consenting to the contract or representation as to incur liability, otherwise separately.

(2) When a person has been thus represented to be a partner in an existing partnership, or with one or more persons not actual partners, he is an agent of the persons consenting to such representation to bind them to the same extent and in the same manner as though he were a partner in fact, with respect to persons who rely upon the representation. Where all the members of the existing partnership consent to the representation, a partnership act or obligation results; but in all other cases it is the joint act or obligation of the person acting and the persons consenting to the representation.

§17 Liability of Incoming Partner

A person admitted as a partner into an existing partnership is liable for all the obligations of the partnership arising before his admission as though he had been a partner when such obligations were incurred, except that this liability shall be satisfied only out of partnership property.

Part IV. Relations of Partners to One Another

§18 Rules Determining Rights and Duties of Partners

The rights and duties of the partners in relation to the partnership shall be determined, subject to any agreement between them, by the following rules:

(a) Each partner shall be repaid his contributions, whether by way of capital or advances to the partnership property and share equally in the profits and surplus remaining after all liabilities, including those to partners, are satisfied; and must contribute towards the losses, whether of capital or otherwise, sustained by the partnership according to his share in the profits.

(b) The partnership must indemnify every partner in respect

of payments made and personal liabilities reasonably incurred by him in the ordinary and proper conduct of its business, or for the preservation of its business or property.

(c) A partner, who in aid of the partnership makes any payment or advance beyond the amount of capital which he agreed to contribute, shall be paid interest from the date of the payment or advance.

(d) A partner shall receive interest on the capital contributed by him only from the date when repayment should be made.

(e) All partners have equal rights in the management and conduct of the partnership business.

(f) No partner is entitled to remuneration for acting in the partnership business, except that a surviving partner is entitled to reasonable compensation for his services in winding up the partnership affairs.

(g) No person can become a member of a partnership without the consent of all the partners.

(h) Any difference arising as to ordinary matters connected with the partnership business may be decided by a majority of the partners; but no act in contravention of any agreement between the partners may be done rightfully without the consent of all the partners.

§19 Partnership Books

The partnership books shall be kept, subject to any agreement between the partners, at the principal place of business of the partnership, and every partner shall at all times have access to and may inspect and copy any of them.

§20 Duty of Partners to Render Information

Partners shall render on demand true and full information of all things affecting the partnership to any partner or the legal representative of any deceased partner or partner under legal disability.

§21 Partner Accountable as a Fiduciary

(1) Every partner must account to the partnership for any benefit, and hold as trustee for it any profits derived by him without the consent of the other partners from any transaction connected with the formation, conduct, or liquidation of the partnership or from any use by him of its property.

(2) This section applies also to the representatives of a deceased partner engaged in the liquidation of the affairs of the partnership as the personal representatives of the last surviving partner.

§22 Right to an Account

Any partner shall have the right to a formal account as to partnership affairs:

(a) If he is wrongfully excluded from the partnership business or possession of its property by his co-partners,

(b) If the right exists under the terms of any agreement,

(c) As provided by section 21,

(d) Whenever other circumstances render it just and reasonable.

§23 Continuation of Partnership Beyond Fixed Term

(1) When a partnership for a fixed term or particular undertaking is continued after the termination of such term or particular undertaking without any express agreement, the rights and duties of the partners remain the same as they were at such termination, so far as is consistent with a partnership at will.

(2) A continuation of the business by the partners or such of them as habitually acted therein during the term, without any settlement or liquidation of the partnership affairs, is prima facie evidence of a continuation of the partnership.

Part V. Property Rights of a Partner

§24 Extent of Property Rights of a Partner

The property rights of a partner are (1) his rights in specific partnership property, (2) his interest in the partnership, and (3) his right to participate in the management.

§25 Nature of a Partner's Right in Specific Partnership Property

(1) A partner is co-owner with his partners of specific partnership property holding as a tenant in partnership.

(2) The incidents of this tenancy are such that:

(a) A partner, subject to the provisions of this act and to any agreement between the partners, has an equal right with his partners to possess specific partnership property for partnership purposes; but he has no right to possess such property for any other purpose without the consent of his partners.

(b) A partner's right in specific partnership property is not assignable except in connection with the assignment of rights of all the partners in the same property.

(c) A partner's right in specific partnership property is not subject to attachment or execution, except on a claim against the partnership. When partnership property is attached for a partnership debt the partners, or any of them, or the representatives of a deceased partner, cannot claim any right under the homestead or exemption laws.

(d) On the death of a partner his right in specific partnership property vests in the surviving partner or partners, except where the deceased was the last surviving partner, when his right in such property vests in his legal representative. Such surviving partner or partners, or the legal representative of the last surviving partner, has no right to possess the partnership property for any but a partnership purpose.

(e) A partner's right in specific partnership property is not subject to dower, curtesy, or allowances to widows, heirs, or next of kin.

§26 Nature of Partner's Interest in the Partnership

A partner's interest in the partnership is his share of the profits and surplus, and the same is personal property.

§27 Assignment of Partner's Interest

(1) A conveyance by a partner of his interest in the partnership does not of itself dissolve the partnership, nor, as against the other partners in the absence of agreement, entitle the assignee, during the continuance of the partnership, to interfere in the management or administration of the partnership business or affairs, or to require any information or account of partnership transactions, or to inspect the partnership books; but it merely entitles the assignee to receive in accordance with his contract the profits to which the assigning partner would otherwise be entitled.

(2) In case of a dissolution of the partnership, the assignee is entitled to receive his assignor's interest and may require an account from the date only of the last account agreed to by all the partners.

§28 Partner's Interest Subject to Charging Order

(1) On due application to a competent court by any judgment creditor of a partner, the court which entered the judgment, order, or decree, or any other court, may charge the interest of the debtor partner with payment of the unsatisfied amount of such judgment debt with interest thereon; and may then or later appoint a receiver of his share of the profits, and of any other money due or to fall due to him in respect of the partnership, and make all other orders, directions, accounts and inquiries which the debtor partner might have made, or which the circumstances of the case may require.

(2) The interest charged may be redeemed at any time before

foreclosure, or in case of a sale being directed by the court may be purchased without thereby causing a dissolution:

(a) With separate property, by any one or more of the partners, or

(b) With partnership property, by any one or more of the partners with the consent of all the partners whose interests are not so charged or sold.

(3) Nothing in this act shall be held to deprive a partner of his right, if any, under the exemption laws, as regards his interest in the partnership.

Part VI. Dissolution and Winding Up

§29 Dissolution Defined

The dissolution of a partnership is the change in the relation of the partners caused by any partner ceasing to be associated in the carrying on as distinguished from the winding up of the business.

§30 Partnership Not Terminated by Dissolution

On dissolution the partnership is not terminated, but continues until the winding up of partnership affairs is completed.

§31 Causes of Dissolution

Dissolution is caused:

(1) Without violation of the agreement between the partners,

(a) By the termination of the definite term or particular undertaking specified in the agreement,

(b) By the express will of any partner when no definite term or particular undertaking is specified,

(c) By the express will of all the partners who have not assigned their interests or suffered them to be charged for their separate debts, either before or after the termination of any specified term or particular undertaking.

(d) By the expulsion of any partner from the business bona fide in accordance with such a power conferred by the agreement between the partners;

(2) In contravention of the agreement between the partners, where the circumstances do not permit a dissolution under any other provision of this section, by the express will of any partner at any time;

(3) By any event which makes it unlawful for the business of the partnership to be carried on or for the members to carry it on in partnership;

(4) By the death of any partner;

(5) By the bankruptcy of any partner or the partnership;

(6) By decree of court under section 32.

§32 Dissolution by Decree of Court

(1) On application by or for a partner the court shall decree a dissolution whenever:

(a) A partner has been declared a lunatic in any judicial proceeding or is shown to be of unsound mind,

(b) A partner becomes in any other way incapable of performing his part of the partnership contract,

(c) A partner has been guilty of such conduct as tends to affect prejudicially the carrying on of the business,

(d) A partner wilfully or persistently commits a breach of the partnership agreement, or otherwise so conducts himself in matters relating to the partnership business that it is not reasonably practicable to carry on the business in partnership with him,

(e) The business of the partnership can only be carried on at a loss,

(f) Other circumstances render a dissolution equitable.

(2) On the application of the purchaser of a partner's interest under sections 28 or 29 [should read 27 or 28];

(a) After the termination of the specified term or particular undertaking,

(b) At any time if the partnership was a partnership at will when the interest was assigned or when the charging order was issued.

§33 General Effect of Dissolution on Authority of Partner

Except so far as may be necessary to wind up partnership affairs or to complete transactions begun but not then finished, dissolution terminates all authority of any partner to act for the partnership,

(1) With respect to the partners,

(a) When the dissolution is not by the act, bankruptcy or death of a partner; or

(b) When the dissolution is by such act, bankruptcy or death of a partner, in cases where section 34 so requires.

(2) With respect to persons not partners, as declared in section 35.

§34 Rights of Partner to Contribution from Co-partners after Dissolution

Where the dissolution is caused by the act, death or bankruptcy of a partner, each partner is liable to his co-partners for his share of any liability created by any partner acting for the partnership as if the partnership had not been dissolved unless

(a) The dissolution being by act of any partner, the partner acting for the partnership had knowledge of the dissolution, or

(b) The dissolution being by the death or bankruptcy of a partner, the partner acting for the partnership had knowledge or notice of the death or bankruptcy.

§35 Power of Partner to Bind Partnership to Third Persons after Dissolution

(1) After dissolution a partner can bind the partnership except as provided in Paragraph (3).

(a) By any act appropriate for winding up partnership affairs or completing transactions unfinished at dissolution;

(b) By any transaction which would bind the partnership if dissolution had not taken place, provided the other party to the transaction

(I) Had extended credit to the partnership prior to dissolution and had no knowledge or notice of the dissolution; or

(II) Though he had not so extended credit, had nevertheless known of the partnership prior to dissolution, and, having no knowledge or notice of dissolution, the fact of dissolution had not been advertised in a newspaper of general circulation in the place (or in each place if more than one) at which the partnership business was regularly carried on.

(2) The liability of a partner under Paragraph (1b) shall be satisfied out of partnership assets alone when such partner had been prior to dissolution

(a) Unknown as a partner to the person with whom the contract is made; and

(b) So far unknown and inactive in partnership affairs that the business reputation of the partnership could not be said to have been in any degree due to his connection with it.

(3) The partnership is in no case bound by any act of a partner after dissolution

(a) Where the partnership is dissolved because it is unlawful to carry on the business, unless the act is appropriate for winding up partnership affairs; or

(b) Where the partner has become bankrupt; or

(c) Where the partner has no authority to wind up partnership affairs; except by a transaction with one who

(I) Had extended credit to the partnership prior to dissolution and had no knowledge or notice of his want of authority; or

(II) Had not extended credit to the partnership prior to dissolution, and; having no knowledge or notice of his want of authority, the fact of his want of authority has not been advertised in the manner provided for advertising the fact of dissolution in Paragraph (1b II).

(4) Nothing in this section shall affect the liability under Section 16 of any person who after dissolution represents himself or consents to another representing him as a partner in a partnership engaged in carrying on business.

§36 Effect of Dissolution on Partner's Existing Liability

(1) The dissolution of the partnership does not of itself discharge the existing liability of any partner.

(2) A partner is discharged from any existing liability upon dissolution of the partnership by an agreement to that effect between himself, the partnership creditor and the person or partnership continuing the business; and such agreement may be inferred from the course of dealing between the creditor having knowledge of the dissolution and the person or partnership continuing the business.

(3) Where a person agrees to assume the existing obligations of a dissolved partnership, the partners whose obligations have been assumed shall be discharged from any liability to any creditor of the partnership who, knowing of the agreement, consents to a material alteration in the nature or time of payment of such obligations.

(4) The individual property of a deceased partner shall be liable for all obligations of the partnership incurred while he was a partner but subject to the prior payment of his separate debts.

§37 Right to Wind Up

Unless otherwise agreed the partners who have not wrongfully dissolved the partnership or the legal representative of the last surviving partner, not bankrupt, has the right to wind up the partnership affairs; provided, however, that any partner, his legal representative or his assignee, upon cause shown, may obtain winding up by the court.

§38 Rights of Partners to Application of Partnership Property

(1) When dissolution is caused in any way, except in contravention of the partnership agreement, each partner, as against his co-partners and all persons claiming through them in respect of their interests in the partnership, unless otherwise agreed, may have the partnership property applied to discharge its liabilities, and the surplus applied to pay in cash the net amount owing to the respective partners. But if dissolution is caused by expulsion of a partner, bona fide under the partnership agreement and if the expelled partner is discharged from all partnership liabilities, either by payment or agreement under section 36(2), he shall receive in cash only the net amount due him from the partnership.

(2) When dissolution is caused in contravention of the partnership agreement the rights of the partners shall be as follows:

(a) Each partner who has not caused dissolution wrongfully shall have,

I. All the rights specified in paragraph (1) of this section, and

II. The right, as against each partner who has caused the dissolution wrongfully, to damages for breach of the agreement.

(b) The partners who have not caused the dissolution wrongfully, if they all desire to continue the business in the same name, either by themselves or jointly with others, may do so, during the agreed term for the partnership and for that purpose may possess the partnership property, provided they secure the payment by bond approved by the court, or pay to any partner who has caused the dissolution wrongfully, the value of his interest in the partnership at the dissolution, less any damages recoverable under clause (2a II) of this section, and in like manner indemnify him against all present or future partnership liabilities.

(c) A partner who has caused the dissolution wrongfully shall have:

I. If the business is not continued under the provisions of paragraph (2b) all the rights of a partner under paragraph (1), subject to clause (2a II), of this section,

II. If the business is continued under paragraph (2b) of this section the right as against his co-partners and all claiming through them in respect of their interests in the partnership, to have the value of his interest in the partnership, less any damages caused to his co-partners by the dissolution, ascertained and paid to him in cash, or the payment secured by bond approved by the court, and to be released from all existing liabilities of the partnership; but in ascertaining the value of the partner's interest the value of the good-will of the business shall not be considered.

§39 Rights Where Partnership Is Dissolved for Fraud or Misrepresentation

Where a partnership contract is rescinded on the ground of the fraud or misrepresentation of one of the parties thereto, the party entitled to rescind is, without prejudice to any other right, entitled,

(a) To a lien on, or a right of retention of, the surplus of the partnership property after satisfying the partnership liabilities to third persons for any sum of money paid by him for the purchase of an interest in the partnership and for any capital or advances contributed by him; and

(b) To stand, after all liabilities to third persons have been satisfied, in the place of the creditors of the partnership for any payments made by him in respect of the partnership liabilities; and

(c) To be indemnified by the person guilty of the fraud or making the representation against all debts and liabilities of the partnership.

§40   Rules for Distribution

In settling accounts between the partners after dissolution, the following rules shall be observed, subject to any agreement to the contrary:

(a) The assets of the partnership are:

I. The partnership property,

II. The contributions of the partners necessary for the payment of all the liabilities specified in clause (b) of this paragraph.

(b) The liabilities of the partnership shall rank in order of payment, as follows:

I. Those owing to creditors other than partners,

II. Those owing to partners other than for capital and profits,

III. Those owing to partners in respect of capital,

IV. Those owing to partners in respect of profits.

(c) The assets shall be applied in the order of their declaration in clause (a) of this paragraph to the satisfaction of the liabilities.

(d) The partners shall contribute, as provided by section 18 (a) the amount necessary to satisfy the liabilities; but if any, but not all, of the partners are insolvent, or, not being subject to process, refuse to contribute, the other partners shall contribute their share of the liabilities, and, in the relative proportions in which they share the profits, the additional amount necessary to pay the liabilities.

(e) An assignee for the benefit of creditors or any person appointed by the court shall have the right to enforce the contributions specified in clause (d) of this paragraph.

(f) Any partner or his legal representative shall have the right to enforce the contributions specified in clause (d) of this paragraph, to the extent of the amount which he has paid in excess of his share of the liability.

(g) The individual property of a deceased partner shall be liable for the contributions specified in clause (d) of this paragraph.

(h) When partnership property and the individual properties of the partners are in possession of a court for distribution, partnership creditors shall have priority on partnership property and separate creditors on individual property, saving the rights of lien or secured creditors as heretofore.

(i) Where a partner has become bankrupt or his estate insolvent the claims against his separate property shall rank in the following order:

I. Those owing to separate creditors,

II. Those owing to partnership creditors,

III. Those owing to partners by way of contribution.

§41 Liability of Persons Continuing the Business in Certain Cases

(1) When any new partner is admitted into an existing partnership, or when any partner retires and assigns (or the representative of the deceased partner assigns) his rights in partnership property to two or more of the partners, or to one or more of the partners and one or more third persons, if the business is continued without liquidation of the partnership affairs, creditors of the first or dissolved partnership are also creditors of the partnership so continuing the business.

(2) When all but one partner retire and assign (or the representative of a deceased partner assigns) their rights in partnership property to the remaining partner, who continues the business without liquidation of partnership affairs, either alone or with others, creditors of the dissolved partnership are also creditors of the person or partnership so continuing the business.

(3) When any partner retires or dies and the business of the dissolved partnership is continued as set forth in paragraphs (1) and (2) of this section, with the consent of the retired partners or the representative of the deceased partner, but without any assignment of his right in partnership property, rights of creditors of the dissolved partnership and of the creditors of the person or partnership continuing the business shall be as if such assignment had been made.

(4) When all the partners or their representatives assign their rights in partnership property to one or more third persons who promise to pay the debts and who continue the business of the dissolved partnership, creditors of the dissolved partnership are also creditors of the person or partnership continuing the business.

(5) When any partner wrongfully causes a dissolution and the remaining partners continue the business under the provisions of section 38(2b), either alone or with others, and without liquidation of the partnership affairs, creditors of the dissolved partnership are also creditors of the person or partnership continuing the business.

(6) When a partner is expelled and the remaining partners continue the business either alone or with others, without liquidation of the partnership affairs, creditors of the dissolved partnership are also creditors of the person or partnership continuing the business.

(7) The liability of a third person becoming a partner in the partnership continuing the business, under this section, to the creditors of the dissolved partnership shall be satisfied out of partnership property only.

(8) When the business of a partnership after dissolution is continued under any conditions set forth in this section the creditors of the dissolved partnership, as against the separate creditors of the retiring or deceased partner or the representative of the deceased partner, have a prior right to any claim of the retired partner or the representative of the deceased partner against the person or partnership continuing the business, on account of the retired or deceased partner's interest in the dissolved partnership or on account of any consideration promised for such interest or for his right in partnership property.

(9) Nothing in this section shall be held to modify any right of creditors to set aside any assignment on the ground of fraud.

(10) The use by the person or partnership continuing the business of the partnership name, or the name of a deceased partner as part thereof, shall not of itself make the individual property of the deceased partner liable for any debts contracted by such person or partnership.

§42 Rights of Retiring or Estate of Deceased Partner When the Business Is Continued

When any partner retires or dies, and the business is continued under any of the conditions set forth in section 41 (1, 2, 3, 5, 6), or section 38(2b) without any settlement of accounts as between him or his estate and the person or partnership continuing the business, unless otherwise agreed, he or his legal representative as against such persons or partnership may have the value of his interest at the date of dissolution ascertained, and shall receive as an ordinary creditor an amount equal to the value of his interest in the dissolved partnership with interest, or, at his option or at the option of his legal representative, in lieu of interest, the profits attributable to the use of his right in the property of the dissolved partnership; provided that the creditors of the dissolved partnership as against the separate creditors, or the representative of the retired or deceased partner, shall have priority on any claim arising under this section, as provided by section 41(8) of this act.

§43 Accrual of Actions

The right to an account of his interest shall accrue to any partner, or his legal representative, as against the winding up partners or the surviving partners or the person or partnership continuing the business, at the date of dissolution, in the absence of any agreement to the contrary.

Part VII. Miscellaneous Provisions

§44 When Act Takes Effect

This act shall take effect on the _____ day of _____ one thousand nine hundred and _____.

§45 Legislation Repealed

All acts or parts of acts inconsistent with this act are hereby repealed.

Appendix B
SELECTED PROVISIONS FROM THE MODEL RULES OF PROFESSIONAL CONDUCT

Rule 1.1 Competence

A lawyer shall provide competent representation to a client. Competent representation requires the legal knowledge, skill, thor-

oughness and preparation reasonably necessary for the representation.

Comment:

Legal Knowledge and Skill

In determining whether a lawyer employs the requisite knowledge and skill in a particular matter, relevant factors include the
relative complexity and specialized nature of the matter, the lawyer's
general experience, the lawyer's training and experience in the field
in question, the preparation and study the lawyer is able to give the
matter and whether it is feasible to refer the matter to, or associate or
consult with, a lawyer of established competence in the field in
question. In many instances, the required proficiency is that of a
general practitioner. Expertise in a particular field of law may be
required in some circumstances.

A lawyer need not necessarily have special training or prior
experience to handle legal problems of a type with which the lawyer
is unfamiliar. A newly admitted lawyer can be as competent as a
practitioner with long experience. Some important legal skills, such
as the analysis of precedent, the evaluation of evidence and legal
drafting, are required in all legal problems. Perhaps the most funda-
mental legal skill consists of determining what kind of legal problems a situation may involve, a skill that necessarily transcends any
particular specialized knowledge. A lawyer can provide adequate
representation in a wholly novel field through necessary study.
Competent representation can also be provided through the association of a lawyer of established competence in the field in question.

In an emergency a lawyer may give advice or assistance in a
matter in which the lawyer does not have the skill ordinarily required
where referral to or consultation or association with another lawyer
would be impractical. Even in an emergency, however, assistance
should be limited to that reasonably necessary in the circumstances,
for ill considered action under emergency conditions can jeopardize
the client's interest.

A lawyer may accept representation where the requisite level of competence can be achieved by reasonable preparation. This applies as well to a lawyer who is appointed as counsel for an unrepresented person. See also Rule 6.2.

Thoroughness and Preparation

Competent handling of a particular matter includes inquiry into and analysis of the factual and legal elements of the problem, and use of methods and procedures meeting the standards of competent practitioners. It also includes adequate preparation. The required attention and preparation are determined in part by what is at stake; major litigation and complex transactions ordinarily require more elaborate treatment than matters of lesser consequence.

Maintaining Competence

To maintain the requisite knowledge and skill, a lawyer should engage in continuing study and education. If a system of peer review has been established, the lawyer should consider making use of it in appropriate circumstances.

Model Code Comparison

DR 6-101(A)(1) provided that a lawyer shall not handle a matter "which he knows or should know that he is not competent to handle, without associating himself with a lawyer who is competent to handle it;" DR 6-101(A)(2) required "preparation adequate in the circumstances." Rule 1.1 more fully particularizes the elements of competence. Whereas DR 6-101(A)(3) prohibited the "[n]eglect of a legal matter," Rule 1.1 does not contain such a prohibition. Instead, Rule 1.1 affirmatively requires the lawyer to be competent.

Rule 1.3 Diligence

A lawyer shall act with reasonable diligence and promptness in representing a client.

Comment:

A lawyer should pursue a matter on behalf of a client despite opposition, obstruction or personal inconvenience to the lawyer, and may take whatever lawful and ethical measures are required to vindicate a client's cause or endeavor. A lawyer should act with commitment and dedication to the interests of the client and with zeal in advocacy upon the client's behalf. However, a lawyer is not bound to press for every advantage that might be realized for a client. A lawyer has professional discretion in determining the means by which a matter should be pursued. See Rule 1.2. A lawyer's workload should be controlled so that each matter can be handled adequately.

Perhaps no professional shortcoming is more widely resented than procrastination. A client's interests often can be adversely affected by the passage of time or the change of conditions; in extreme instances, as when a lawyer overlooks a statute of limitations, the client's legal position may be destroyed. Even when the client's interests are not affected in substance, however, unreasonable delay can cause a client needless anxiety and undermine confidence in the lawyer's trustworthiness.

Unless the relationship is terminated as provided in Rule 1.16, a lawyer should carry through to conclusion all matters undertaken for a client. If a lawyer's employment is limited to a specific matter, the relationship terminates when the matter has been resolved. If a lawyer has served a client over a substantial period in a variety of matters, the client sometimes may assume that the lawyer will continue to serve on a continuing basis unless the lawyer gives notice of withdrawal. Doubt about whether a client-lawyer relationship still exists should be clarified by the lawyer, preferably in writing, so that the client will not mistakenly suppose the lawyer is looking after the client's affairs when the lawyer has ceased to do so. For example, if a lawyer has handled a judicial or administrative proceeding that produced a result adverse to the client but has not been specifically instructed concerning pursuit of an appeal, the lawyer should advise the client of the possibility of appeal before relinquishing responsibility for the matter.

Model Code Comparison

DR 6-101(A)(3) required that a lawyer not "[n]eglect a legal matter entrusted to him." EC 6-4 stated that a lawyer should "give appropriate attention to his legal work." Canon 7 stated that "a lawyer should represent a client zealously within the bounds of the law." DR 7-101(A)(1) provided that a lawyer "shall not intentionally . . . fail to seek the lawful objectives of his client through reasonably available means permitted by law and the Disciplinary Rules. . . ." DR 7-101(A)(3) provided that a lawyer "shall not intentionally . . . [p]rejudice or damage his client during the course of the relationship. . . ."

Rule 1.4   Communication

(a) A lawyer shall keep a client reasonably informed about the status of a matter and promptly comply with reasonable requests for information.

(b) A lawyer shall explain a matter to the extent reasonably necessary to permit the client to make informed decisions regarding the representation.

Comment:

The client should have sufficient information to participate intelligently in decisions concerning the objectives of the representation and the means by which they are to be pursued, to the extent the client is willing and able to do so. For example, a lawyer negotiating on behalf of a client should provide the client with facts relevant to the matter, inform the client of communications from another party and take other reasonable steps that permit the client to make a decision regarding a serious offer from another party. A lawyer who receives from opposing counsel an offer of settlement in a civil controversy or a proffered plea bargain in a criminal case should promptly inform the client of its substance unless prior discussions with the client have left it clear that the proposal will be unacceptable. See Rule 1.2(a). Even when a client delegates authority to the lawyer, the client should be kept advised of the status of the matter.

Adequacy of communication depends in part on the kind of advice or assistance involved. For example, in negotiations where there is time to explain a proposal, the lawyer should review all important provisions with the client before proceeding to an agreement. In litigation a lawyer should explain the general strategy and prospects of success and ordinarily should consult the client on tactics that might injure or coerce others. On the other hand, a lawyer ordinarily cannot be expected to describe trial or negotiation strategy in detail. The guiding principle is that the lawyer should fulfill reasonable client expectations for information consistent with the duty to act in the client's best interests, and the client's overall requirements as to the character of representation.

Ordinarily, the information to be provided is that appropriate for a client who is a comprehending and responsible adult. However, fully informing the client according to this standard may be impracticable, for example, where the client is a child or suffers from mental disability. See Rule 1.14. When the client is an organization or group, it is often impossible or inappropriate to inform every one of its members about its legal affairs; ordinarily, the lawyer should address communications to the appropriate officials of the organization. See Rule 1.13. Where many routine matters are involved, a system of limited or occasional reporting may be arranged with the client. Practical exigency may also require a lawyer to act for a client without prior consultation.

Withholding Information

In some circumstances, a lawyer may be justified in delaying transmission of information when the client would be likely to react imprudently to an immediate communication. Thus, a lawyer might withhold a psychiatric diagnosis of a client when the examining psychiatrist indicates that disclosure would harm the client. A lawyer may not withhold information to serve the lawyer's own interest or convenience. Rules or court orders governing litigation may provide that information supplied to a lawyer may not be disclosed to the client. Rule 3.4(c) directs compliance with such rules or orders.

Model Code Comparison

Rule 1.4 has no direct counterpart in the Disciplinary Rules of the Model Code. DR 6-101(A)(3) provided that a lawyer shall not "[n]eglect a legal matter entrusted to him." DR 9-102(B)(1) provided that a lawyer shall "[p]romptly notify a client of the receipt of his funds, securities, or other properties." EC 7-8 stated that a lawyer "should exert his best efforts to insure that decisions of his client are made only after the client has been informed of relevant considerations." EC 9-2 stated that "a lawyer should fully and promptly inform his client of material developments in the matters being handled for the client."

Rule 1.5 Fees

(a) A lawyer's fee shall be reasonable. The factors to be considered in determining the reasonableness of a fee include the following:

(1) the time and labor required, the novelty and difficulty of the questions involved, and the skill requisite to perform the legal service properly;

(2) the likelihood, if apparent to the client, that the acceptance of the particular employment will preclude other employment by the lawyer;

(3) the fee customarily charged in the locality for similar legal services;

(4) the amount involved and the results obtained;

(5) the time limitations imposed by the client or by the circumstances;

(6) the nature and length of the professional relationship with the client;

(7) the experience, reputation, and ability of the lawyer or lawyers performing the services; and

(8) whether the fee is fixed or contingent.

(b) When the lawyer has not regularly represented the client, the basis or rate of the fee shall be communicated to the client, preferably in writing, before or within a reasonable time after commencing the representation.

(c) A fee may be contingent on the outcome of the matter for which the service is rendered, except in a matter in which a contingent fee is prohibited by paragraph (d) or other law. A contingent fee agreement shall be in writing and shall state the method by which the fee is to be determined, including the percentage or percentages that shall accrue to the lawyer in the event of settlement, trial or appeal, litigation and other expenses to be deducted from the recovery, and whether such expenses are to be deducted before or after the contingent fee is calculated. Upon conclusion of a contingent fee matter, the lawyer shall provide the client with a written statement stating the outcome of the matter and, if there is a recovery, showing the remittance to the client and the method of its determination.

(d) A lawyer shall not enter into an arrangement for, charge, or collect:

(1) any fee in a domestic relations matter, the payment or amount of which is contingent upon the securing of a divorce or upon the amount of alimony or support, or property settlement in lieu thereof; or

(2) a contingent fee for representing a defendant in a criminal case.

(e) A division of fee between lawyers who are not in the same firm may be made only if:

(1) the division is in proportion to the services performed by each lawyer or, by written agreement with the client, each lawyer assumes joint responsibility for the representation;

(2) the client is advised of and does not object to the participation of all the lawyers involved; and

(3) the total fee is reasonable.

Comment:

Basis or Rate of Fee

When the lawyer has regularly represented a client, they ordinarily will have evolved an understanding concerning the basis or rate of the fee. In a new client-lawyer relationship, however, an understanding as to the fee should be promptly established. It is not necessary to recite all the factors that underlie the basis of the fee, but only those that are directly involved in its computation. It is sufficient, for example, to state that the basic rate is an hourly charge or a fixed amount or an estimated amount, or to identify the factors that may be taken into account in finally fixing the fee. When developments occur during the representation that render an earlier estimate substantially inaccurate, a revised estimate should be provided to the client. A written statement concerning the fee reduces the possibility of misunderstanding. Furnishing the client with a simple memorandum or a copy of the lawyer's customary fee schedule is sufficient if the basis or rate of the fee is set forth.

Terms of Payment

A lawyer may require advance payment of a fee, but is obliged to return any unearned portion. See Rule 1.16(d). A lawyer may accept property in payment for services, such as an ownership interest in an enterprise, providing this does not involve acquisition of a proprietary interest in the cause of action or subject matter of the litigation contrary to Rule 1.8(j). However, a fee paid in property instead of money may be subject to special scrutiny because it involves questions concerning both the value of the services and the lawyer's special knowledge of the value of the property.

An agreement may not be made whose terms might induce the lawyer improperly to curtail services for the client or perform them in a way contrary to the client's interest. For example, a lawyer should not enter into an agreement whereby services are to be provided only up to a stated amount when it is foreseeable that more extensive services probably will be required, unless the situation is adequately explained to the client. Otherwise, the client might have to bargain for further assistance in the midst of a proceeding or transaction. However, it is proper to define the extent of services in light of the client's ability to pay. A lawyer should not exploit a fee arrangement based primarily on hourly charges by using wasteful procedures. When there is doubt whether a contingent fee is consistent with the client's best interest, the lawyer should offer the client alternative bases for the fee and explain their implications. Applicable law may impose limitations on contingent fees, such as a ceiling on the percentage.

Division of Fee

A division of fee is a single billing to a client covering the fee of two or more lawyers who are not in the same firm. A division of fee facilitates association of more than one lawyer in a matter in which neither alone could serve the client as well, and most often is used when the fee is contingent and the division is between a referring lawyer and a trial specialist. Paragraph (e) permits the lawyers to divide a fee on either the basis of the proportion of services they render or by agreement between the participating lawyers if all assume responsibility for the representation as a whole and the client is advised and does not object. It does not require disclosure to the client of the share that each lawyer is to receive. Joint responsibility for the representation entails the obligations stated in Rule 5.1 for purposes of the matter involved.

Disputes over Fees

If a procedure has been established for resolution of fee disputes, such as an arbitration or mediation procedure established by the bar, the lawyer should conscientiously consider submitting to it. Law may prescribe a procedure for determining a lawyer's fee, for example, in representation of an executor or administrator, a class or a person entitled to a reasonable fee as part of the measure of damages. The lawyer entitled to such a fee and a lawyer representing another party concerned with the fee should comply with the prescribed procedure.

Model Code Comparison

DR 2-106(A) provided that a lawyer "shall not enter into an agreement for, charge, or collect an illegal or clearly excessive fee." DR 2-106(B) provided that a fee is "clearly excessive when, after a review of the facts, a lawyer of ordinary prudence would be left with a definite and firm conviction that the fee is in excess of a reasonable fee." The factors of a reasonable fee in Rule 1.5(a) are substantially identical to those listed in DR 2-106(B). EC 2-17 states that a lawyer "should not charge more than a reasonable fee. . . ."

There was no counterpart to paragraph (b) in the Disciplinary

Rules of the Model Code. EC 2-19 stated that it is "usually beneficial to reduce to writing the understanding of the parties regarding the fee, particularly when it is contingent."

There was also no counterpart to paragraph (c) in the Disciplinary Rules of the Model Code. EC 2-20 provided that "[c]ontingent fee arrangements in civil cases have long been commonly accepted in the United States," but that "a lawyer generally should decline to accept employment on a contingent fee basis by one who is able to pay a reasonable fixed fee. . . ."

With regard to paragraph (d), DR 2-106(C) prohibited "a contingent fee in a criminal case." EC 2-20 provided that "contingent fee arrangements in domestic relation cases are rarely justified."

With regard to paragraph (e), DR 2-107(A) permitted division of fees only if: "(1) The client consents to employment of the other lawyer after a full disclosure that a division of fees will be made. (2) The division is in proportion to the services performed and responsibility assumed by each. (3) The total fee does not exceed clearly reasonable compensation. . . ." Paragraph (e) permits division without regard to the services rendered by each lawyer if they assume joint responsibility for the representation.

Rule 1.7 Conflict of Interest: General Rule

(a) A lawyer shall not represent a client if the representation of that client will be directly adverse to another client, unless:

(1) the lawyer reasonably believes the representation will not adversely affect the relationship with the other client; and

(2) each client consents after consultation.

(b) A lawyer shall not represent a client if the representation of that client may be materially limited by the lawyer's responsibilities to another client or to a third person, or by the lawyer's own interests, unless:

(1) the lawyer reasonably believes the representation will not be adversely affected; and

(2) the client consents after consultation. When representation of multiple clients in a single matter is undertaken, the consultation shall include explanation of the implications of the common representation and the advantages and risks involved.

Comment:

Loyalty to a Client

Loyalty is an essential element in the lawyer's relationship to a client. An impermissible conflict of interest may exist before representation is undertaken, in which event the representation should be declined. The lawyer should adopt reasonable procedures, appropriate for the size and type of firm and practice, to determine in both litigation and non-litigation matters the parties and issues involved and to determine whether there are actual or potential conflicts of interest.

If such a conflict arises after representation has been undertaken, the lawyer should withdraw from the representation. See Rule 1.16. Where more than one client is involved and the lawyer withdraws because a conflict arises after representation, whether the lawyer may continue to represent any of the clients is determined by Rule 1.9. See also Rule 2.2(c). As to whether a client-lawyer relationship exists or, having once been established, is continuing, see Comment to Rule 1.3 and Scope.

As a general proposition, loyalty to a client prohibits undertaking representation directly adverse to that client without that client's consent. Paragraph (a) expresses that general rule. Thus, a lawyer ordinarily may not act as advocate against a person the lawyer represents in some other matter, even if it is wholly unrelated. On the other hand, simultaneous representation in unrelated matters of clients whose interests are only generally adverse, such as competing economic enterprises, does not require consent of the respective clients. Paragraph (a) applies only when the representation of one client would be directly adverse to the other.

Loyalty to a client is also impaired when a lawyer cannot consider, recommend or carry out an appropriate course of action for the client because of the lawyer's other responsibilities or interests. The conflict in effect forecloses alternatives that would otherwise be available to the client. Paragraph (b) addresses such situations. A possible conflict does not itself preclude the representation. The critical questions are the likelihood that a conflict will eventuate and, if it does, whether it will materially interfere with the lawyer's independent professional judgment in considering alternatives or foreclose courses of action that reasonably should be pursued on behalf of the client. Consideration should be given to whether the client wishes to accommodate the other interest involved.

Consultation and Consent

A client may consent to representation notwithstanding a conflict. However, as indicated in paragraph (a)(1)with respect to representation directly adverse to a client, and paragraph (b)(1) with respect to material limitations on representation of a client, when a disinterested lawyer would conclude that the client should not agree to the representation under the circumstances, the lawyer involved cannot properly ask for such agreement or provide representation on the basis of the client's consent. When more than one client is involved, the question of conflict must be resolved as to each client. Moreover, there may be circumstances where it is impossible to make the disclosure necessary to obtain consent. For example, when the lawyer represents different clients in related matters and one of the clients refuses to consent to the disclosure necessary to permit the other client to make an informed decision, the lawyer cannot properly ask the latter to consent.

Lawyer's Interests

The lawyer's own interests should not be permitted to have adverse effect on representation of a client. For example, a lawyer's need for income should not lead the lawyer to undertake matters that cannot be handled competently and at a reasonable fee. See Rules 1.1 and 1.5. If the probity of a lawyer's own conduct in a transaction is in serious question, it may be difficult or impossible for the lawyer to give a client detached advice. A lawyer may not allow related business interests to affect representation, for example, by referring clients to an enterprise in which the lawyer has an undisclosed interest.

Conflicts in Litigation

Paragraph (a) prohibits representation of opposing parties in litigation. Simultaneous representation of parties whose interests in litigation may conflict, such as co-plaintiffs or co-defendants, is governed by paragraph (b). An impermissible conflict may exist by reason of substantial discrepancy in the parties' testimony, incompatibility in positions in relation to an opposing party or the fact that there are substantially different possibilities of settlement of the claims or liabilities in question. Such conflicts can arise in criminal cases as well as civil. The potential for conflict of interest in representing multiple defendants in a criminal case is so grave that ordinarily a lawyer should decline to represent more than one co-defendant. On the other hand, common representation of persons having similar interests is proper if the risk of adverse effect is minimal and the requirements of paragraph (b) are met. Compare Rule 2.2 involving intermediation between clients.

Ordinarily, a lawyer may not act as advocate against a client the lawyer represents in some other matter, even if the other matter is wholly unrelated. However, there are circumstances in which a lawyer may act as advocate against a client. For example, a lawyer representing an enterprise with diverse operations may accept employment as an advocate against the enterprise in an unrelated matter if doing so will not adversely affect the lawyer's relationship with the enterprise or conduct of the suit and if both clients consent upon consultation. By the same token, government lawyers in some circumstances may represent government employees in proceedings in which a government agency is the opposing party. The propriety of concurrent representation can depend on the nature of the litigation. For example, a suit charging fraud entails conflict to a degree not involved in a suit for a declaratory judgment concerning statutory interpretation.

A lawyer may represent parties having antagonistic positions on a legal question that has arisen in different cases, unless representation of either client would be adversely affected. Thus, it is ordinarily not improper to assert such positions in cases pending in different trial courts, but it may be improper to do so in cases pending at the same time in an appellate court.

Interest of Person Paying for a Lawyer's Service

A lawyer may be paid from a source other than the client, if the client is informed of that fact and consents and the arrangement does not compromise the lawyer's duty of loyalty to the client. See Rule 1.8(f). For example, when an insurer and its insured have conflicting interests in a matter arising from a liability insurance agreement, and the insurer is required to provide special counsel for the insured, the arrangement should assure the special counsel's professional independence. So also, when a corporation and its directors or employees are involved in a controversy in which they have conflicting interests, the corporation may provide funds for separate legal representation of the directors or employees, if the clients consent after consultation and the arrangement ensures the lawyer's professional independence.

Other Conflict Situations

Conflicts of interest in contexts other than litigation sometimes may be difficult to assess. Relevant factors in determining whether there is potential for adverse effect include the duration and intimacy of the lawyer's relationship with the client or clients involved, the functions being performed by the lawyer, the likelihood that actual conflict will arise and the likely prejudice to the client from the conflict if it does arise. The question is often one of proximity and degree.

For example, a lawyer may not represent multiple parties to a negotiation whose interests are fundamentally antagonistic to each other, but common representation is permissible where the clients are generally aligned in interest even though there is some difference of interest among them.

Conflict questions may also arise in estate planning and estate administration. A lawyer may be called upon to prepare wills for several family members, such as husband and wife, and, depending upon the circumstances, a conflict of interest may arise. In estate administration the identity of the client may be unclear under the law of a particular jurisdiction. Under one view, the client is the fiduciary; under another view the client is the estate or trust, including its beneficiaries. The lawyer should make clear the relationship to the parties involved.

A lawyer for a corporation or other organization who is also a member of its board of directors should determine whether the responsibilities of the two roles may conflict. The lawyer may be called on to advise the corporation in matters involving actions of the directors. Consideration should be given to the frequency with which such situations may arise, the potential intensity of the conflict, the effect of the lawyer's resignation from the board and the possibility of the corporation's obtaining legal advice from another lawyer in such situations. If there is material risk that the dual role will compromise the lawyer's independence of professional judgment, the lawyer should not serve as a director.

Conflict Charged by an Opposing Party

Resolving questions of conflict of interest is primarily the responsibility of the lawyer undertaking the representation. In litigation, a court may raise the question when there is reason to infer that the lawyer has neglected the responsibility. In a criminal case, inquiry by the court is generally required when a lawyer represents multiple defendants. Where the conflict is such as clearly to call in question the fair or efficient administration of justice, opposing counsel may properly raise the question. Such an objection should be viewed with caution, however, for it can be misused as a technique of harassment. See Scope.

Model Code Comparison

DR 5-101(A) provided that "[e]xcept with the consent of his client after full disclosure, a lawyer shall not accept employment if the exercise of his professional judgment on behalf of the client will be or reasonably may be affected by his own financial, business, property, or personal interests." DR 5-105(A) provided that a lawyer "shall decline proffered employment if the exercise of his independent professional judgment in behalf of a client will be or is likely to be adversely affected by the acceptance of the proffered employment, or if it would be likely to involve him in representing differing interests, except to the extent permitted under DR 5-105(C)." DR 5-105(C) provided that "a lawyer may represent multiple clients if it is obvious that he can adequately represent the interest of each and if each consents to the representation after full disclosure of the possible effect of such representation on the exercise of his independent professional judgment on behalf of each." DR 5-107(B) provided that a lawyer "shall not permit a person who recommends, employs, or pays him to render legal services for another to direct or regulate his professional judgment in rendering such services.

Rule 1.7 clarifies DR 5-105(A) by requiring that, when the lawyer's other interests are involved, not only must the client consent after consultation but also that, independent of such consent, the representation reasonably appears not to be adversely affected by the lawyer's other interests. This requirement appears to be the intended meaning of the provision in DR 5-105(C) that "it is obvious that he can adequately represent" the client, and was implicit in EC 5-2, which stated that a lawyer "should not accept proffered employment if his personal interests or desires will, or there is a reasonable probability that they will, affect adversely the advice to be given or services to be rendered the prospective client."

Rule 1.8 Conflict of Interest: Prohibited Transactions

(a) A lawyer shall not enter into a business transaction with a client or knowingly acquire an ownership, possessory, security or other pecuniary interest adverse to a client unless:

(1) the transaction and terms on which the lawyer acquires the interest are fair and reasonable to the client and are fully disclosed and transmitted in writing to the client in a manner which can be reasonably understood by the client;

(2) the client is given a reasonable opportunity to seek the advice of independent counsel in the transaction; and

(3) the client consents in writing thereto.

(b) A lawyer shall not use information relating to representation of a client to the disadvantage of the client unless the client consents after consultation, except as permitted or required by Rule 1.6 or Rule 3.3.

(c) A lawyer shall not prepare an instrument giving the lawyer or a person related to the lawyer as parent, child, sibling, or spouse any substantial gift from a client, including a testamentary gift, except where the client is related to the donee.

(d) Prior to the conclusion of representation of a client, a lawyer shall not make or negotiate an agreement giving the lawyer literary or media rights to a portrayal or account based in substantial part on information relating to the representation.

(e) A lawyer shall not provide financial assistance to a client in connection with pending or contemplated litigation, except that:

(1) a lawyer may advance court costs and expenses of litigation, the repayment of which may be contingent on the outcome of the matter; and

(2) a lawyer representing an indigent client may pay court costs and expenses of litigation on behalf of the client.

(f) A lawyer shall not accept compensation for representing a client from one other than the client unless:

(1) the client consents after consultation;

(2) there is no interference with the lawyer's independence of professional judgment or with the client-lawyer relationship; and

(3) information relating to representation of a client is protected as required by Rule 1.6.

(g) A lawyer who represents two or more clients shall not participate in making an aggregate settlement of the claims of or against the clients, or in a criminal case an aggregated agreement as to guilty or nolo contendere pleas, unless each client consents after consultation, including disclosure of the existence and nature of all the claims or pleas involved and of the participation of each person in the settlement.

(h) A lawyer shall not make an agreement prospectively limiting the lawyer's liability to a client for malpractice unless permitted by law and the client is independently represented in making the agreement, or settle a claim for such liability with an unrepresented client or former client without first advising that person in writing that independent representation is appropriate in connection therewith.

(i) A lawyer related to another lawyer as parent, child, sibling or spouse shall not represent a client in a representation directly adverse to a person who the lawyer knows is represented by the other lawyer except upon consent by the client after consultation regarding the relationship.

(j) A lawyer shall not acquire a proprietary interest in the cause of action or subject matter of litigation the lawyer is conducting for a client, except that the lawyer may:

(1) acquire a lien granted by law to secure the lawyer's fee or expenses; and

(2) contract with a client for a reasonable contingent fee in a civil case.

Comment:

Transactions Between Client and Lawyer

As a general principle, all transactions between client and lawyer should be fair and reasonable to the client. In such transactions a review by independent counsel on behalf of the client is often advisable. Furthermore, a lawyer may not exploit information relating to the representation to the client's disadvantage. For example, a lawyer who has learned that the client is investing in specific real estate may not, without the client's consent, seek to acquire nearby property where doing so would adversely affect the client's plan for investment. Paragraph (a) does not, however, apply to standard commercial transactions between the lawyer and the client for products or services that the client generally markets to others, for example, banking or brokerage services, medical services, products manufactured or distributed by the client, and utilities services. In such transactions, the lawyer has no advantage in dealing with the client, and the restrictions in paragraph (a) are unnecessary and impracticable.

A lawyer may accept a gift from a client, if the transaction meets general standards of fairness. For example, a simple gift such as a present given at a holiday or as a token of appreciation is permitted. If effectuation of a substantial gift requires preparing a legal instrument such as a will or conveyance, however, the client should have the detached advice that another lawyer can provide. Paragraph (c) recognizes an exception where the client is a relative of the donee or the gift is not substantial.

Literary Rights

An agreement by which a lawyer acquires literary or media rights concerning the conduct of the representation creates a conflict between the interests of the client and the personal interests of the lawyer. Measures suitable in the representation of the client may detract from the publication value of an account of the representation. Paragraph (d) does not prohibit a lawyer representing a client in a transaction concerning literary property from agreeing that the lawyer's fee shall consist of a share in ownership in the property, if the arrangement conforms to Rule 1.5 and paragraph (j).

Person Paying for Lawyer's Services

Rule 1.8(f) requires disclosure of the fact that the lawyer's services are being paid for by a third party. Such an arrangement must also conform to the requirements of Rule 1.6 concerning confidentiality and Rule 1.7 concerning conflict of interest. Where the client is a class, consent may be obtained on behalf of the class by court-supervised procedure.

Family Relationships Between Lawyers

Rule 1.8(i) applies to related lawyers who are in different firms. Related lawyers in the same firm are governed by Rules 1.7, 1.9, and 1.10. The disqualification stated in Rule 1.8(i) is personal and is not imputed to members of firms with whom the lawyers are associated.

Acquisition of Interest in Litigation

Paragraph (j) states the traditional general rule that lawyers are prohibited from acquiring a proprietary interest in litigation. This general rule, which has its basis in common law champerty and maintenance, is subject to specific exceptions developed in decisional law and continued in these Rules, such as the exception for reasonable contingent fees set forth in Rule 1.5 and the exception for certain advances of the costs of litigation set forth in paragraph (e).

This Rule is not intended to apply to customary qualification and limitations in legal opinions and memoranda.

Model Code Comparison

With regard to paragraph (a), DR 5-104(A) provided that a lawyer "shall not enter into a business transaction with a client if they have differing interests therein and if the client expects the lawyer to exercise his professional judgment therein for the protection of the client, unless the client has consented after full disclosure." EC 5-3 stated that a lawyer "should not seek to persuade his client to permit him to invest in an undertaking of his client nor make improper use of his professional relationship to influence his client to invest in an enterprise in which the lawyer is interested."

With regard to paragraph (b), DR 4-101(B)(3) provided that a lawyer should not use "a confidence or secret of his client for the advantage of himself, or of a third person, unless the client consents after full disclosure."

There was no counterpart to paragraph (c) in the Disciplinary Rules of the Model Code. EC 5-5 stated that a lawyer "should not suggest to his client that a gift be made to himself or for his benefit. If a lawyer accepts a gift from his client, he is peculiarly susceptible to the charge that he unduly influenced or overreached the client. If a client voluntarily offers to make a gift to his lawyer, the lawyer may accept the gift, but before doing so, he should urge that the client secure disinterested advice from an independent, competent person who is cognizant of all the circumstances. Other than in exceptional circumstances, a lawyer should insist that an instrument in which his client desires to name him beneficially be prepared by another lawyer selected by the client."

Paragraph (d) is substantially similar to DR 5-104(B), but refers to "literary or media" rights, a more generally inclusive term than "publication" rights.

Paragraph (e)(1) is similar to DR 5-103(B), but eliminates the requirement that "the client remains ultimately liable for such expenses."

Paragraph (e)(2) has no counterpart in the Model Code.

Paragraph (f) is substantially identical to DR 5-107(A)(1).

Paragraph (g) is substantially identical to DR 5-106.

The first clause of paragraph (h) is similar to DR 6-102(A). There was no counterpart in the Model Code to the second clause of paragraph (h).

Paragraph (i) has no counterpart in the Model Code.

Paragraph (j) is substantially identical to DR 5-103(A).

Rule 1.9 Conflict of Interest: Former Client

(a) A lawyer who has formerly represented a client in a matter shall not thereafter represent another person in the same or a substantially related matter in which that person's interests are materially adverse to the interests of the former client unless the former client consents after consultation.

(b) A lawyer shall not knowingly represent a person in the same or a substantially related matter in which a firm with which the lawyer formerly was associated had previously represented a client

(1) whose interests are materially adverse to that person; and

(2) about whom the lawyer had acquired information protected by Rules 1.6 and 1.9(c) that is material to the matter;

unless the former client consents after consultation.

(c) A lawyer who has formerly represented a client in a matter or whose present or former firm has formerly represented a client in a matter shall not thereafter:

(1) use information relating to the representation to the disadvantage of the former client except as Rule 1.6 or Rule 3.3 would permit or require with respect to a client, or when information has become generally known; or

(2) reveal information relating to the representation except as Rule 1.6 or Rule 3.3 would permit or require with respect to a client.

Comment:

After termination of a client-lawyer relationship, a lawyer may not represent another client except in conformity with this Rule. The principles in Rule 1.7 determine whether the interests of the present and former client are adverse. Thus, a lawyer could not properly seek to rescind on behalf of a new client a contract drafted on behalf of the former client. So also a lawyer who has prosecuted an accused person could not properly represent the accused in a subsequent civil action against the government concerning the same transaction.

The scope of a "matter" for the purposes of this Rule may depend on the facts of a particular situation or transaction. The lawyer's involvement in a matter can also be a question of degree. When a lawyer has been directly involved in a specific transaction, subsequent representation of other clients with materially adverse interests clearly is prohibited. On the other hand, a lawyer who recurrently handled a type of problem for a former client is not precluded from later representing another client in a wholly distinct problem of that type even though a subsequent representation involves a position adverse to the prior client. Similar considerations can apply to the reassignment of military lawyers between defense and prosecution functions within the same military jurisdiction. The underlying question is whether the lawyer was so involved in the matter that the subsequent representation can be justly regarded as a changing of sides in the matter in question.

Lawyers Moving Between Firms

When lawyers have been associated within a firm but then end their association, the question of whether a lawyer should undertake representation is more complicated. There are several competing considerations. First, the client previously represented by the former firm must be reasonably assured that the principle of loyalty to the client is not compromised. Second, the rule should not be so broadly cast as to preclude other persons from having reasonable choice of legal counsel. Third, the rule should not unreasonably hamper lawyers from forming new associations and taking on new clients after having left a previous association. In this connection, it should be recognized that today many lawyers practice in firms, that many lawyers to some degree limit their practice to one field or another, and that many move from one association to another several times in their careers. If the concept of imputation were applied with unqualified rigor, the result would be radical curtailment of the opportunity of lawyers to move from one practice setting to another and of the opportunity of clients to change counsel.

Reconciliation of these competing principles in the past has been attempted under two rubrics. One approach has been to seek per se rules of disqualification. For example, it has been held that a partner in a law firm is conclusively presumed to have access to all confidences concerning all clients of the firm. Under this analysis, if a lawyer has been a partner in one law firm and then becomes a partner in another law firm, there may be a presumption that all confidences known by the partner in the first firm are known to all partners in the second firm. This presumption might properly be applied in some circumstances, especially where the client has been extensively represented, but may be unrealistic where the client was represented only for limited purposes. Furthermore, such a rigid rule exaggerates the difference between a partner and an associate in modern law firms.

The other rubric formerly used for dealing with disqualification is the appearance of impropriety proscribed in Canon 9 of the ABA Model Code of Professional Responsibility. This rubric has a two fold problem. First, the appearance of impropriety can be taken to include any new client-lawyer relationship that might make a former client feel anxious. If that meaning were adopted, disqualification would become little more than a question of subjective judgment by the former client. Second, since "impropriety" is undefined, the term "appearance of impropriety" is question-begging. It therefore has to be recognized that the problem of disqualification cannot be properly resolved either by simple analogy to a lawyer practicing alone or by the very general concept of appearance of impropriety.

Confidentiality

Preserving confidentiality is a question of access to information. Access to information, in turn, is essentially a question of fact in particular circumstances, aided by inferences, deductions or working presumptions that reasonably may be made about the way in which lawyers work together. A lawyer may have general access to files of all clients of a law firm and may regularly participate in discussions of their affairs; it should be inferred that such a lawyer in fact is privy to all information about all the firm's clients. In contrast, another lawyer may have access to the files of only a limited number of clients and participate in discussions of the affairs of no other clients; in the absence of information to the contrary, it should be inferred that such a lawyer in fact is privy to information about the clients actually served but not those of other clients.

Application of paragraph (b) depends on a situation's particular facts. In such an inquiry, the burden of proof should rest upon the firm whose disqualification is sought.

Paragraph (b) operates to disqualify the lawyer only when the lawyer involved has actual knowledge of information protected by Rules 1.6 and 1.9(b). Thus, if a lawyer while with one firm acquired no knowledge or information relating to a particular client of the firm, and that lawyer later joined another firm, neither the lawyer individually nor the second firm is disqualified from representing another client in the same or a related matter even though the interests of the two clients conflict. See Rule 1.10(b) for the restrictions on a firm once a lawyer has terminated association with the firm.

Independent of the question of disqualification of a firm, a lawyer changing professional association has a continuing duty to preserve confidentiality of information about a client formerly represented. See Rules 1.6 and 1.9.

Adverse Positions

The second aspect of loyalty to a client is the lawyer's obligation to decline subsequent representations involving positions adverse to a former client arising in substantially related matters. This obligation requires abstention from adverse representation by the individual lawyer involved, but does not properly entail abstention of other lawyers through imputed disqualification. Hence, this aspect of the problem is governed by Rule 1.9(a). Thus, if a lawyer left one firm for another, the new affiliation would not preclude the firms involved from continuing to represent clients with adverse interests in the same or related matters, so long as the conditions of paragraphs (b) and (c) concerning confidentiality have been met.

Information acquired by the lawyer in the course of representing a client may not subsequently be used or revealed by the lawyer to the disadvantage of the client. However, the fact that a lawyer has once served a client does not preclude the lawyer from using generally known information about that client when later representing another client.

Disqualification from subsequent representation is for the protection of former clients and can be waived by them. A waiver is effective only if there is disclosure of the circumstances, including the lawyer's intended role in behalf of the new client.

With regard to an opposing party's raising a question of conflict of interest, see Comment to Rule 1.7. With regard to disqualification of a firm with which a lawyer is or was formerly associated, see Rule 1.10.

Model Code Comparison

There was no counterpart to this Rule in the Disciplinary Rules of the Model Code. Representation adverse to a former client was sometimes dealt with under the rubric of Canon 9 of the Model Code, which provided: "A lawyer should avoid even the appearance of impropriety." Also applicable were EC 4-6 which stated that the "obligation of a lawyer to preserve the confidences and secrets of his client continues after the termination of his employment" and Canon 5 which stated that "[a] lawyer should exercise independent professional judgment on behalf of a client."

The provision for waiver by the former client in paragraphs (a) and (b) is similar to DR 5-105(C).

The exception in the last clause of paragraph (c)(1) permits a lawyer to use information relating to a former client that is in the "public domain," a use that was also not prohibited by the Model Code, which protected only "confidences and secrets." Since the scope of paragraphs (a) and (b) is much broader than "confidences and secrets," it is necessary to define when a lawyer may make use of information about a client after the client-lawyer relationship has terminated.

Rule 1.10 Imputed Disqualification: General Rule

(a) While lawyers are associated in a firm, none of them shall knowingly represent a client when any one of them practicing alone would be prohibited from doing so by Rules 1.7, 1.8(c), 1.9 or 2.2.

(b) When a lawyer has terminated an association with a firm, the firm is not prohibited from thereafter representing a person with interests materially adverse to those of a client represented by the formerly associated lawyer and not currently represented by the firm, unless:

(1) the matter is the same or substantially related to that in which the formerly associated lawyer represented the client; and

(2) any lawyer remaining in the firm has information protected by Rules 1.6 and 1.9(c) that is material to the matter.

(c) A disqualification prescribed by this rule may be waived by the affected client under the conditions stated in Rule 1.7.

Comment:

Definition of "Firm"

For purposes of the Rules of Professional Conduct, the term "firm" includes lawyers in a private firm, and lawyers in the legal department of a corporation or other organization, or in a legal services organization. Whether two or more lawyers constitute a firm within this definition can depend on the specific facts. For example, two practitioners who share office space and occasionally consult or assist each other ordinarily would not be regarded as constituting a firm. However, if they present themselves to the public in a way suggesting that they are a firm or conduct themselves as a firm, they should be regarded as a firm for the purposes of the Rules. The terms of any formal agreement between associated lawyers are relevant in determining whether they are a firm, as is the fact that they have mutual access to information concerning the clients they serve. Furthermore, it is relevant in doubtful cases to consider the underlying purpose of the Rule that is involved. A group of lawyers could be regarded as a firm for purposes of the rule that the same lawyer should not represent opposing parties in litigation, while it might not be so regarded for purposes of the rule that information acquired by one lawyer is attributed to the other.

With respect to the law department of an organization, there is ordinarily no question that the members of the department constitute a firm within the meaning of the Rules of Professional Conduct. However, there can be uncertainty as to the identity of the client. For example, it may not be clear whether the law department of a corporation represents a subsidiary or an affiliated corporation, as well as the corporation by which the members of the department are directly employed. A similar question can arise concerning an unincorporated association and its local affiliates.

Similar questions can also arise with respect to lawyers in legal aid. Lawyers employed in the same unit of a legal service organization constitute a firm, but not necessarily those employed in separate units. As in the case of independent practitioners, whether the lawyers should be treated as associated with each other can depend on the particular rule that is involved, and on the specific facts of the situation.

Where a lawyer has joined a private firm after having represented the government, the situation is governed by Rule 1.11(a) and (b); where a lawyer represents the government after having served private clients, the situation is governed by Rule 1.11(c)(1). The individual lawyer involved is bound by the Rules generally, including Rules 1.6, 1.7 and 1.9.

Different provisions are thus made for movement of a lawyer from one private firm to another and for movement of a lawyer between a private firm and the government. The government is entitled to protection of its client confidences and, therefore, to the protections provided in Rules 1.6, 1.9 and 1.11. However, if the more extensive disqualification in Rule 1.10 were applied to former government lawyers, the potential effect on the government would be unduly burdensome. The government deals with all private citizens and organizations and, thus, has a much wider circle of adverse legal interests than does any private law firm. In these circumstances, the government's recruitment of lawyers would be seriously impaired if Rule 1.10 were applied to the government. On balance, therefore, the government is better served in the long run by the protections stated in Rule 1.11.

Principles of Imputed Disqualification

The rule of imputed disqualification stated in paragraph (a) gives effect to the principle of loyalty to the client as it applies to lawyers who practice in a law firm. Such situations can be considered from the premise that a firm of lawyers is essentially one lawyer for purposes of the rules governing loyalty to the client, or from the premise that each lawyer is vicariously bound by the obligation of loyalty owed by each lawyer with whom the lawyer is associated. Paragraph (a) operates only among the lawyers currently associated in a firm. When a lawyer moves from one firm to another, the situation is governed by Rules 1.9(b) and 1.10(b).

Rule 1.10(b) operates to permit a law firm, under certain circumstances, to represent a person with interests directly adverse to those of a client represented by a lawyer who formerly was associated with the firm. The Rule applies regardless of when the formerly associated lawyer represented the client. However, the law firm may not represent a person with interests adverse to those of a present client of the firm, which would violate Rule 1.7. Moreover, the firm may not represent the person where the matter is the same or substantially related to that in which the formerly associated lawyer represented the client and any other lawyer currently in the firm has material information protected by Rules 1.6 and 1.9(c).

Model Code Comparison

DR 5-105(D) provided that "[i]f a lawyer is required to decline or to withdraw from employment under a Disciplinary Rule, no partner, or associate, or any other lawyer affiliated with him or his firm, may accept or continue such employment."

Rule 1.16 Declining or Terminating Representation

(a) Except as stated in paragraph (c), a lawyer shall not represent a client or, where representation has commenced, shall withdraw from the representation of a client if:

(1) the representation will result in violation of the Rules of Professional Conduct or other law;

(2) the lawyer's physical or mental condition materially impairs the lawyer's ability to represent the client; or

(3) the lawyer is discharged.

(b) Except as stated in paragraph (c), a lawyer may withdraw from representing a client if withdrawal can be accomplished without material adverse effect on the interests of the client, or if:

(1) the client persists in a course of action involving the lawyer's services that the lawyer reasonably believes is criminal or fraudulent;

(2) the client has used the lawyer's services to perpetrate a crime or fraud;

(3) a client insists upon pursuing an objective that the lawyer considers repugnant or imprudent;

(4) the client fails substantially to fulfill an obligation to the lawyer regarding the lawyer's services and has been given reasonable warning that the lawyer will withdraw unless the obligation is fulfilled;

(5) the representation will result in an unreasonable financial burden on the lawyer or has been rendered unreasonably difficult by the client; or

(6) other good cause for withdrawal exists.

(c) When ordered to do so by a tribunal, a lawyer shall continue representation notwithstanding good cause for terminating the representation.

(d) Upon termination of representation, a lawyer shall take steps to the extent reasonably practicable to protect a client's interests, such as giving reasonable notice to the client, allowing time for employment of other counsel, surrendering papers and property to which the client is entitled and refunding any advance payment of fee that has not been earned. The lawyer may retain papers relating to the client to the extent permitted by other law.

Comment:

A lawyer should not accept representation in a matter unless it can be performed competently, promptly, without improper conflict of interest and to completion.

Mandatory Withdrawal

A lawyer ordinarily must decline or withdraw from representation if the client demands that the lawyer engage in conduct that is illegal or violates the Rules of Professional Conduct or other law. The lawyer is not obliged to decline or withdraw simply because the client suggests such a course of conduct; a client may make such a suggestion in the hope that a lawyer will not be constrained by a professional obligation.

When a lawyer has been appointed to represent a client, withdrawal ordinarily requires approval of the appointing authority. See also Rule 6.2. Difficulty may be encountered if withdrawal is based on the client's demand that the lawyer engage in unprofessional conduct. The court may wish an explanation for the withdrawal, while the lawyer may be bound to keep confidential the facts that would constitute such an explanation. The lawyer's statement that professional considerations require termination of the representation ordinarily should be accepted as sufficient.

Discharge

A client has a right to discharge a lawyer at any time, with or without cause, subject to liability for payment for the lawyer's services. Where future dispute about the withdrawal may be anticipated, it may be advisable to prepare a written statement reciting the circumstances.

Whether a client can discharge appointed counsel may depend on applicable law. A client seeking to do so should be given a full explanation of the consequences. These consequences may include a decision by the appointing authority that appointment of successor counsel is unjustified, thus requiring the client to represent himself.

If the client is mentally incompetent, the client may lack the legal capacity to discharge the lawyer, and in any event the discharge may be seriously adverse to the client's interests. The lawyer should make special effort to help the client consider the consequences and, in an extreme case, may initiate proceedings for a conservatorship or similar protection of the client. See Rule 1.14.

Optional Withdrawal

A lawyer may withdraw from representation in some circumstances. The lawyer has the option to withdraw if it can be accomplished without material adverse effect on the client's interests. Withdrawal is also justified if the client persists in a course of action that the lawyer reasonably believes is criminal or fraudulent, for a lawyer is not required to be associated with such conduct even if the lawyer does not further it. Withdrawal is also permitted if the lawyer's services were misused in the past even if that would materially prejudice the client. The lawyer also may withdraw where the client insists on a repugnant or imprudent objective.

A lawyer may withdraw if the client refuses to abide by the terms of an agreement relating to the representation, such as an agreement concerning fees or court costs or an agreement limiting the objectives of the representation.

Assisting the Client Upon Withdrawal

Even if the lawyer has been unfairly discharged by the client, a lawyer must take all reasonable steps to mitigate the consequences to the client. The lawyer may retain papers as security for a fee only to the extent permitted by law.

Whether or not a lawyer for an organization may under certain unusual circumstances have a legal obligation to the organization after withdrawing or being discharged by the organization's highest authority is beyond the scope of these Rules.

Model Code Comparison

With regard to paragraph (a), DR 2-109(A) provided that a lawyer "shall not accept employment . . . if he knows or it is obvious that [the prospective client] wishes to . . . [b]ring a legal action . . . or otherwise have steps taken for him, merely for the purpose of harassing or maliciously injuring any person. . . ." Nor may a lawyer accept employment if the lawyer is aware that the prospective client wishes to "[p]resent a claim or defense . . . that is not warranted under existing law, unless it can be supported by good faith argument for an extension, modification, or reversal of existing law." DR 2-110(B) provided that a lawyer

> shall withdraw from employment . . . if:
> (1) He knows or it is obvious that his client is bringing the legal action . . . or is otherwise having steps taken for him, merely for the purpose of harassing or maliciously injuring any person.

(2) He knows or it is obvious that his continued employment will result in violation of a Disciplinary Rule.

(3) His mental or physical condition renders it unreasonably difficult for him to carry out the employment effectively.

(4) He is discharged by his client.

With regard to paragraph (b), DR 2-110(C) permitted withdrawal regardless of the effect on the client if:

(1) His Client: (a) Insists upon presenting a claim or defense that is not warranted under existing law and cannot be supported by good faith argument for an extension, modification, or reversal of existing law; (b) Personally seeks to pursue an illegal course of conduct; (c) Insists that the lawyer pursue a course of conduct that is illegal or that is prohibited under the Disciplinary Rules; (d) By other conduct renders it unreasonably difficult for the lawyer to carry out his employment effectively; (e) Insists, in a matter not pending before a tribunal, that the lawyer engage in conduct that is contrary to the judgment and advice of the lawyer but not prohibited under the Disciplinary Rules; (f) Deliberately disregards an agreement or obligation to the lawyer as to expenses and fees.

(2) His continued employment is likely to result in a violation of a Disciplinary Rule.

(3) His inability to work with cocounsel indicates that the best interest of the client likely will be served by withdrawal.

(4) His mental or physical condition renders it difficult for him to carry out the employment effectively.

(5) His client knowingly and freely assents to termination of his employment.

(6) He believes in good faith, in a proceeding pending before a tribunal, that the tribunal will find the existence of other good cause for withdrawal.

With regard to paragraph (c), DR 2-110(A)(1) provided: "If permission for withdrawal from employment is required by the rules of a tribunal, the lawyer shall not withdraw . . . without its permission."

The provisions of paragraph (d) are substantially identical to DR 2-110(A)(2) and (3).

Rule 5.1 Responsibilities of a Partner or Supervisory Lawyer

(a) A partner in a law firm shall make reasonable efforts to ensure that the firm has in effect measures giving reasonable assurance that all lawyers in the firm conform to the Rules of Professional Conduct.

(b) A lawyer having direct supervisory authority over another lawyer shall make reasonable efforts to ensure that the other lawyer conforms to the Rules of Professional Conduct.

(c) A lawyer shall be responsible for another lawyer's violation of the Rules of Professional Conduct if:

(1) the lawyer orders or, with knowledge of the specific conduct, ratifies the conduct involved; or

(2) the lawyer is a partner in the law firm in which the other lawyer practices, or has direct supervisory authority over the other lawyer, and knows of the conduct at a time when its consequences can be avoided or mitigated but fails to take reasonable remedial action.

Comment:

Paragraphs (a) and (b) refer to lawyers who have supervisory authority over the professional work of a firm or legal department of a government agency. This includes members of a partnership and the shareholders in a law firm organized as a professional corporation; lawyers having supervisory authority in the law department of an enterprise or government agency; and lawyers who have intermediate managerial responsibilities in a firm.

The measures required to fulfill the responsibility prescribed in paragraphs (a) and (b) can depend on the firm's structure and the nature of its practice. In a small firm, informal supervision and occasional admonition ordinarily might be sufficient. In a large firm, or in practice situations in which intensely difficult ethical problems frequently arise, more elaborate procedures may be necessary. Some firms, for example, have a procedure whereby junior lawyers can make confidential referral of ethical problems directly to a designated senior partner or special committee. See Rule 5.2. Firms, whether large or small, may also rely on continuing legal education in professional ethics. In any event, the ethical atmosphere of a firm can influence the conduct of all its members and a lawyer having authority over the work of another may not assume that the subordinate lawyer will inevitably conform to the Rules.

Paragraph (c)(1) expresses a general principle of responsibility for acts of another. See also Rule 8.4(a).

Paragraph (c)(2) defines the duty of a lawyer having direct supervisory authority over performance of specific legal work by another lawyer. Whether a lawyer has such supervisory authority in particular circumstances is a question of fact. Partners of a private firm have at least indirect responsibility for all work being done by the firm, while a partner in charge of a particular matter ordinarily has direct authority over other firm lawyers engaged in the matter. Appropriate remedial action by a partner would depend on the immediacy of the partner's involvement and the seriousness of the misconduct. The supervisor is required to intervene to prevent avoidable consequences of misconduct if the supervisor knows that the misconduct occurred. Thus, if a supervising lawyer knows that a subordinate misrepresented a matter to an opposing party in negotiation, the supervisor as well as the subordinate has a duty to correct the resulting misapprehension.

Professional misconduct by a lawyer under supervision could reveal a violation of paragraph (b) on the part of the supervisory lawyer even though it does not entail a violation of paragraph (c) because there was no direction, ratification or knowledge of the violation.

Apart from this Rule and Rule 8.4(a), a lawyer does not have disciplinary liability for the conduct of a partner, associate or subordinate. Whether a lawyer may be liable civilly or criminally for another lawyer's conduct is a question of law beyond the scope of these Rules.

Model Code Comparison

There was no direct counterpart to this Rule in the Model Code. DR 1-103(A) provided that a lawyer "possessing unprivileged knowledge of a violation of DR 1-102 shall report such knowledge to . . . authority empowered to investigate or act upon such violation."

Rule 5.6 Restrictions on Right to Practice

A lawyer shall not participate in offering or making:
(a) a partnership or employment agreement that restricts the rights of a lawyer to practice after termination of the relationship, except an agreement concerning benefits upon retirement; or
(b) an agreement in which a restriction on the lawyer's right to practice is part of the settlement of a controversy between private parties.

Comment:

An agreement restricting the right of partners or associates to practice after leaving a firm not only limits their professional autonomy but also limits the freedom of clients to choose a lawyer. Paragraph (a) prohibits such agreements except for restrictions incident to provisions concerning retirement benefits for service with the firm.

Paragraph (b) prohibits a lawyer from agreeing not to represent other persons in connection with settling a claim on behalf of a client.

Model Code Comparison

This Rule is substantially similar to DR 2-108.

Rule 7.1 Communications Concerning a Lawyer's Services

A lawyer shall not make a false or misleading communication about the lawyer or the lawyer's services. A communication is false or misleading if it:
(a) contains a material misrepresentation of fact or law, or

omits a fact necessary to make the statement considered as a whole not materially misleading;

(b) is likely to create an unjustified expectation about results the lawyer can achieve, or states or implies that the lawyer can achieve results by means that violate the Rules of Professional Conduct or other law; or

(c) compares the lawyer's services with other lawyers' services, unless the comparison can be factually substantiated.

Comment:

This Rule governs all communications about a lawyer's services, including advertising permitted by Rule 7.2. Whatever means are used to make known a lawyer's services, statements about them should be truthful. The prohibition in paragraph (b) of statements that may create "unjustified expectations" would ordinarily preclude advertisements about results obtained on behalf of a client, such as the amount of a damage award or the lawyer's record in obtaining favorable verdicts, and advertisements containing client endorsements. Such information may create the unjustified expectation that similar results can be obtained for others without reference to the specific factual and legal circumstances.

Model Code Comparison

DR 2-101 provided that "[a] lawyer shall not . . . use . . . any form of public communication containing a false, fraudulent, misleading, deceptive, self-laudatory or unfair statement or claim." DR 2-101(B) provided that a lawyer "may publish or broadcast . . . the following information . . . in the geographic area or areas in which the lawyer resides or maintains offices or in which a significant part of the lawyer's clientele resides, provided that the information . . . complies with DR 2-101(A), and is presented in a dignified manner. . . ." DR 2-101(B) then specified twenty-five categories of information that may be disseminated. DR 2-101(C) provided that "[a]ny person desiring to expand the information authorized for disclosure in DR 2-101(B), or to provide for its dissemination through other forums may apply to [the agency having jurisdiction under state law]. . . . The relief granted in response to any such application shall be promulgated as an amendment to DR 2-101(B), universally applicable to all lawyers."

Rule 7.2 Advertising

(a) Subject to the requirements of Rules 7.1 and 7.3, a lawyer may advertise services through public media, such as a telephone directory, legal directory, newspaper or other periodical, outdoor advertising, radio or television, or through written or recorded communication.

(b) A copy or recording of an advertisement or communication shall be kept for two years after its last dissemination along with a record of when and where it was used.

(c) A lawyer shall not give anything of value to a person for recommending the lawyer's services, except that a lawyer may pay the reasonable cost of advertisements or communications permitted by this rule and may pay the usual charges of a not-for-profit lawyer referral service or other legal service organization.

(d) Any communication made pursuant to this rule shall include the name of at least one lawyer responsible for its content.

Comment:

To assist the public in obtaining legal services, lawyers should be allowed to make known their services not only through reputation but also through organized information campaigns in the form of advertising. Advertising involves an active quest for clients, contrary to the tradition that a lawyer should not seek clientele. However, the public's need to know about legal services can be fulfilled in part through advertising. This need is particularly acute in the case of persons of moderate means who have not made extensive use of legal services. The interest in expanding public information about legal services ought to prevail over considerations of tradition. Nevertheless, advertising by lawyers entails the risk of practices that are misleading or overreaching.

This Rule permits public dissemination of information concerning a lawyer's name or firm name, address and telephone number; the kinds of services the lawyer will undertake; the basis on which the lawyer's fees are determined, including prices for specific services and payment and credit arrangements; a lawyer's foreign language ability; names of references and, with their consent, names of clients regularly represented; and other information that might invite the attention of those seeking legal assistance.

Questions of effectiveness and taste in advertising are matters of speculation and subjective judgment. Some jurisdictions have had extensive prohibitions against television advertising, against advertising going beyond specified facts about a lawyer, or against "undignified" advertising. Television is now one of the most powerful media for getting information to the public, particularly persons of low and moderate income; prohibiting television advertising, therefore, would impede the flow of information about legal services to many sectors of the public. Limiting the information that may be advertised has a similar effect and assumes that the bar can accurately forecast the kind of information that the public would regard as relevant.

Neither this Rule nor Rule 7.3 prohibits communications authorized by law, such as notice to members of a class in class action litigation.

Record of Advertising

Paragraph (b) requires that a record of the content and use of advertising be kept in order to facilitate enforcement of this Rule. It does not require that advertising be subject to review prior to dissemination. Such a requirement would be burdensome and expensive relative to its possible benefits, and may be of doubtful constitutionality.

Paying Others to Recommend a Lawyer

A lawyer is allowed to pay for advertising permitted by this Rule, but otherwise is not permitted to pay another person for channeling professional work. This restriction does not prevent an organization or person other than the lawyer from advertising or recommending the lawyer's services. Thus, a legal aid agency or prepaid legal services plan may pay to advertise legal services provided under its auspices. Likewise, a lawyer may participate in not-for-profit lawyer referral programs and pay the usual fees charged by such programs. Paragraph (c) does not prohibit paying regular compensation to an assistant, such as a secretary, to prepare communications permitted by this Rule.

Model Code Comparison

With regard to paragraph (a), DR 2-101(B) provided that a lawyer "may publish or broadcast, subject to DR 2-103, . . . in print media . . . or television or radio. . . ."

With regard to paragraph (b), DR 2-101(D) provided that if the advertisement is "communicated to the public over television or radio, . . . a recording of the actual transmission shall be retained by the lawyer."

With regard to paragraph (c), DR 2-103(B) provided that a lawyer "shall not compensate or give anything of value to a person or organization to recommend or secure his employment . . . except that he may pay the usual and reasonable fees or dues charged by any of the organizations listed in DR 2-103(D)." (DR 2-103(D) referred to legal aid and other legal services organizations.) DR 2-101(I) provided that a lawyer "shall not compensate or give anything of value to representatives of the press, radio, television, or other communication medium in anticipation of or in return for professional publicity in a news item."

There was no counterpart to paragraph (d) in the Model Code.

Rule 7.3 Direct Contact with Prospective Clients

(a) A lawyer shall not by in-person or live telephone contact solicit professional employment from a prospective client with whom the lawyer has no family or prior professional relationship when a significant motive for the lawyer's doing so is the lawyer's pecuniary gain.

(b) A lawyer shall not solicit professional employment from a prospective client by written or recorded communication or by in-person or telephone contact even when not otherwise prohibited by paragraph (a), if:

(1) the prospective client has made known to the lawyer a desire not to be solicited by the lawyer; or

(2) the solicitation involves coercion, duress or harassment.

(c) Every written or recorded communication from a lawyer soliciting professional employment from a prospective client known to be in need of legal services in a particular matter, and with whom the lawyer has no family or prior professional relationship, shall include the words "Advertising Material" on the outside envelope and at the beginning and ending of any recorded communication.

(d) Notwithstanding the prohibitions in paragraph (a), a lawyer may participate with a prepaid or group legal service plan operated by an organization not owned or directed by the lawyer which uses in-person or telephone contact to solicit memberships or subscriptions for the plan from persons who are not known to need legal services in a particular matter covered by the plan.

Comment:

There is a potential for abuse inherent in direct in-person or live telephone contact by a lawyer with a prospective client known to need legal services. These forms of contact between a lawyer and a prospective client subject the layperson to the private importuning of the trained advocate in a direct interpersonal encounter. The prospective client, who may already feel overwhelmed by the circumstances giving rise to the need for legal services, may find it difficult fully to evaluate all available alternatives with reasoned judgment and appropriate self-interest in the face of the lawyer's presence and insistence upon being retained immediately. The situation is fraught with the possibility of undue influence, intimidation, and over-reaching.

This potential for abuse inherent in direct in-person or live telephone solicitation of prospective clients justifies its prohibition, particularly since lawyer advertising and written and recorded communication permitted under Rule 7.2 offer alternative means of conveying necessary information to those who may be in need of legal services. Advertising and written and recorded communications which may be mailed or autodialed make it possible for a prospective client to be informed about the need for legal services, and about the qualifications of available lawyers and law firms, without subjecting the prospective client to direct in-person or telephone persuasion that may overwhelm the client's judgment.

The use of general advertising and written and recorded communications to transmit information from lawyer to prospective client, rather than direct in-person or live telephone contact, will help to assure that the information flows cleanly as well as freely. The contents of advertisements and communications permitted under Rule 7.2 are permanently recorded so that they cannot be disputed and may be shared with others who know the lawyer. This potential for informal review is itself likely to help guard against statements and claims that might constitute false and misleading communications, in violation of Rule 7.1. The contents of direct in-person or live telephone conversations between a lawyer to a prospective client can be disputed and are not subject to third-party scrutiny. Consequently, they are much more likely to approach (and occasionally cross) the dividing line between accurate representations and those that are false and misleading.

There is far less likelihood that a lawyer would engage in abusive practices against an individual with whom the lawyer has a prior personal or professional relationship or where the lawyer is motivated by considerations other than the lawyer's pecuniary gain. Consequently, the general prohibition in Rule 7.3(a) and the requirements of Rule 7.3(c) are not applicable in those situations.

But even permitted forms of solicitation can be abused. Thus, any solicitation which contains information which is false or misleading within the meaning of Rule 7.1, which involves coercion, duress or harassment within the meaning of Rule 7.3(b)(2), or which involves contact with a prospective client who has made known to the lawyer a desire not to be solicited by the lawyer within the meaning of Rule 7.3(b)(1) is prohibited. Moreover, if after sending a letter or other communication to a client as permitted by Rule 7.2 the lawyer receives no response, any further effort to communicate with the prospective client may violate the provisions of Rule 7.3(b).

This Rule is not intended to prohibit a lawyer from contacting representatives of organizations or groups that may be interested in establishing a group or prepaid legal plan for their members, insureds, beneficiaries or other third parties for the purpose of informing such entities of the availability of and details concerning the plan or arrangement which the lawyer or lawyer's firm is willing to offer. This form of communication is not directed to a prospective client. Rather, it is usually addressed to an individual acting in a fiduciary capacity seeking a supplier of legal services for others who may, if they choose, become prospective clients of the lawyer. Under these circumstances, the activity which the lawyer undertakes in communicating with such representatives and the type of information transmitted to the individual are functionally similar to and serve the same purpose as advertising permitted under Rule 7.2.

The requirement in Rule 7.3(c) that certain communications be marked "Advertising Material" does not apply to communications sent in response to requests of potential clients or their spokespersons or sponsors. General announcements by lawyers, including changes in personnel or office location, do not constitute communications soliciting professional employment from a client known to be in need of legal services within the meaning of this Rule.

Paragraph (d) of this Rule would permit an attorney to participate with an organization which uses personal contact to solicit members for its group or prepaid legal service plan, provided that the personal contact is not undertaken by any lawyer who would be a provider of legal services through the plan. The organization referred to in paragraph (d) must not be owned by or directed (whether as manager or otherwise) by any lawyer or law firm that participates in the plan. For example, paragraph (d) would not permit a lawyer to create an organization controlled directly or indirectly by the lawyer and use the organization for the in-person or telephone solicitation of legal employment of the lawyer through memberships in the plan or otherwise. The communication permitted by these organizations also must not be directed to a person known to need legal services in a particular matter, but is to be designed to inform potential plan members generally of another means of affordable legal services. Lawyers who participate in a legal service plan must reasonably assure that the plan sponsors are in compliance with Rules 7.1, 7.2 and 7.3(b). See 8.4(a).

Model Code Comparison

DR 2-104(A) provided with certain exceptions that "[a] lawyer who has given in-person unsolicited advice to a layperson that he should obtain counsel or take legal action shall not accept employment resulting from that advice. . . ." The exceptions include DR 2-104(A)(1), which provided that a lawyer "may accept employment by a close friend, relative, former client (if the advice is germane to the former employment), or one whom the lawyer reasonably believes to be a client." DR 2-104(A)(2) through DR 2-104(A)(5) provided other exceptions relating, respectively, to employment resulting from public educational programs, recommendation by a legal assistance organization, public speaking or writing and representing members of a class in class action litigation.

Appendix C
SELECTED PROVISIONS FROM THE MODEL CODE OF PROFESSIONAL RESPONSIBILITY

DR 2-103 *Recommendation of Professional Employment*

(A) A lawyer shall not, except as authorized in DR 2-101 (B), recommend employment as a private practitioner, of himself, his partner, or associate to a layperson who has not sought his advice regarding employment of a lawyer.

(B) A lawyer shall not compensate or give anything of value to a person or organization to recommend or secure his employment by a client, or as a reward for having made a recommendation resulting in his employment by a client, except that he may pay the usual and reasonable fees or dues charged by any of the organizations listed in DR 2-103(D).

(C) A lawyer shall not request a person or organization to recommend or promote the use of his services or those of his partner or associate, or any other lawyer affiliated with him or his firm, as a private practitioner, except as authorized in DR 2-101, and except that

(1) He may request referrals from a lawyer referral service operated, sponsored, or approved by a bar association and may pay its fees incident thereto.

(2) He may cooperate with the legal service activities of any of the offices or organizations enumerated in DR 2-103(D)(1) through (4) and may perform legal services for those to whom he was recommended by it to do such work if:

(a) The person to whom the recommendation is made is a member or beneficiary of such office or organization; and

(b) The lawyer remains free to exercise his independent professional judgment on behalf of his client.

(D) A lawyer or his partner or associate or any other lawyer affiliated with him or his firm may be recommended, employed or paid by, or may cooperate with, one of the following offices or organizations that promote the use of his services or those of his partner or associate or any other lawyer affiliated with him or his firm if there is no interference with the exercise of independent professional judgment in behalf of his client:

(1) A legal aid office or public defender office:

(a) Operated or sponsored by a duly accredited law school.

(b) Operated or sponsored by a bona fide nonprofit community organization.

(c) Operated or sponsored by a governmental agency.

(d) Operated, sponsored, or approved by a bar association.

(2) A military legal assistance office.

(3) A lawyer referral service operated, sponsored, or approved by a bar association.

(4) Any bona fide organization that recommends, furnishes

or pays for legal services to its members or beneficiaries provided the following conditions are satisfied:

(a) Such organization, including any affiliate, is so organized and operated that no profit is derived by it from the rendition of legal services by lawyers, and that, if the organization is organized for profit, the legal services are not rendered by lawyers employed, directed, supervised or selected by it except in connection with matters where such organization bears ultimate liability of its member or beneficiary.

(b) Neither the lawyer, nor his partner, nor associate, nor any other lawyer affiliated with him or his firm, nor any nonlawyer, shall have initiated or promoted such organization for the primary purpose of providing financial or other benefit to such lawyer, partner, associate or affiliated lawyer.

(c) Such organization is not operated for the purpose of procuring legal work or financial benefit for any lawyer as a private practitioner outside of the legal services program of the organization.

(d) The member or beneficiary to whom the legal services are furnished, and not such organization, is recognized as the client of the lawyer in the matter.

(e) Any member or beneficiary who is entitled to have legal services furnished or paid for by the organization may, if such member or beneficiary so desires, select counsel other than that furnished, selected or approved by the organization for the particular matter involved; and the legal service plan of such organization provides appropriate relief for any member or beneficiary who asserts a claim that representation by counsel furnished, selected or approved would be unethical, improper, or inadequate under the circumstances of the matter involved and the plan provides an appropriate procedure for seeking such relief.

(f) The lawyer does not know or have cause to know that such organization is in violation of applicable laws, rules of court and other legal requirements that govern its legal service operations.

(g) Such organization has filed with the appropriate disciplinary authority at least annually a report with respect to its legal service plan, if any, showing its terms, its schedule of benefits, its subscription charges, agreements with counsel, and financial results of its legal service activities or, if it has failed to do so, the lawyer does not know or have cause to know of such failure.

(E) A lawyer shall not accept employment when he knows or it is obvious that the person who seeks his services does so as a result of conduct prohibited under this Disciplinary Rule.

DR 2-104 *Suggestion of Need of Legal Services*

(A) A lawyer who has given in-person unsolicited advice to a layperson that he should obtain counsel or take legal action shall not accept employment resulting from that advice, except that:

(1) A lawyer may accept employment by a close friend, relative, former client (if the advice is germane to the former employment), or one whom the lawyer reasonably believes to be a client.

(2) A lawyer may accept employment that results from his participation in activities designed to educate laypersons to recognize legal problems, to make intelligent selection of counsel, or to utilize available legal services if such activities are conducted or sponsored by a qualified legal assistance organization.

(3) A lawyer who is recommended, furnished or paid by a qualified legal assistance organization enumerated in DR 2-103(D)(1) through (4) may represent a member or beneficiary thereof, to the extent and under the conditions prescribed therein.

(4) Without affecting his right to accept employment, a lawyer may speak publicly or write for publication on legal topics so long as he does not emphasize his own professional experience or reputation and does not undertake to give individual advice.

(5) If success in asserting rights or defenses of his client in litigation in the nature of a class action is dependent upon the joinder of others, a lawyer may accept, but shall not seek, employment from those contacted for the purpose of obtaining their joinder.

DR 2-107 *Division of Fees Among Lawyers*

(A) A lawyer shall not divide a fee for legal services with another lawyer who is not a partner in or associate of his law firm or law office, unless:

(1) The client consents to employment of the other lawyer after a full disclosure that a division of fees will be made.

(2) The division is made in proportion to the services performed and responsibility assumed by each.

(3) The total fee of the lawyers does not clearly exceed reasonable compensation for all legal services they rendered the client.

(B) This Disciplinary Rule does not prohibit payment to a former partner or associate pursuant to a separation or retirement agreement.

DR 2-108 *Agreements Restricting the Practice of a Lawyer*

(A) A lawyer shall not be a party to or participate in a partnership or employment agreement with another lawyer that restricts the right of a lawyer to practice law after the termination of a relationship created by the agreement, except as a condition to payment of retirement benefits.

(B) In connection with the settlement of a controversy or suit, a lawyer shall not enter into an agreement that restricts his right to practice law.

DR 2-110 *Withdrawal from Employment*

(A) In General

(1) If permission for withdrawal from employment is required by the rules of a tribunal, a lawyer shall not withdraw from

employment in a proceeding before that tribunal without its permission.

(2) In any event, a lawyer shall not withdraw from employment until he has taken reasonable steps to avoid foreseeable prejudice to the rights of his client, including giving due notice to his client, allowing time for employment of other counsel, delivering to the client all papers and property to which the client is entitled, and complying with applicable laws and rules.

(3) A lawyer who withdraws from employment shall refund promptly any part of a fee paid in advance that has not been earned.

(B) Mandatory Withdrawal

A lawyer representing a client before a tribunal, with its permission if required by its rules, shall withdraw from employment, and a lawyer representing a client in other matters shall withdraw from employment, if:

(1) He knows or it is obvious that his client is bringing the legal action, conducting the defense, or asserting a position in the litigation, or is otherwise having steps taken for him, merely for the purpose of harassing or maliciously injuring any person.

(2) He knows or it is obvious that his continued employment will result in violation of a Disciplinary Rule.

(3) His mental or physical condition renders it unreasonably difficult for him to carry out the employment effectively.

(4) He is discharged by his client.

(C) Permissive Withdrawal

If DR 2-110 (B) is not applicable, a lawyer may not request permission to withdraw in matters pending before a tribunal, and may not withdraw in other matters, unless such request or such withdrawal is because:

(1) His client:

(a) Insists upon presenting a claim or defense that is not

warranted under existing law and cannot be supported by good faith argument for an extension, modification, or reversal of existing law.

(b) Personally seeks to pursue an illegal course of conduct.

(c) Insists that the lawyer pursue a course of conduct that is illegal or that is prohibited under the Disciplinary Rules

(d) By other conduct renders it unreasonably difficult for the lawyer to carry out his employment effectively.

(e) Insists, in a matter not pending before a tribunal, that the lawyer engage in conduct that is contrary to the judgment and advice of the lawyer but not prohibited under the Disciplinary Rules.

(f) Deliberately disregards an agreement or obligation to the lawyer as to expenses or fees.

(2) His continued employment is likely to result in a violation of a Disciplinary Rule.

(3) His inability to work with co-counsel indicates that the best interests of the client likely will be served by withdrawal.

(4) His mental or physical condition renders it difficult for him to carry out the employment effectively.

(5) His client knowingly and freely assents to termination of his employment.

(6) He believes in good faith, in a proceeding pending before a tribunal, that the tribunal will find the existence of other good cause for withdrawal.

DR 5-105 *Refusing to Accept or Continue Employment if the Interests of Another Client May Impair the Independent Professional Judgment of the Lawyer*

(A) A lawyer shall decline proffered employment if the exercise of his independent professional judgment in behalf of a client will be or is likely to be adversely affected by the acceptance of the proffered employment, or if it would be likely to involve him in representing differing interests, except to the extent permitted under DR 5-105(C).

(B) A lawyer shall not continue multiple employment if the exercise of his independent professional judgment in behalf of a client will be or is likely to be adversely affected by his representation of another client, or if it would be likely to involve him in representing differing interests, except to the extent permitted under DR 5-105(C).

(C) In the situations covered by DR 5-105 (A) and (B), a lawyer may represent multiple clients if it is obvious that he can adequately represent the interest of each and if each consents to the representation after full disclosure of the possible effect of such representation on the exercise of his independent professional judgment on behalf of each.

(D) If a lawyer is required to decline employment or to withdraw from employment under a Disciplinary Rule, no partner, or associate, or any other lawyer affiliated with him or his firm, may accept or continue such employment.

DR 5-107 *Avoiding Influence by Others Than the Client*

(A) Except with the consent of his client after full disclosure, a lawyer shall not:

(1) Accept compensation for his legal services from one other than his client.

(2) Accept from one other than his client any thing of value related to his representation of or his employment by his client.

(B) A lawyer shall not permit a person who recommends, employs, or pays him to render legal services for another to direct or regulate his professional judgment in rendering such legal services.

(C) A lawyer shall not practice with or in the form of a professional corporation or association authorized to practice law for a profit, if:

(1) A non-lawyer owns any interest therein, except that a

fiduciary representative of the estate of a lawyer may hold the stock or interest of the lawyer for a reasonable time during administration;

(2) A non-lawyer is a corporate director or officer thereof; or

(3) A non-lawyer has the right to direct or control the professional judgment of a lawyer.

Appendix D
SELECTED ETHICS OPINIONS

Formal Opinion   300
Informal Opinion 428
                    521
                    522
                    1072

Formal Opinion 300 (Aug. 7, 1961)

It is unethical for an attorney employing another attorney to include as part of the employment contract a restrictive covenant prohibiting the employee from practicing law in the city and county for two years after the termination of employment.

Canon Interpreted: Professional Ethics 7

The opinion of our Committee has been requested by a member of the Association on whether or not it is ethical for an attorney to insert a restrictive covenant in a contract of employment with another attorney. It is stated that the restrictive covenant would be directed toward prohibiting the employee from practicing law in the city and county in which the lawyer practices for a period of two years after termination of the employment. This appears to be a question of first impression with the Committee.

Restrictive covenants of the type described are sometimes used in connection with commercial transactions such as the sale of a business, often being associated with the sale of the "good will" or "going concern value" of the enterprise.

The practice of law, however, is a profession, not a business or commercial enterprise. The relations between attorney and client are personal and individual relationships (Canon 35). The practice of law is not a business which can be bought or sold.

It was held by this Committee in Opinion 266, issued June 21, 1945, that it would be improper for a lawyer to purchase the practice and good will of a deceased lawyer who was not his partner. In this opinion the Committee said:

> The good will of the practice of a lawyer is not, however, of itself an asset, which either he or his estate can sell. As said by the Committee on Professional Ethics of the New York County Lawyer's Association in its Opinion 109 (October 6, 1943):
> Clients are not merchandise. Lawyers are not tradesmen. They have nothing to sell but personal service. An attempt, therefore, to barter in clients, would appear to be inconsistent with the best concepts of our professional status.

It appears to this Committee that a restrictive covenant of the type described would be an attempt to "barter in clients." In this connection, we call attention to that part of Canon 7, reading as follows:

> Efforts, direct or indirect, in any way to encroach upon the business of another lawyer, are unworthy of those who should be brethren at the Bar; . . .

Canon 27 prohibits every form of solicitation of employment. A former employee of a lawyer or law firm would be bound by these canons to refrain from any effort to secure the work of clients of his former employer.

Furthermore, he would be bound, under Canons 6 and 37 to preserve the confidences, and not to divulge the secrets, of any client of his former employer, which he may have received or learned as an associate of such former employer.

Obviously, no restrictive covenant in an employment contract is needed to enforce these provisions of the Canons of Professional Ethics; and a general covenant restricting an employed lawyer, after leaving the employment, from practicing in the community for a stated period, appears to this Committee to be an unwarranted restriction on the right of a lawyer to choose where he will practice and inconsistent with our professional status. Accordingly, the Committee is of the opinion it would be improper for the employing lawyer to require the covenant and likewise for the employed lawyer to agree to it.

The opinion of the Committee is concurred in by Messrs. Casner, Enersen, Johnson, Jones, McCown, Miller and Shepherd.

Mr. Pettengill dissents, stating his reasons as follows:

> I do not consider the covenant an *unwarranted restriction* or inconsistent "with our professional status." Under certain circumstances, a law firm and its clients might be entitled to such protection. If so, a restrictive covenant would be more effective than depending on the claim that the employee-lawyer was violating a Canon of Ethics. An injunction to prevent a breach of a restrictive covenant affords a speedier and much more effective remedy.

Informal Opinion 428: Advertisement by Corporate Counsel for Patent Lawyer (Mar. 29, 1961)

You have asked the views of the Committee on Professional Ethics of the American Bar Association; the pertinent facts you state as follows:

An attorney who is a member of the association, and who is employed on a full-time basis by a manufacturer of electronic equipment, has sent the following circular letter simultaneously to a number of patent attorneys and patent agents employed on a full-time basis by competing manufacturers of electronic equipment:

Dear Mr. Doe:

XYZ Company has an opening on its staff for a patent attorney who would handle patent matters for the company. The work would primarily concern the field of electronics.

A brochure that explains the activities of the Company, its major fields of interest, and which provides other pertinent information is enclosed.

If you are interested in associating with us, we would like to have you come to our city and see our facilities. At that time we can discuss the position more fully.

Very truly yours,

Richard Roe
Staff Attorney

These letters have in every case been sent without the knowledge or consent of the employers of the attorneys and agents to whom they have been addressed.

You state that the propriety of the attorney's conduct in sending such letters has been questioned on the ground that, since every patent attorney or agent has knowledge of confidential matters disclosed in his client's patent applications, any employment in a similar capacity by a competitor "may involve the . . . use" if not the actual disclosure of such matters, and that the sending of such letters tends to induce breach of Canon 37. At the same time you state that such conduct has been defended on the ground that any attorney considering employment must himself be the sole judge whether such employment might involve the use by him of confidential matters learned during previous employment by another.

Canon 37 in part states as follows:

It is the duty of a lawyer to preserve his client's confidences. This duty outlasts the lawyer's employment, and extends as well to his employees; and neither of them should accept employment which involves or may involve the disclosure or use of these confidences, either for the private advantage of the lawyer or his employees or to the disadvantage of the client, without his knowledge and consent, and even though there are other available sources of such information, a lawyer should not continue employment when he discovers that this obligation prevents the performance of his full duty to his former or to his new client.

From the foregoing Canon, it is to be observed that the obligation is upon the lawyer who might be employed to consider whether he can accept employment in view of confidential information he may have received from past employment. Thus, it is the latter lawyer, and not the one who seeks to employ lawyers, that must make the determination.

A basic weakness of the case you present appears to us to be that of an assumption that the employing lawyer has for his purpose getting a new lawyer-employee to disclose confidences, and the further assumption that the new lawyer-employee would do so. From the letter that you quote, we consider that there is no basis for such assumptions. But accepting your assumption as correct, then it could be said that the employer-lawyer would be violating Canons 32 and 15. With respect to Canon 15, such conduct of the employer-lawyer would be in violation of that provision which states: "The office of attorney does not permit, much less does it demand of him for any client, violation of law or any manner of fraud or chicane." Generally, such conduct would be a failure of the lawyer to perform his duty as described in Canon 32.

Informal Opinion 521: Restrictive Covenant in Lawyer's Employment Contract (Dec. 12, 1962)

This is in response to your request for an opinion on the above subject. You call our attention to the fact that our formal Opinion No. 300, released August 7, 1961, held that it was improper for a contract of employment between a lawyer or law firm and another lawyer restricting the employee from practicing law in the locality for some stated period after termination of his employment; and you have asked our opinion whether this rule would be extended to a restriction against the handling of legal work of any person or firm who was an established client of the firm at the time the employee terminated his employment.

In our formal Opinion No. 300 we called attention to Canon No. 7, reading as follows: "Efforts, direct or indirect, in any way to encroach upon the business of another lawyer, are unworthy of those who would be brethren at the Bar; . . ." and also to Canon 27, which prohibits every form of solicitation of employment. We expressed the view that a former employee of a lawyer or law firm would be bound by these Canons to refrain from any effort to secure the work of clients of his former employer.

You have advised, however, that in instances which have come to your attention where the former employee upon leaving the employment of the law firm, or shortly thereafter, he took over the work of a client of the firm which he had handled while he was employed by that firm. You call attention to the fact that local representatives of corporations, particularly insurance company clients, maintain a close relationship in the handling of personal injury cases with the lawyer in the firm assigned to handle the work; that they necessarily know of the lawyer's leaving the firm; and you point out the difficulty of enforcing the Canon against solicitation in such a situation.

Notwithstanding these considerations, the Committee is of the opinion that the rule announced in Formal Opinion 300 would be equally applicable to a covenant of the type you suggest in a contract of employment of a lawyer.

In your letter you also make reference to the Partnership Agreements. We call your attention to the fact that we were not attempting to pass on restrictive covenants in Partnership Agreements in writing formal Opinion 300. There the parties are dealing on an equal footing and we believe restrictive covenants within reasonable and legal limits as between the partners do not involve any questions of ethics.

Informal Opinion: 522 Holiday Greetings to Clients (May 31, 1962)

You have inquired as to whether there is any opinion of this Committee that frowns upon an attorney sending holiday greetings to his clients. In Informal Opinion C-213, dated November 27, 1959, we had before us the question of whether it would be ethical for a lawyer or firm to send Christmas greetings to clients. The Committee referred to statement of Henry Drinker, in his book on Legal Ethics, page 247, where he said: "Under Canon 27 every indirect form of advertising, designed to sell professional employment is improper. Typical instances of such indirect advertising, condemned by the Committee, are . . . the sending out of Christmas books or greetings; . . ." In said Informal Opinion of November 27, 1959, this Committee said:

> It is the opinion of our Committee that it is unethical for a lawyer to send Christmas greetings to clients as such.
>
> This, of course, would not prevent an attorney from sending greetings to persons who happen to be clients (or employees or officers of clients) whom he knows socially or with whom he has had close personal contacts, just as he would do with friends who are not clients or associated with clients. Our Committee is further of the opinion that a lawyer's Christmas greeting cards or letters should make no reference to the sender's profession, and that he should avoid cards which depict a lawyer, a judge, scales of justice, etc. In this connection we call attention to Opinion 107, in which the Committee held it was improper for a lawyer, designated as such, to join other persons in the insertion of Christmas greetings in a local newspaper.

Applying these rules, in an opinion dated March 14, 1961, we disapproved sending out of greeting cards by lawyers.

Informal Opinion: 1072 Restrictive Covenant in Partnership Agreement (Oct. 8, 1968)

You have requested an opinion of this Committee on the propriety of incorporating in a partnership agreement a restrictive covenant upon the individual practice of law by a withdrawing partner within the county where the firm is engaged in practice for suggested period of five years. You state:

> We represent a firm of five attorneys here in _____ , New York, four of whom are members pursuant to a written partnership agreement. The partners wish to amend the agreement in several respects, including the incorporation of a restrictive covenant upon the individual practice of law by a withdrawing partner within our county for a period of perhaps five years.
>
> . . . The intention of the partners in imposing restrictive covenants upon themselves is not only to prevent a withdrawing partner from opening an office within the county in competition with the remaining partners, but also to prevent a withdrawing partner (should he open an office elsewhere) from performing any services or practicing in any manner within the County of _____ . . . .
>
> Informal Opinion 300 of the American Bar Association Committee on Professional Ethics stated that it is unethical for an attorney employing another attorney to include as part of the employment contract a restrictive covenant prohibiting the employee from practicing law in the city and county for two years after the termination of employment. Informal Opinion 521, however, indicates that a restrictive covenant within reasonable and legal limits as between partners dealing on an equal footing does not involve a question of ethics. Our situation, of course, involves partners dealing on equal footing, and the critical verbiage would appear to be 'within reasonable . . . limits.'
>
> We would appreciate the Committee's advice as to whether the covenant suggested would be permissible. If not, would it be permissible if limited to a shorter period of time? Might it be permissible for a period of ten years? If the suggested covenant is not permissible, would it be permissible under the circumstances to prevent a withdrawing partner from opening an office within _____ County but not preventing him from practicing here in the event that he opened an office in another County?

We believe that what we have stated in Formal Opinion 300 has like application to partnerships, notwithstanding what our Committee has heretofore said in Informal Opinion 521, which is specifically overruled by this opinion. We quote from so much of Formal Opinion 300 as we believe here applicable, to wit:

Restrictive covenants of the type described are sometimes used in connection with commercial transactions, such as the sale of a business, often being associated with the sale of the "good will" or "going concern value" of the enterprise.

The practice of law, however, is a profession, not a business or commercial enterprise. The relations between attorney and client are personal and individual relationships (Canon 35). The practice of law is not a business which can be bought or sold.

It was held by this Committee in Opinion 266, issued June 21, 1945, that it would be improper for a lawyer to purchase the practice and good will of a deceased lawyer who was not his partner. In this opinion the Committee said: "The good will of the practice of a lawyer is not, however, of itself an asset which either he or his estate can sell. As said by the Committee on Professional Ethics of the New York County Lawyers Association in its opinion 109, (October 6, 1943): 'Clients are not merchandise. Lawyers are not tradesmen. They have nothing to sell but personal service. An attempt, therefore, to barter in clients would appear to be inconsistent with the best concepts of our professional status.'

It appears to this Committee that a restrictive covenant of the type described would be an attempt to "barter in clients."

Somewhat analogous is Opinion 633 of the Committee on Professional Ethics of The Association of the Bar of the City of New York. There the question arose as to whether an attorney may sell his interest in a law partnership to another lawyer, the only issue being whether there was any violation of professional ethics in the sale of one's practice or interest in the legal practice. The Committee held: ". . . Clients are not merchandise. Lawyers are not tradesmen. They have nothing to sell but personal service. An attempt, therefore, to barter in clients would appear to be inconsistent with the best concepts of our professional status. . . ."

To the same effect is that Committee's Opinion 688, in which an opinion was requested involving the propriety and ethics of the following clause in a partnership agreement between a law firm and a lawyer who was to become a member thereof, the provision reading:

Throughout the partnership term, and for two years thereafter, John Doe is not, for his own account, or for or with others (except the partnership), to solicit, cause to be solicited, or accept any legal work appertaining to the legal profession, from any of the clients of the partnership, or from others with whom he came into contact directly or indirectly as a result of the partnership or from those recommended by such clients or others. Nor is he, without consent of the partnership to solicit, cause to be solicited or accept any private employment from such clients or others. For this purpose, the sending out of an announcement to clients of the partnership, or to such others of his establishment in his own practice or his association with others, shall be regarded as solicitation.

The Committee on Professional Ethics of The Association of the Bar of the City of New York, in Opinion 688, held in part, to wit: "The Committee does not pass on the questions of law inherent in this inquiry. In rendering the following opinion, the Committee assumes that the solicitation referred to in the quoted clause is not intended to include any solicitation which would in any respect violate Canon 27 of the Canons of Professional Ethics:

1. The quoted provisions impose conditions and limitations on the relations between partners of a law firm and between the clients of the firm and of the individual partners which by their very expression tend to derogate from the trust and confidence necessarily inherent in such relations.

2. The quoted provisions treat the practice of law as a commercial business rather than as a profession, and base the relations of the partners on a commercial as distinguished from a professional basis.

3. The quoted provisions tend to interfere with and obstruct the freedom of the client in choosing and dealing with his lawyer."

We believe the above principles applicable to the present inquiry and see no difference, so far as the ethical question is concerned, whether the restrictive covenant is an agreement between a lawyer-employer and a lawyer-employee or is an agreement between lawyer-partners on equal footing. It seems to the Committee that the ultimate questions and considerations are the same. The right to practice law is a privilege granted by the State, and so long as a lawyer holds his license to practice, this right cannot and should not be restricted by such an agreement. The attorneys should not engage in an attempt to barter in clients, nor should their practice be restricted. The attorney must remain free to practice when and where he will and to be available to prospective clients who might desire to engage his services.

We, therefore, conclude that a restrictive covenant that you contemplate, as between partners and the law firm, would be unethical and it would be improper for the firm and the attorneys to enter into such an arrangement.

Appendix E
MATERIALS CONCERNING THE INSOLVENCY AND REORGANIZATION OF PROFESSIONAL ASSOCIATIONS AND CORPORATIONS—LEGAL, ETHICAL, AND PRACTICAL CONSIDERATIONS

Meeting of the Business Bankruptcy Committee
of the Section of Business Law,
Held at the National Conference of Bankruptcy Judges
at San Diego, California on October 3, 1988

Nathan B. Feinstein, Esq.
Piper & Marbury
Baltimore, Maryland

Stephen P. Feldman, Esq.
Stutman, Treister & Glatt
Professional Corporation
Los Angeles, California

Arthur S. Olick, Esq.
Anderson Russell Kill & Olick, P.C.
New York, New York

Michael L. Temin, Esq.
Wolf, Block, Schlor & Solis-Cohen
Philadelphia, Pennsylvania

Introduction

With the recent demise of several major law firms, one of which was the fourth largest firm in the United States, interest has been sparked among bankruptcy specialists and other lawyers in the subject of the insolvency of professionals. Unlike other insolvency cases, those involving professionals — in particular lawyers — may present unique clashes between rules of law and of ethics. Hence, they should be of special interest to all of us.

Despite the recent level of interest in the insolvency of professionals, there are relatively few reported cases on such insolvencies and these involve only some of the issues which could arise when a law firm, for example, goes under. Hence, this program will be just as much about questions not yet considered by the courts as it will be about questions they have attempted to answer.

Selected Considerations

I. Protections for individuals against the risk of the insolvency of the business which includes their practice

A. Protections created by the choice of business structure

1. Sole proprietorship — the individual is liable for all of the debts of his or her business.

2. Partnership — Under the Uniform Partnership Act, adopted by forty-eight states, all general partners are liable (a) jointly and severally for the torts or breaches of trust for which the partnership is liable and (b) jointly for all other debts and obligations of the partnership. See, e.g., §26 of the New York Partnership Law. This was also the case at common law. Francis v. McNeal, 228 U.S. 695 (1913) (liability imposed for a tortious act not only upon the partner who committed it but equally on those partners who were innocent of any wrongdoing). Based upon these principles, the New York Court of Appeals made it clear recently that the innocent partner of a

dishonest lawyer can be required to repay the state's Clients' Security Fund for money it paid out to 373 clients who were the victims of the dishonest lawyer's misconduct. Clients' Security Fund of the State of New York v. Grandeau, N.Y. Ct. App., No. 194 (6/30/88), reported in ABA/BNA Lawyers Manual at 235. See generally Vicarious Liability of Lawyer for Tort of Partner in Law Firm, 70 A.L.R.3d 1298 (1976); Derivative Liability of a Partner for Punitive Damages for Wrongful Act of Co-Partner, 14 A.L.R.4th 1336 (1982).

a. Can this liability be avoided by practice through a limited partnership?

b. Can the individual's liability be avoided if the practitioner incorporates and the corporation becomes the partner?

c. Is application of these principles justified in the world of the modern multi-tiered partnership? If not, should there be a legislative answer?

3. The professional service corporation — Unlike the proprietorship and the general partnership, the professional corporation, depending on the laws of a particular state, may offer some protection to its principals against certain claims. In New York, for example, §11505 of its Business Corporations Law has been strictly construed so as to impose personal liability on shareholders "only in connection with the rendition of professional services" and not for the ordinary business debts of such corporation. We're Associates v. Cohen, Stracher & Bloom, P.C., 490 N.Y.S.2d 743, 75 (N.Y. 1985). New York offers no protection from liability on *clients'* claims even for principals who are not culpable of a wrongful act. By contrast for example, California and Pennsylvania do offer some protection from clients' claims — at least in theory. Since October, 1971, the obligation of each shareholder of a California legal services corporation who guarantees payment of clients' claims can be limited on an annual basis to $50,000 per claim (multiplied by the number of attorneys) and $100,000 per year (multiplied by the number of attorneys), with absolute ceilings of $500,000 per claim and $5 million per year regardless of the number of attorneys. Part IV-B, Law Corporation Rules of the State Bar

of California. (Of course, no limit is enjoyed by the perpetrator of the wrong since his or her liability is not based on a guaranty.) In Pennsylvania, the liability of a shareholder is limited for negligent or wrongful acts or misconduct "committed by him or by any person under his direct supervision and control."

B. Protections available through use of exemption laws or spendthrift trusts — There is nothing unique to professionals here, but a device frequently utilized by professionals to protect their earnings — the retirement plan — has been the subject of considerable controversy.

1. The use of state created exemptions — In terms of exemptions, the treatment of such retirement plans by the states has ranged from a total lack of any exemption, to a total grant of the exemption, to a partial or conditional grant. Not long ago, California changed its policy from one of total exemption to a policy that fully exempts an individual's interest in all "private retirement plans" but exempts an interest in a self-employed retirement plan and in an individual retirement account only to the extent it can be shown that the interest is necessary to provide for the support of the individual and his or her spouse upon the debtor's retirement. See, Cal. Code Civ. Proc. §704.115. The provisions of §704.115 have been strictly construed so as to deny the exemption where the plan was used for a purpose other than just retirement, e.g., as a source for borrowing by the debtor. In re Bloom, 68 Bankr. 455 (Bankr. 9th Cir. 1986).

2. The use of spendthrift trusts — A true spendthrift trust is effective and the debtor's interest in such is not property of the estate by virtue of §541(c)(2) of the Bankruptcy Code. The question has arisen whether an ERISA-qualified plan constitutes a valid spendthrift trust or whether an interest in such a pla' is exempt under §522(b)(2)(A) of the Code, which exempts, among other interests, "any property that is exempt under Federal law." Section 541(c)(2) excludes from "property of the estate" the beneficial interest of a debtor in a trust that is enforceable under applicable non-bankruptcy law. A number of cases have held that the anti-alienation provisions contained in a retirement plan in order to obtain qualification under ERISA

do not alone place a debtor's interest in such plans within the exclusion contained in §541(c)(2). See, e.g., Matter of Goff, 706 F.2d 574, 582 (1983). Similar reasoning has led to such interests being held not exempt under §522(b)(2)(A). In re Graham, 726 F.2d 1268 (8th Cir. 1984).

A recent and rather thorough discussion of the spendthrift trust issue is found in the Fifth Circuit's recent opinion in the case of In re Brooks, 844 F.2d 258 (1988). Brooks, one of 32 doctors holding shares in a professional corporation, filed for relief under chapter 11 and sought to have declared as protected from the reach of his creditors his interest ($645,123.09) in the corporation's ERISA-qualified pension trust. Because Texas law at the time did not exempt the assets of such qualified plans (as it did commencing in 1987), Dr. Brooks based his claim for protection on the contention that the trust was a valid spendthrift trust under Texas law and, accordingly, his interest was not "property of the estate" under §541(c)(2). Like the other 31 doctors who held a share in the professional corporation, Brooks was eligible to serve on the corporation's board of directors and on its executive committee. (Indeed, Brooks had served on both). Under the terms of the retirement plan adopted by the corporation, the contributions made to the plan were for the exclusive benefit of the participants and could not revert to the corporation. Each participant could direct into which of a number of mutual investment plans his interest be placed, could direct that contributions be used to pay premiums on a policy insuring his life, and could borrow from the plan under certain circumstances. If, after three years of employment a participant terminated his employment, he was entitled to withdraw his entire interest. Given all of the debtor's power over his interest, the court held that Brooks was a "settlor" creating a trust for his own benefit and, as such, a provision purporting to shelter his beneficial interest against the claims of creditors was not effective to create a spendthrift trust under Texas law. In support of its decision, the Fifth Circuit cited other cases denying professionals the right to shield part of their earnings by establishing profit-sharing or pension plans through their solo practices, partnerships or associations. In re

Lichstrahl, 750 F.2d 1488 (11th Cir. 1985); In re Daniel, 771
F.2d 1352 (9th Cir. 1985), *cert. denied*, 475 U.S. 1016 (1986);
In re Graham, 726 F.2d 1268 (8th Cir. 1984). However, the
Fifth Circuit left open the possibility for a different result under
different facts, e.g., a larger entity in which the participant has
less control over the employer and the plan. 844 F.2d at 264.

Other cases in accord with *Brooks:*

In re Slezak, 63 Bankr. 625 (W.D. Ky. 1986) (doctor's
interest in a plan established by a large professional association)

In re Ridenour, 45 Bankr. 72 (E.D. Tenn. 1984) (lawyer's interest in a plan adopted by a three-member firm)

Other cases contra to *Brooks:*

In re Threewitt, 24 Bankr. 927 (D. Kan. 1982) (holding
an interest in an ERISA-qualified plan protected by
§541(c)(2) and reversing an opinion of the Bankruptcy
Court to the contrary)

In re Pruitt, 30 Bankr. 330 (Bankr. Colo. 1983)

In re Phillips, 34 Bankr. 543 (Bankr. S.D. Ohio 1983)

C. Protection of future earnings by filing under the Code

1. Such protection is available in chapter 7 cases under
§541(a)(6) and, perhaps to a more limited extent, in chapter
11. Compare in re FitzSimmons, 725 F.2d 1208 (9th Cir.
1984), with In re Cooley, 87 Bankr. 432 (Bankr. S.D. Tex.
1988), discussed infra at pp. 10-13.

II. Administering the insolvent estate of the professional association

A. Alternative Methods of Administration: The choice over
how a law firm goes about breaking up may not be that of its
members. Creditors may determine the method of administration. Some or all of the following criteria should be useful to both
principals and creditors in deciding which method of administration best for a particular case.

1. Informal — usually impracticable due to distrust among
principals, their desire not to "dwell on the past" and creditor
distrust. See, e.g., In re Finley, Kumble, Wagner, Heine, Underberg, Manley, Meyerson & Casey, 17 Bankr. Ct. Dec. 583
(S.D.N.Y. 1988) (hereinafter "In re Finley, Kumble").

2. Assignment for the Benefit of Creditors

3. Dissolution proceedings under state law, administered by a receiver

a. Article 6 of the Uniform Partnership Act ("UPA") governs the "dissolution and winding up" of a partnership.

"Dissolution" is the change in the relation of the partners caused by any partner ceasing to be associated in the "carrying on" of the business. (UPA §29) On dissolution, the partnership is not "terminated" but continues until the "winding up" of partnership affairs is completed. (UPA §30) Dissolution is caused by — among other things — the end of the term of the partnership, the will of any partner (when no term is stated), the will of all (before or after the end of the term), expulsion of a partner, the express will of any partner at any time, the death of a partner, the bankruptcy of the partnership, or by court decree. (UPA §31) A decree of dissolution may be entered on application by or for a partner whenever "(e) The business of the partnership can only be carried on at a loss" or "(f) Other circumstances render a dissolution equitable." (UPA §32) Dissolution terminates the authority of any partner to act for the partnership except so far as may be necessary to wind up partnership affairs or to complete unfinished transactions. (UPA §33)

The dissolution of the partnership does not "of itself" discharge the existing liability of any partner, absent agreement by a partnership creditor, express or inferred by course of conduct. (UPA §§36(1) and (2)). Unless otherwise agreed, the partners who have not wrongfully dissolved the partnership may "wind up" the partnership affairs. However, any partner may "for cause" obtain winding up by the court. (UPA §37) ("Cause" includes fraud, mismanagement, waste of assets or their commingling, failure to account, etc.) In aid of winding up, a receiver may be appointed.

Partners entitled to rescind have rights superior to those who do not *but not as against third parties*. They are entitled to indemnification. (UPA §39)

As to the "settling of accounts between partners," §40 of the UPA sets forth the following rules *subject to any agreement to the contrary*": The assets of the partnership consist of

(1) the partnership property and (2) the contributions necessary to pay liabilities owing in the following rank: (a) creditors other than partners; (b) partners other than for capital and profits; (c) partners in respect of capital; and (d) partners in respect of profits. The proceeds of the partnership property are to be distributed in that order. Partners are required to contribute the amount necessary to satisfy *liabilities* to the extent not covered by the proceeds. If some partners are themselves insolvent, the solvent partners bear the burden proportionately. Either an assignee for the benefit of creditors or a person appointed by the Court may enforce these obligations. (Section 40 of the UPA also sets forth priorities among partnership creditors and individual creditors in the sharing of partnership property and individual property.

    b. Dissolution of a corporation is likewise governed by statute, e.g., Cal. Corp. Code §1800 *et seq*.

    4. Proceedings under title 11

        a. Chapter 7 (or chapter 13 for an individual who qualifies)

        b. Chapter 11, e.g., In re FitzSimmons, 725 F.2d 1208 (9th Cir. 1984); In re Cooley, 87 Bankr. 432 (Bankr. S.D. Tex. 1988); In re Finley, Kumble, supra, discussed infra at pp. 10-13.

    B. Choosing between a filing under the Bankruptcy Code and the state court receivership — Criteria to be considered may include:

        1. Stigma and concern over credit reporting

        2. Jurisdiction of the court and reach of its process

        3. Availability of discovery devices

        4. Relative clarity and scope of governing law — the "preci᷄ :ness" of the Bankruptcy Code versus the apparent flexibility of the state court receivership

        5. Powers of the fiduciary

        a. Like a trustee in bankruptcy, a receiver has the power to bring or defend actions, to take possession of property, to collect debts, to compromise controversies, to make transfers and "generally do such acts respecting the property as the court may authorize." See, e.g., Calif. Code Civ. Proc. §568.

b. However, unless granted by statute, the receiver lacks the avoiding powers of a trustee. (For example, in California a receiver may set aside transfers without delivery. Calif. Civ. Code §3440(b), but is not granted the powers given to a bankruptcy trustee under the Bankruptcy Code or to an assignee for the benefit of creditors under California law to avoid preferences and fraudulent transfers. See Cal. Civ. Code §3439.07.)

6. Availability of injunctive relief to protect principals of the firm while the assets of the firm are being administrated

a. Orders enjoining the prosecution of suits against principals have been obtained in recent state court dissolution proceedings for professional associations. See "Order Staying Commencement, Prosecution, Continuation of Any Suit, Proceeding or Lien Against Any of the Entities) entered in the case of Kadison, Pfaelzer, Woodard, Quinn & Rossi v. Kadison, et al., Los Angeles Superior Court Case No. C654974. Such orders appear to conflict with older cases holding that the filing of a dissolution proceeding and the appointment of a receiver does not operate to prevent actions by creditors against the principals of the firm. Bogert v. Turner, 120 N.Y.S. 420, 135 App. Div. 530 (1909); Ex parte Planter's Bank, 115 S.E. 229 (S.C. 1922); Adams v. Woods, 8 Cal. 152 (1857); Naglee v. Minturn, 8 Cal. 540 (1857); Adams v. Hackett, 7 Cal. 187 (1857). Hence, the more recent rulings cast doubt on the continuing applicability of these old decisions.

b. In a case under the Bankruptcy Code, the filing of a petition does not automatically stay the actions of creditors against general partners, and hence creditors are free to pursue their state-based claims or to file involuntary petitions against the general partners. See, In re Aboussie Brothers Construction Company, 8 Bankr. 302 (E.D. Mo. 1981); In re Lamb, 40 Bankr. 689 (Bankr. E.D. Tenn. 1984). Nevertheless, both before the Code and since its enactment, some courts have held that debts of the partnership must first be satisfied from partnership assets before creditors will be permitted to proceed against the general partners and have enjoined creditor action against principals of the firm accordingly. See, e.g., In re Hurley Mercantile Co., 56 F.2d 1023 (5th Cir. 1932), *cert. denied, sub norm.*, Atacosa County State Bank v. Coppard, 286 U.S. 555 (1932); Vegetable Kingdom, Inc. v. Katzen, 653 F. Supp. 917 (N.D.N.Y. 1987); In re Elemar Associates, 3 Bankr. Ct. Dec. 958 (Bankr. S.D.N.Y. 1977); Wisnouse v. Telsey, 367 F. Supp. 855 (S.D.N.Y. 1973). In the *Elemar* case, for example, the court, while acknowledging the ultimate liability of a non-debtor partner for the debts of a partnership filing under Chapter XI of the Bankruptcy Act, granted an injunction restraining a partnership creditor from enforcing a judgment against the general partner. As the court explained,

> New York Courts have held, just as Section 5g [of the Bankruptcy Act] requires without limitation, that on a joint liability creditors will look first to partnership property. Any deficiency is to be made up from the partner's individual property. . . . Of course, exhaustion of the partnership's assets in satisfaction of the partnership's debts must be had before invocation by the creditor of the partner's property.

Id. at 960 (citations omitted).

In reaching the conclusion, the court relied upon the case of Seligman v. Friedlander, 199 N.Y. 373 *reh'g denied,* 200 N.Y. 505 (1910), in which the New York Court of Appeals stated:

> When a partnership debt is incurred it presumptively creates partnership assets and should in reason be paid therefrom and not until they are exhausted should individual property be proceeded against. . . . The inconvenience and injustice of suing half a dozen partners individually in as many separate actions without suing the partnership proper . . . is so obvious as to enjoin upon the courts extreme caution in construing a statute alleged to permit that result.

Id. at 380-81.

Most recently, in In re Finley, Kumble, Bankruptcy Judge Abram invoked Section 105(a) of the Code to temporarily enjoin suits against individual partners in order to facilitate the marshalling of partnership assets and to prevent the dissipation of the efforts and assets of the general partners. Dozens of creditors had instituted lawsuits against individual partners and groups of partners in that case, which threatened the efforts of the trustee to collect accounts receivable and seek a resolution with creditors. The continuation of separate litigation was deemed by the court to be an interference with the orderly administration of the debtor's estate. See also In re Old Orchard Investment Co., 31 Bankr. 599, 601-03 (W.D. Mich. 1983).

c. In a corporate context, §105 of the Code has been invoked by courts to justify injunctions precluding creditors from proceeding against principals. See, e.g., In re Arrow Huss, Inc., 51 Bankr. 853 (Bankr. D. Utah 1985) (suit against officers and employees restrained); In re Original Wild West Foods, Inc., 45 Bankr. 202 (Bankr. W.D. Tex 1984); In re Kipps, 34 Bankr. 91 (Bankr. S.D.N.Y. 1983) (suit against debtor's president restrained); In re Lahman Mfg. Co., 33 Bankr. 681 (Bankr. D.S.D. 1983) (suit against corp. officers restrained); and In re Steel Products, Inc., 47 Bankr. 44 (Bankr. W.D. Wash. 1984). (IRS restrained from collecting pre-petition withholding taxes); In re TRS, Inc., 16 Bankr. Ct. Dec. 865 (D. Kan. 1987); In re Johns-Manville Corp., 26 Bankr. 420 (S.D.N.Y. 1983), *aff'd in part,* 40 Bankr. 219 (S.D.N.Y. 1984).

Cases contra:

In re United Department Stores, Inc., 39 Bankr. 54 (Bankr. S.D.N.Y. 1984)

In re Booth Tow Services, Inc., 53 Bankr. 1014 (W.D. Mo. 1985)

In re United States v. Huckabee Auto Co., 46 Bankr. 741 (W.D. Ga. 1985)

In re Dickenson Lines, Inc., 47 Bankr. 653 (Bankr. D. Minn. 1985)

In re Precision Colors, Inc. 36 Bankr. 429 (Bankr. S.D. Ohio 1984)

7. Representation of principal's interest in the insolvency case

a. Individual principals can appear either in a dissolution case under state law or as a "party in interest" in a title 11 case. See, e.g., In re Amatex Corp., 755 F.2d 1034, 1042 (3d Cir. 1985); In re Citizens Loan & Thrift Co., 7 Bankr. 88 (Bankr. N.D. Iowa 1980).

b. Whether a committee of principals would be permitted to appear in a state court dissolution action depends upon local law.

c. In a case under chapter 11 for a professional corporation, an equity holders committee could be appointed under §1102(a)(2) of the Bankruptcy Code.

d. However, where the chapter 11 debtor is a partnership the appointment of an "official" committee of general partners appears unavailable.

The Code defines an "equity security holder" as a "holder of an equity security of the debtor." 11 U.S.C. §101(6). An equity security with respect to a partnership is defined in Section 101(15)(B) of the Code as the "interest of a *limited* partner in a *limited partnership*." (emphasis supplied) Accordingly, it has been observed that:

> [an] equity security under the Code does not expressly include the interest of a general partner in a debtor-partnership and by clear implication the inclusion in the definition of an equity security of the interest of a limited partner in a limited partnership excludes the interest of a general partner in a partnership.

In re Westgate General Partnership, 55 Bankr. 560, 561 (Bankr. E.D. Pa. 1985) (denying motion of general partners of partnership debtor for appointment of "official" committee of equity security holders, and stating that even if such committee were formed, "general partners would be ineligible for membership"). Id. at 562.

In her recent decision in the *Finley, Kumble* case, Bankruptcy Judge Abram stated:

> The concept of a committee member as a class representative cannot be applied to a general partners' committee. Fundamentally, it is each partner for himself in the race to avoid or minimize personal liability to the debtor's creditors.

In re Finley, Kumble, supra. At least as a matter of policy, as opposed to statutory interpretation, this result seems questionable.

By contrast, an official *limited* partners' committee has been found to be proper under Code §1102(a). See, e.g., In re Nashua Trust Co., 73 Bankr. 423 (Bankr. D.N.J. 1987); In re 1981 Equidyne Properties, Inc., 59 Bankr. 930 (Bankr. S.D.N.Y. 1986); In re Amarex, Inc., 53 Bankr. 888 (Bankr. W.D. Okla. 1985).

8. Ability to continue operations under supervision of a fiduciary: Compare 11 U.S.C. §108 and 28 U.S.C. §959(b) with Cal. Corp. Code §13045. See discussion at pp. _____ infra.

9. Pursuit of principals for deficiency; retention by principals of post-petition income

a. In the case of the partnership, a receiver in a state court dissolution proceeding may pursue the principals for the deficiency, UPA §40(e), as may the trustee in a chapter 7 case under §723(a) of the Code which provides:

> [i]f there is a deficiency of property of the estate to pay in full all claims which are allowed in a case under this chapter concerning a partnership and with respect to which a general partner of the partnership is personally liable, the trustee shall have a claim against such general partner for the full amount of the deficiency.

However, in keeping with the "separate entity" treatment of partnerships, as illustrated in the case of In re Elemar Associates, supra, §723(b) of the Code requires a trustee to first seek recovery from those general partners who are not themselves debtors under title 11. Pending determination of the extent of the deficiency, the Bankruptcy Court may order such partner to provide to the trustee indemnity for, or assurance of payment of, such deficiency.

b. Section 723 is inapplicable to chapter 11 cases for a partnership, even where a trustee has been appointed or where the partnership is involved in a liquidation under that chapter. 11 U.S.C. §103(b) (1978); In re The Monetary

Group, et al., 55 Bankr. 297, 298-99 (Bankr. M.D. Fla. 1985); In re I-37 Gulf Limited Partnership, 48 Bankr. 647, 649 (Bankr. S.D. Tex. 1985). The inapplicability of §723 in chapter 11 suggests the conclusion that in chapter 11 cases, a trustee cannot force contribution or indemnification from general partners in chapter 11 cases. However, in the *Finley, Kumble* case, the court ordered the general partners to each file a statement of personal assets and liabilities (order entered 5/16/88) as did the court in the case of In re Monetary Group, et al., 55 Bankr. 297 Bankr. M.D. Fla. 1985). See Bankruptcy Rules 2004 and 1007(g).

c. In connection with the pursuit of partners, the issue arises concerning the so-called "unfinished business" of the firm. This relates to how fees on cases pending on the date of dissolution are to be divided between the estate and the partners who handle the cases after that date. The issue will be discussed in more detail, especially from the ethical perspective, in a subsequent portion of these materials. (See pp. 21-28, infra). In the present context, it is worth reporting that *absent an agreement to the contrary specifically dealing with such unfinished business,* the courts have imposed a duty on the respective members of the dissolving firm to complete *without compensation* matters pending at dissolution which they take. Jewel v. Boxer, 156 Cal. App. 3d 171 (1984); Rosenfeld, Meyer & Susman v. Cohen, 146 Cal. App. 3d 200 (1983); see Resnick v. Kaplan, 49 Md. 499 (1981); Frates v. Nichols, 167 S.2d 77 (Fla. 1964). However, to avoid undue hardship, apparently only the *net* proceeds collected need be turned over. Jewel v. Boxer, supra at 180. (Contra Hawkesworth v. Ponzoli, 388 So. 2d 299, 301 (Fla. App. 1980).) The burden is on the partner collecting the fee to establish the propriety of the items chargeable against gross proceeds. Rosenfeld, Meyer & Susman v. Cohen, 191 Cal. App. 3d 1035 (1987).

d. Although the "unfinished business" doctrine was based on the duty partners have to one another to wind up and complete the business of the firm, it has been extended to professional corporations. Fox v. Abrams, 163 Cal. App. 3d

610 (1985). Since the doctrine is based on the principal's fiduciary duty to the firm and the other principals, could a trustee for a professional corporation sue shareholders to complete pending cases they took? Is their duty to the firm property of the estate under §541(a) of the Code? In a chapter 11 case for a partnership, could this be used by a trustee to force contributions from partners despite the inapplicability of §723?

e. Courts rejecting the "unfinished business" rule as to law firms include the Texas Court of Civil Appeals. Cofer v. Hearne, 459 S.W.2d 877 (1970).

f. In the context of the proprietorship, state "dissolution proceedings" as such are not available. However, title 11 is, so the question arises as to what extent may the individual proprietor retain post-petition income free of the rights of the estate and of creditors. In a chapter 7 case, §541(a)(6) of the Code excludes from the estate "earnings from services performed by an individual debtor after the commencement of the case." Section 541(a)(6) has been held applicable in chapter 11 by virtue of §103(a) of the Code. In re Fitz-Simmons, 725 F.2d 1208 (9th Cir. 1984); In re Cooley, 87 Bankr. 432 (Bankr. S.D. Tex. 1988). However, the question of to what extent receipts are the result of "services performed by an individual" rather than the result of the services of others or of the property of the estate has been a matter of disagreement between the two courts which have considered the issue to date.

In the *FitzSimmons* case, the chapter 11 debtor was an attorney engaged in practice as a sole proprietor. In his office he employed other attorneys and staff. Curiously, a trustee was appointed for "FitzSimmons' estate, with the exception of his law practice" which the debtor was allowed to continue to operate as DIP subject to an order regulating his operation. That order allowed the DIP to pay himself $3,500/month and required him to remit to the trustee at the end of the month all funds in excess of $15,000 plus all fees received on a particular contingent fee case. FitzSimmons appealed this order. The Bankruptcy Appellate Panel reversed insofar as the order held that an individual's post-petition earnings were property of the estate. The trustee appealed to the Court of Appeals for the Ninth Circuit. The debtor contended that since he operated as a sole proprietorship, all post-petition earnings from the practice fell within the earnings exception. The trustee argued that all earnings were property of the estate, with only the salary set by the Bankruptcy Court excepted under §541(a)(6). The trustee based this contention on the proposition that in a case under chapter 11, where operation of the business is authorized as part of the reorganization effort, §§1107 and 1108 of the Code override §541(a)(6) and compel a turnover of post-petition earnings. Rejecting the trustee's argument, the Court of Appeals observed that, pursuant to §103 of the Code, the provisions of chapter 5, including §541(a)(6), apply to chapter 11 cases. If Congress intended otherwise, the Court observed, it could have provided for such as it did for chapter 13 cases in §1306(a)(2). However, the Court did not fully agree with the debtor, holding that §541(a)(6) only excepts earnings from services performed "personally" by the debtor. Profits earned by the proprietorship other than from services personally performed by the debtor were property of the estate. Hence, to the extent the earnings are attributable to the proprietorship's invested capital, accounts receivable, goodwill, employment contracts with its staff, client relationships, fee arrangements or the like, the earnings are property of the estate. The Court remanded for a determination of allocation in accordance with its ruling.

The *Cooley* case involved a world renowned heart surgeon, who filed for relief under chapter 11. Together with the petition, a plan of reorganization and disclosure statement were filed. The plan proposed a liquidation of the assets over a period of time which would result in the payment of claims in full. Most of the debtor's post-petition income was derived from his medical practice, which he operated as a sole proprietor. He employed four other surgeons plus additional staff. He was the "rainmaker"; it was his reputation and referral network that provided "a continuous patient pool" for the business. In addition to his surgical services, Cooley contributed managerial services as well. In 1987, Cooley performed 41% of all surgeries, resulting in 48% of net receipts. After the filing, one of the creditors moved to limit the operation of the debtor's business, thus raising the issue of to what extent profits generated by the sole proprietorship were excluded as property of the estate under §541(a)(6) of the Code.

Like the *FitzSimmons* court, the court in *Cooley* observed that chapter 11 contained no restriction on the applicability of §541(a)(6) as did chapter 13. Unlike chapter 13, chapter 11 could be commenced involuntarily — a fact which to the court raised 13th Amendment concerns of involuntary servitude absent the exclusion of post-petition earnings. On these considerations and on its perception that chapter 11 offered a chance at a fresh start from the *outset* of the case, the court ruled in favor of the debtor.

The court, however, was troubled by the Ninth Circuit's ruling in *FitzSimmons,* feeling that that court had improperly engrafted the world "personally" into §541(a)(6) so that it read "earnings from services performed [personally] by an individual debtor." Bankruptcy Judge Mahoney found the Ninth Circuit's rational "unpersuasive" as well as unfaithful to the directives of §541, concluding that "valuation of an individual's personal services is neither mandated under Section 541 nor practicable." Accordingly, she held that the burden was on the creditor to demonstrate which property interests of the estate generate revenues accruable to the estate under §541(a)(6).

> Instead, I hold that once the debtor has met his burden of going forward with evidence to show that under the earnings exception: (1) the debtor is an individual, (2) who performs services, (3) which generates earnings,(4) postpetition, the burden of proof rests upon the creditor as movant to show that the purported individual debtor's earnings are in actuality '[p]roceeds, product, offspring, rents [or] profits' derived from those assets or other property interests which have previously accrued to the estate by operation of Section 541. This

approach seems best to guard against the potential conflict with the prohibition against involuntary servitude and to ensure protection of an individual's fresh start. I am also convinced that such an approach is more faithful to the plan meaning of Section 541(a)(6)."

With this in mind, Judge Mahoney ruled that:

(1) To the extent invested capital as of the commencement of the case (i.e., fixed assets of $149,000) generated post-petition profits, the estate was entitled to a return equal to the ratio borne by the capital to the other contributions generating the profits (in *Cooley,* 12%).

(2) There was no distinction between "business" good will and "personal" good will that could be made and hence no return to the estate on that item was warranted.

(3) Post-petition income attributable to the associate surgeons ($3,403,315 the year prior to filing) did constitute "profits" from property of the estate and accordingly belonged to the estate and not to Dr. Cooley so long as they are "affiliated with the estate."

Based on the foregoing the sum of (a) 12% × 149,482 ($18.938) and (b) $3,403,315 divided by the 1987 income from the practice ($9,747,599) gave "the approximate percentage to be applied to post-petition income in order to determine the amounts accruing to the estate."

The Court, in this opinion, refused to reach the issue of what effect on the foregoing the expiration of the contracts with the associate surgeons would have if the surgeons relocated thereafter. However, it reached the issue in a subsequent opinion decided after the plan of reorganization was confirmed. In re Cooley, 11988 WL 81115 (Bankr. S.D. Tex 1988). A creditor sought injunctive relief compelling Cooley to turn over any subsequent income realized from the efforts of these associate surgeons should they resume a relationship with Cooley in his new location. The court denied the requested injunction since the only interest of the estate was the contracts with the surgeons. When those contracts expired, there was no property interest giving use to "profits of or from property of the estate." The court rejected the argument that the "advantageous relationship" between Cooley and the associates was property of the estate, stating that a ruling otherwise would conflict with the Code's policy favoring a fresh start.

    10. Availability of a discharge and its scope

      a. Availability

        (1) Unavailable in a state court dissolution case

        (2) Available in a case under title 11:

          (a) in a chapter 7 case for an individual as provided in §727 of the Code;

          (b) in a chapter 11 case for an individual, a partnership, or a corporation within the limitations of §1141 of the Code. A discharge is unavailable where the plan provides for liquidation of substantially all the property of the estate, the debtor does not engage in business after the plan's consummation, and the debtor would be denied a discharge under §727(a). Even in chapter 11, confirmation will not discharge an individual from non-dischargeable debts. §1141(d)(2)

      b. Scope — To what extent can an order of confirmation for the firm discharge the principal's liability?

        (1) A general partner may secure a discharge from both partnership and non-partnership debts in his or her individual case subject to §727 of the Code. Absent a personal filing, the principal remains liable for debts of the firm unless he or she is able to secure a voluntary release of the claims of individual creditors. Section 1141(d) limits the discharge incident to the confirmation of a plan to the "debtor." Debtor is defined in Section 101(12) of the Code as a person concerning whom a title 11 case has been instituted. (Moreover, §524(e) of the Code provides that a "discharge of a debt of the debtor does not affect the liability of any other entity on" such debts. 11 U.S.C. §524(e).) Hence, the language of the Code supports the view that, at least with respect to dissenting creditors, principals may not be discharged from firm debts simply by reason of a confirmed plan for the firm. See In re

Consolidated Motor Inns, 666 F.2d 189 (5th Cir. 1982) (debts of non-debtor general partners to non-assenting creditors cannot be discharged by a partnership debtor's Chapter XII reorganization plan). Nevertheless, some courts have confirmed plans which purport to bind non-assenting creditors to a release of principals from their individual liability for the firm's debts. In re CCA Partnership, 70 Bankr. 694 (Bankr. D. Del. 1986). Moreover, where a confirmed plan does provide for the discharge of general partners of a debtor partnership, creditors may find that the doctrine of *res judicata* prevents them from later pursuing their claims against the principals. Levy v. Cohen, 561 P.2d 252, 37 Cal. Rptr. 162, *cert. denied,* 434 U.S. 833 (S. Ct. Cal. 1977). See also Stoll v. Gottlieb, 305 U.S. 165, 171-72, *reh'g denied,* 305 U.S. 675 (1938) (confirmation order releasing debtor's guarantor from further liability under the guarantee was *res judicata* on issue of guarantor's liability, even if bankruptcy court did not have jurisdiction to grant such release); Republic Supply Co. v. Shoaf, 815 F.2d 1046 (5th Cir. 1987). Contra Underhill v. Royal, 769 F.2d 426 (9th Cir. 1985); Union Carbide Corp. v. Newboles, 686 F.2d 593, 595 (7th Cir. 1982) (confirmed chapter XI plan does not operate to discharge debtor's guarantors, despite language in plan to the contrary).

(2) A difficult issue arises in the case of contribution claims which may be asserted among general partners of a chapter 11 debtor. Where one or more general partners contributes voluntarily to a chapter 11 plan in exchange for a release of any further deficiency claims by assenting creditors, see, e.g., In re AOV Industries, Inc. et al., 792 F.2d 1140 (D.C. Cir. 1986), can non-contributing partners successfully sue the released partners if they are ultimately forced to pay a larger share of the partnership's debts than the released partners? This was the issue faced by Bankruptcy Judge Proctor in the case of In re The Securities Group 1980, (Bankr. M.D. Fla. 1988) Case No. 84-431-BK-J-GP [Lowin v. Dayton Securities Assoc., Adversary

Proceeding No. 85-214]. In that case, the trustee sued a limited partner of the debtor for contributions to the partnership estate. Thereafter, the limited partner impleaded the other partners, including those who had contributed to the plan in return for releases from derivative causes of action and other claims. The court dismissed the action as to the released partners, holding that its prior approval of the contributions made by the "settling partners" would act as a bar to any action by other non-settling general or limited partners for contribution. (Additionally, the court held that third parties' claims for indemnification would be similarly barred.)

Although your authors have not found another case on point, the result in *Securities Group* should be open to question. Releases may occasionally be the only way to achieve adequate plan funding and creditor acceptance, see, e.g., In re Johns-Manville Corp., 843 F.2d 636, 640 (2d Cir. 1988). The dollars paid in for the benefit of creditors can be seen as adequate consideration for a release which precludes such creditors from pursuing those principals who provide the funds. However, in the case of claims for contribution held by other principals, is there consideration? Those principals who settle with the estate in return for a release from further claims arguably do not give value to non-settling principals, except in the case in which a settling partner pays more than his or her aliquot share of the deficiency. While the threat of a result as occurred in the *Securities Group* case may be a great impetus to reach a settlement with the estate, it may be unfair to so affect the rights of principals who do not settle to seek contribution and/or indemnity from their co-principals, regardless of such co-principal's rights or obligations vis-a-vis firm creditors. Indeed, it can be argued that the right of contribution does not arise until such time as overpayment has been made by a particular principal in excess of his or her "fair share." To bar such claims merely by dint of the timing of a principal's payment (whether while the estate's "settlement window" is open or thereafter) or by virtue of to whom such payment is made (to the trustee or to actual creditors) may lead to inconsistent and unjust results.

(3) If the partners together have sufficient net worth to make up any shortfall estimated to occur from a liquidation of the firm's assets, could a plan that does not pay creditors in full meet the "best interests" requirement of §1129(a)(7)(A)(ii)? In the view of at least one court, "no." In re I-37 Gulf Limited Partnership, 48 Bankr. 647 (Bankr. S.D. Tex. 1985). *Accord* H.R. Rep. No. 595, 95th Cong., 1st Sess. 412, reprinted in 1977 U.S. Code Cong. & Admin. News 6368.

(4) In dealing with claims under a plan, can clients' claims be separately classified?

Some courts have stated that all unsecured claims are to be singularly classified. Granada Wines v. New England Teamsters and Trucking Industry Pension Fund, 748 F.2d 42, 46 (1st Cir. 1984); In re Fantastic Homes Enterprises, Inc., 44 Bankr. 999 (Bankr. M.D. Fla. 1984) ("Congress intended all unsecured claims of a similar nature to be grouped within one class, unless a separate classification is established under [Code] §1122(b).") (However, whenever a plan proponent has classified claims for the purpose of manipulating and defeating the Code's goal of equal treatment of similarly situated creditors, the court may not condone classification. In re Mastercraft Record Plating, Inc., 32 Bankr. 106, 108 (Bankr. S.D.N.Y. 1983), *rev'd on other grounds,* 39 Bankr. 654 (1984); In re Pine Lake Village Apartment Co., 19 Bankr. 819, 831 (Bankr. S.D.N.Y. 1982).

Other courts have recognized Congressional intent to provide a flexible scheme of classification, holding that "[Code §1122(a)] does not require that similar claims must be grouped together, but merely that any group created must be homogenous." Barnes v. Whelan, 689 F.2d 193, 201 (D.C. Cir. 1982). In cases specifically concerned with the application of §1122(a) of the Code, the *Barnes* rationale has been heartily embraced. See In re Mason & Dixon Lines, Inc., 63 Bankr. 176, 181 (Bankr.

N.D. Ga. 1985); In re U.S. Truck Co., Inc., 42 Bankr. 790, 794-96 (Bankr. E.D. Mich. 1984) (dictum); In re Huckabee Auto Co., 33 Bankr. 132, 137 (Bankr. M.D. Ga. 1981); Matter of Martin's Point Limited Partnership, 12 Bankr. 721, 726 (Bankr. N.D. Ga. 1981); Teamsters Natl. Freight Indus. Negotiating Comm. v. U.S. Truck Co., Inc., 800 F.2d 581 (6th Cir. 1986) (separate classification of union claims arising from debtor rejection of a collective bargaining agreement approved because of the substantially dissimilar interests involved).

(5) Can the feasibility requirement of §1129(a)(11) be met for a law firm given the absolute right of a client to change counsel?

III. Attorney-client conflicts raised by the insolvency of the law firm.

A. Pre-filing

1. In the period preceding the filing of either a dissolution case or a case under the Bankruptcy Code, the members of a firm are subject to conflicting pressures arising from their duty to their firm and their duty to their clients.

a. The need to increase billings in an effort to save the firm can lead to "churning" or "loading" (doing work that might be avoided or postponed; devoting resources to a matter beyond what is required).

b. On the other hand, if the professional perceives the demise inevitable, the pressures to retain the client as "one's own" can lead to unjustified write-offs or failures to bill.

2. When is an attorney required to tell a client about the firm's troubles? When is it a breach of duty to do so?

a. Model Rule 1.4 requires that: "A lawyer shall keep a client reasonably informed about the status of the matter. . . ."

b. This Rule has been interpreted to include the obligation to promptly advise a client when the lawyer is unable to perform as anticipated. As noted in ABA/BNA 31:504: "The duty is breached if a law partnership's clients are not advised of the partnership's dissolution and some prejudice thereby results." See Vollgraff v. Block, 117 Misc. 2d 489, 458

N.Y.S.2d 437 (Sup. Ct. 1982). See also Attorney Grievance Commission v. Robinson, 287 Md. 690, 415 A.2d 289 (1980); In re Rabb, 83 N.J. 109, 415 A.2d 1168." And "A lawyer who is unable to carry a matter forward promptly must inform the client of that fact. E.g., Passanante v. Yormark, 139 N.J. Super. 233, 350 A.2d 497 (1975); Committee on Legal Ethics v. Smith, 156 W. Va. 471, 194 S.E.2d 665 (1973)."

c. On the other hand, if the client is told prematurely, the effort to inform may be perceived as an effort of solicitation — a breach of a partner's fiduciary duty to his colleagues. As noted in Matter of Silverberg, 438 N.Y.S.2d 143 (App. Div. 1981):

> The solicitation of a firm's clients by one partner for his own benefit, prior to any decision to dissolve the partnership, is a breach of fiduciary obligation owed to each other and the partnership, and a breach of the partnership agreement in general (cf. Mitchell v. Reed, 61 N.Y. 123, 126; Duane Jones Co. v. Burke, 306 N.Y. 172, 188-89, 117 N.E.2d 237; Adler, Barish, Daniels, Levin & Creskoff v. Epstein, 482 Pa. 416, 393 A.2d 1175, *appeal dismissed* and *cert. denied*, 442 U.S. 907, 99 S. Ct. 2817, 61 L. Ed. 2d 272). Although dissolution occurs when the partners determine to discontinue business (see Chaim Ben-Dashan v. Plitt, 58 A.D.2d 244, 396 N.Y.S.2d 542), the partnership is not terminated until the winding up of partnership affairs is completed (see Partnership Law, §61). However, the fiduciary relation between partners terminates upon notice of dissolution, [footnote omitted] even though the partnership affairs have not been wound up (see Bayer v. Bayer, 215 App. Div. 454, 214 N.Y.S.2d 542). After dissolution, each former partner is free to practice law individually, and has the right to accept retainers from persons who had been clients of the firm (see Talley v. Lamb, Sup., 100 N.Y.S.2d 112, 118; cf. Bayer v. Bayer, supra).

In Adler, Barish, Daniels, Levin & Creskoff v. Epstein, 393 A.2d 1175 (Pa. 1978), former associates of the firm were enjoined from soliciting and continuing to serve former clients of the firm even after they had left the firm. Bray v. Squires, 702 S.W.2d 266 (Tex. 1985).

B. Post-filing

1. Administration of cases belonging to the firm at the time of filing

a. Where the firm seeks to reorganize, can the provisions of §365 allowing assumption of executory contracts be utilized to overcome the right of the client to discharge counsel?

(1) The answer should be "no." Despite the fact that a contract with a client is a personal services contract, it ought to be assumable by the debtor in possession under §365(a) (notwithstanding, that it is not assumable by a trustee by reason of §365(c)(1). Matter of West Electronics, Inc., 852 F.2d 79 (3d Cir. 1988). Whatever the result may be, under state law, the client has an absolute right to discharge an attorney at any time, e.g., Calif. Code Civ. Proc. §284, Fracasse v. Brent, 6 Cal. 3d 784, 790 (1972), and to retain counsel of its choice. ABA Model Rule 1.16(a)(3); ABA Model Code DR 2-110(B)(4). Estate of Cazaurang, 1 Cal. 2d 712 (1934). It is submitted that those rights of the client form part of every contract and, accordingly, even if the contract is assumed, the client remains free "under its terms" to select other counsel. Whatever fees the firm may be entitled to for services provided pre-discharge remain recoverable. Fracasse v. Brent, supra at 791-93; Rosenfeld, Meyer & Susman v. Cohen, 146 Cal. App. 3d at 226-227; see generally Note, Attorney Client — Damages — Breach of Contingent Fee Contract, 1960 Wis. L. Rev. 156. However, to preserve the estate's rights to these fees, care should be taken where possible to avoid rejection of the contract.

(2) As a matter of ethics, the lawyer's right to withdraw is not co-extensive with the client's right to discharge the lawyer. However, "[t]he relationship of attorney and client is one . . . [requiring] absolute confidence in the lawyer by the client and an equal confidence in the client by his lawyer. Shotgun weddings and enforced lawyer-client relationships fall in the same category." Fisher v. State, 248 So. 2d 479, 484 (Fla. 1971). Due to the sensitivity and reciprocity of the lawyer-client relationship, lawyers have generally been permitted to withdraw for good cause from

representation. "What amounts to specific performance by an attorney has been required, but such cases are extremely rare. They fall into two general classifications, that is, situations where the client's rights will be prejudiced by the delay consequent on replacing counsel and cases where the trial calendar . . . will be dislocated, so as to impede the interests of justice [citations omitted]." Goldsmith v. Pyramid Communications, 362 F. Supp. 694, 696 (S.D.N.Y. 1973). See Imhoff v. Hammer, 305 A.2d 325 (Del. 1973).

b. Where the firm is liquidating, can the power to reject executory contracts under §365 of the Code or the power to abandon property under §554 of the Code be used to avoid discontinuance of the representation by members of the firm?

(1) Do considerations of public policy preclude such a result? See Midlantic Natl. Bank v. New Jersey Dept. of Envtl. Protection, 106 S. Ct. 755 (1986) (precluding a trustee from abandoning polluted property when abandonment prohibited under state and federal statutes). Can the harm to the client so outweigh the benefit to the firm that rejection should not be authorized? See Infosystems Technology, Inc. v. Logical Software, Inc., CCH Bankr. L.R. ¶71,899 (D. Mass. 1987).

(2) Even if the firm can escape its duties, it is submitted that individual members may not unless authorized by the court in which the case is pending. See Saravia v. 1736 18th Street, 844 F.2d 823 (D.C. Cir. 1988) (rejection of lease does not excuse debtor landlord from complying with local law compelling landlords to provide certain services). Is the duty of counsel to the court in which an action is pending a "claim" that can be rejected?

c. Duty to continue representation of the client

(1) Where several attorneys have worked on the case, who must retain it?

(a) Is he or she entitled to compensation from the estate for doing so if the client is (i) not obligated to pay or (ii) not able to pay?

(b) If compensation is due, is counsel's claim a general unsecured claim or is it entitled to priority?

(2) If the client's case is "abandoned", must the estate hire other counsel or is the client's only redress to file a claim?

(a) Does the Bankruptcy Code allow for the hiring of counsel at the expense of the estate?

(b) Why isn't this like any other executory contract that is breached?

(c) Does the result change if no other counsel can be found?

(d) The duty to complete the "unfinished business" of the firm.

(i) The rule — As briefly discussed above at pp. _____ , absent an agreement to the contrary that provides for the division of proceeds collected on cases existing at dissolution, each principal will be obliged to conclude without compensation the cases he or she takes to his or her new office. Rosenfeld, Meyer & Susman v. Cohen, 146 Cal. App. 3d 200 (1983) ("*Rosenfeld I*"); Jewel v. Boxer, 156 Cal. App. 3d 203 (1984); Fox v. Abrams, 163 Cal. App. 3d 610 (1985); Champion v. Super. Court, 201 Cal. App. 3d 777 (1988).

(ii) The rationale — The case of *Rosenfeld I* ("RM&S") involved the dissolution of an "at will" partnership cased by the withdrawal from the firm of two partners — Cohen and Riordan ("C&R"). When C&R left, they took with them a major client, International Rectifier, who was plaintiff in a major antitrust case. RM&S had a written contract with Rectifier entitling it, among other things, to one-third of any recovery. C&R had handled the case at RM&S before they left. Their departure resulted from their demand for more compensation (double their percentage) not being met by RM&S. C&R, while still partners at RM&S, had made their deal for Rectifier to go with them. When C&R received more that $2.4 million in fees from a settlement of the case, RM&S sued. As framed by the court, the issue presented by the case was:

Given the facts of the case, does a former partner of a partnership at will owe any fiduciary duty to former partners after dissolving the partnership and subsequently agreeing with former clients of the dissolved partnership to accept and carry on business which was originally a portion of the assets of the dissolved partnership?

In its opinion, the court concluded that the *Rectifier* action constituted the "unfinished business" of the dissolved partnership so that C&R breached their fiduciary duty by failing to complete the case for the dissolved partnership. Accordingly, they must hold the sums received as constructive trustee for the partnership. As set out by the court:

- Each partner has a duty to wind up and complete the business of the dissolved partnership ("executory contracts") existing prior to its dissolution (the "unfinished business"), citing Calif. Corp. Code §§15030 and 15033.
- A partner of a dissolved partnership may not take any action with respect to "unfinished business" which leads to purely personal gain.
- Rectifier's discharge of RM&S after dissolution does not change this since whether or not a matter is "unfinished business" is determined by the "circumstances existing on the date of dissolution." (To wit, was there a contract of employment with the client on the matter at the time of dissolution?)
- The breach of fiduciary duty is not altered by the client's discharge of the dissolved firm. "Though Rectifier had a right to terminate the contract with RM&S and hire C&R, C&R could not avoid what was tantamount to a conflict of interest — i.e., the fiduciary duty it owed to RM&S." 146 Cal. App. 3d at 219. *The discharge by the client is irrelevant.*

- According to the court the "unfinished business" cases strike a balance between a partner's right to pursue his own business after dissolution and his duty of loyalty to his former partners. "The partner may take for his own account *new business* even when emanating from clients of the dissolved partnership *and the partner is entitled to the reasonable value of the services in completing the partnership business but he may not seize for his own account the business which was in existence during the terms of the partnership.* Clearly, the balance between such competing public policies is upset if a partner may dissolve a partnership . . . or if a partner may withhold his necessary services from the dissolved partnership to preclude the completion of unfinished business, or if the partner may complete such business and retain the proceeds for himself." 146 Cal. 3d at 220.

Rosenfeld I involved a situation of a partnership "at will" — one without a partnership agreement. Therefore, it left unanswered whether the result on "unfinished business" would be different if there was an agreement discharging a former partner from any duty to complete "unfinished business" for the partnership. It also left unanswered with any precision the question of how to calculate the "reasonable value" of the ex-partner's services which *Rosenfeld I* in dictum allowed the ex-partner to deduct from the proceeds collected on unfinished business. Two — perhaps three — cases decided after *Rosenfeld I* have shed some light and some confusion on the point. Jewell v. Boxer, supra; Abrams v. Fox; and "*Rosenfeld II*" (Rosenfeld, Meyer & Susman v. Cohen, 191 Cal. App. 3d 1035 (1987). (The California Supreme Court denied petitions for rehearing in *Jewell, Abrams* and *Rosenfeld II.*)

In Jewell v. Boxer, like *Rosenfeld I,* there was no

partnership agreement. At the time of dissolution (by mutual agreement) the firm was handling numerous active cases — workmens compensation cases and other matters. After dissolution, each former partner made arrangements with his client to take over the case. Two of the partners sued the other two for an accounting on fees received on the "unfinished business." The trial court allocated the fees received based on three factors: time spent by each firm (the old and the new); source of each case (always the old firm); and, in personal injury contingency cases, the result achieved by the new firm. The Court awarded:

- 25% to the source of the case;
- 20, 30 or 40% to the new firms for results obtained in contingency cases; and
- the balance, (55-35%) based on hours.

On appeal, the Court of Appeals reversed and, while expressing its admiration to the trial judge for his attempt to achieve an equitable result, held that under the Uniform Partnership Act *all proceeds* from unfinished business — *absent a contrary agreement* — must be allocated among the partners "according to their respective interest in the partnership." No extra compensation was to be awarded to a former partner for finishing the unfinished business. (To the extent that *Rosenfeld I* suggested otherwise, it was labeled as in conflict with established law; the court suggested that all *Rosenfeld I* meant was that the reasonable value which the partner gets for his efforts completing unfinished business in his percentage of the fees the other partners generate on the "unfinished business" they complete.)

To avoid undue hardship, the court stated that "the former partners are obligated to ensure that a disproportionate burden of completing unfinished business does not fall on one partner or one group of partners, unless the former partners agree otherwise. . . . Partners are free to include in a written partnership agreement provisions for completion of unfinished business that ensure a degree of exactness and certainty unattainable by rules of general application." 156 Cal. 3d at 180.

Moreover, to avoid other hardship, the court held that it is the *net income,* not the *gross income,* which must be allocated among the former partners. A reimbursement of overhead expenses attributable to the winding up is "certainly an equitable result." These, the court in a footnote suggests, would include indirect expenses "such as office salaries, rent and library costs." 156 Cal. App. 3d at 180 n.6.

In Fox v. Abrams, the dissolution of a professional corporation was involved. While there was a "Buy-Sell Agreement," the document made no provision for how unfinished business was to be handled. Following Jewel v. Boxer, the Court of Appeals held the proceeds collected on unfinished business were to be divided in proportion to the percentage interest of the members. The court in *Fox* did not disapprove the approach taken in Jewell v. Boxer on the overhead issue.

In the second *Rosenfeld* case, 191 Cal. App. 3d 1035 (1987), no real light was shed on the overhead issue but the criticism of *Rosenfeld I* by Jewel v. Boxer was not refuted. Moreover, the court made it clear that the burden is on the partner collecting the fee to establish items chargeable thereto. 191 Cal. 3d at 1051. Absent the burden being discharged, the court held that the gross proceeds are the basis for the allocation.

(iii) Ethical issued raised by the rule

• In the situation where the firm has no agreement and the rule applies, it can be argued that the rule operates to deny a client the right to counsel of choice by discouraging the attorney from taking pending cases to his or her new shop.

• Suppose, however, that an agreement is executed providing that the withdrawal of a partner does not cause a dissolution and specifying how revenues are to be shared on cases taken by the member who is terminated or withdraws? Here, too, ethical issues are raised, as they were in the case of Champion v. Super. Court, 201 Cal. App. 3d 777 (1988).

Champion involved the Boccardo Law Firm of San Francisco. In March 1985, the firm amended its partnership agreement to change the way pending cases were treated upon termination or withdrawal of a partner. Departing from a text which set forth different formulae for sharing client fees between the partnership and the departing partner depending upon the progress of the cases, the amended agreement set forth a uniform rule: all clients and client files remained the property of the firm; if the client desired the departing partner to take the case, any fees realized remained the property of the firm and the departing partner received the percentage of the fee equal to his percentage at the time of his departure. The revised agreement further provided that the firm was "to have a lien on the case and its proceeds to protect and secure the Partnership's interest in such case. . . ."

At the time of the amendment, James F. Boccardo held a 50% interest in the firm. The other members — some 14 — held interests ranging from 2.8% to 5.4%. Champion held a 1% interest at the time he joined the firm and agreed to be bound by the amended agreement. When he resigned on June 30, 1986, he held a 1.79% interest. Eight clients elected to have Champion represent them. Shortly after he left, the firm and its remaining partners sued Champion and others, seeking, inter alia, a declaration of rights and duties of the partners under the agreement as amended. The trial court rules in favor of the plaints. Champion appealed, contending: (1) under the amended agreement he was entitled to 1.79% of all fees collected on all cases pending at his departure, not just on those he took with him; and (2) the agreement was unenforceable because it conflicted with several of California's Rules of Professional Conduct which, respectively, prohibited unconscionable fees, fee splitting without the consent of the client, and agreements restricting the right of any attorney to practice law beyond the term of his membership in or employment by a law firm. (Rules 1-107, 2-108 and 2-109)

While rejecting Champion's first contention, regarding the interpretation of the agreement, the Court of Appeals agreed with his other argument — that the agreement was [un]enforceable because it violated the prohibition against unconscionable fees: If Champion's clients were required to pay The Boccardo Law Firm 98.021% of the fees on the cases he took, the partnership would be extracting an unconscionable fee. Such a fee to the firm, which bore no relationship to the stage of the litigation at the time of departure, was — in the court's view — unconscionable. "A fee of this size, without any relationship to service rendered, must 'shock the conscience of lawyers of ordinary prudence practicing' in the community." 201 Cal. App. 3d at 783.

The court also agreed with Champion's contention that the agreement was unenforceable because it was in conflict with the public policy allowing a client to discharge an attorney with or without cause and to retain counsel of his choice. Because the amended agreement denied the withdrawing partner reasonable compensation, it, in effect, denied the client the right to elect representation of his or her choosing. "[A]s a practical matter, the client is deprived of representation by the very lawyer most familiar with the case and most desired by the client." Id.

In a rather strange piece of jurisprudence, the court, having struck down ¶9.9 as unenforceable for the reasons stated above and having ruled that the paragraph was not reasonably susceptible to being read to apply its stated percentages to all cases pending at the time Champion withdrew, the court proceeded to comment on an issue not really before it: Could the contract be enforced if ¶9.9 were read contrary to its clear meaning so as to apply the stated percentages to all pending cases? (Apparently this position was advanced by Champion as a "fall back" if he lost on the public policy issues. The position was based on the "unfinished business" doctrine.

While restating that such a "tortured" reading of ¶9.9 would avoid illegality and "create a de facto dissolution," the court offered a less drastic course as available. By declaring ¶9.9 unenforceable, the withdrawing partner may represent a former client under the same terms as would an attorney who had never been a partner, controlled only by the requirement of Fracasse v. Brent, 6 Cal. 3d 784 (1972), that the firm be compensated on the basis of quantum meruit for its contribution to the case. In the court's view, where the withdrawing partner leaves with less than his or her share of lucrative cases, this approach was "better for the partnership than a dissolution and still protects the client's interest." 201 Cal. App. 3d at 785. Where the withdrawing partner leaves with more than his or her share of lucrative cases, the partnership may elect to dissolve [under ¶10] and wind up under the principles of Fox v. Abrams and Jewel v. Boxer.

• However, in Saltzberg v. Fishman, 462

N.E.2d 901 (1984), the court upheld an agreement for division of fees between a firm and a departing associate on the somewhat attenuated reasoning that even after Saltzberg left, the files remained at Fishman & Fishman, with the agreement on fees no more than a retention of Saltzberg's services by the firm for "the limited purpose of disposing of the cases."

• Compare Model Rule of Professional Conduct 5.6 which provides: "A lawyer shall not participate in offering or making: (a) a partnership or employment agreement that restricts the rights of a lawyer to practice after termination of the relationship."

• An agreement between a lawyer and a *client* which restricts the attorney's right to practice subsequent to the termination of their relationship may be unenforceable based on the same considerations which render such agreements between counsel unenforceable. ABA Informal Opinion 1301 (1975).

(iv) Suppose there is an agreement relating to unfinished business that provides for a division of fees on a more "generous" basis, e.g., 75% to the lawyer taking the case, 25% to the firm on fees generated post-dissolution date (with 100% of all fees accrued prior to dissolution belonging to the firm). Does this agreement meet the rule in *Champion?* If the firm, prior to dissolution, voted to replace such a provision with one giving 100% of post-dissolution fees to the lawyer taking the case, would a fraudulent transfer have occurred? Would an agreement that, as originally drafted long before dissolution, gave 100% of such fees to the lawyer taking the case avoid both the problems raised by the finished business rule and the risk of attack under faudulent conveyance laws?

d. Can the court in the title 11 case effect the administration of matters being handled by the debtor?

(1) Section 105(a) of the Code empowers the court to "issue any order, process or judgment that is necessary to carry out the provisions of" title 11. Section 108 provides certain extensions of time for the commencement of actions, the filing of pleadings, notices, etc., or the performance of similar acts. Under either statute can the title 11 court affect deadlines in cases being handled by the professional?

(2) The answer should be "no." Section 108 applies to the "debtor", not to the debtor's client, whereas the deadlines discussed are imposed on the party to the case.

e. The "client's file"

(1) As a general matter, the file is the property of the client although the lawyer may have certain rights of retention. See Model Rule 1.6(d). See also D.R. 2-110(A)(2).

(2) In the event of a title 11 case, §362 would stay the client's exercise of its rights to the file.

(3) Until those rights can be exercised, what can the client do to insure the sanctity of the file's contents?

(a) Request an order from the bankruptcy court under §107(b) protecting the confidences contained in the file. See In re Epic Associates, 54 Bankr. 445 (Bankr. E.D. Va. 1985) (order entered maintaining confidentiality of the identities of holders of the debtors mortgages and mortgage-backed certificates).

(b) Is the trustee entitled to discover privileged communications under CFTC v. Weintraub, 471 U.S. 343 (1985)? It would seem not, since the privilege here is the client's privilege, not the attorney's.

(c) Is the debtor obliged to seek such an order? See Model Rule 1.6.

(4) Assuming that the files are the property of the client, must the estate bear the cost of preservation? For how long? At what point and after what effort may the files be abandoned under §554 of the Code?

(5) It should be noted that the attorney enjoys a "retaining lien" to secure payment of fees. (This is in addition to the "charging lien" the attorney may have in a

judgment he or she obtains for a client.) See generally L'Estrange & Tucker, Avoiding Attorney-Client Fee Disputes: Written Fee Agreements Can Make Sense, 55 Wis. B. Bull. 29 (1982); Thompson, Attorney Fee and Liens, 85 Com. L.J. 4 (1980); Note, The Attorney's Lien in Federal Courts, 39, A.B.A.J. 131 (1953); Note, Attorney's Retaining Lien Over Former Client's Papers, 65 Colum. L. Rev. 296 (1965); Note, Practical Problems in Compensation Liens, 12 Forum 666 (1977); Note, Attorney versus Client Lien Rights and Remedies in Tennessee, 7 Mem. St. U.L. Rev. 435 (1977); Note, Possessory Liens: Due Process, 16 Wm. & Mary L. Rev. 971 (1975). The retaining lien applies to all work a lawyer has performed for a client and generally enables the lawyer to retain papers, money, securities, and property received from the client until the lawyer is compensated or receives security for the claimed fee.

Despite the foregoing, "the *ethical* propriety of asserting a retaining lien is not absolute . . . ," and the burden is on the lawyer to determine whether circumstances justify asserting the lien to which a lawyer may be entitled by law. ABA Informal Opinion 1461 (Nov. 11, 1980).

(Some courts have held that the lawyer must provide copies of the papers necessary to the client's ongoing lawsuit, but may retain the originals as evidence of the lawyer's lien. E.g., Goldsmith v. Pyramid Communications, 362 F. Supp. 694 (S.D.N.Y. 1973). But see Academy of California Optometrists v. Superior Court, 51 Cal. App. 3d 999, 124 Cal. Rptr. 668 (1975); see also City of Hankinson v. Otter Tail Power Co., 294 F. Supp. 249 (D.N.D. 1969).)

(6) Assuming that a trustee can retain the client's file to secure payment of fees, can he do so if the client asserts malpractice as a defense? Under the first clause of Model Rule 1.8(h) and under D.R. 6-102(A), a lawyer may not condition return of a client's documents on the client's release of claims that might arise from the representation. In re Preston, 111 Ariz. 102, 523 P.2d 1303 (1974); In re

Darby, 426 N.E.2d 683 (Ind. 1981). See also Nolan v.
Foreman, 665 F.2d 738 (CA5 1982).

f. Collection of fees

(1) Section 704(1) of the Code provides in part that
the trustee shall "collect and reduce to money the property
of the estate."

(2) Can the trustee make use of the courts to collect
the accounts of a law firm as freely as he would in a case for
a debtor other than a law firm?

(a) Both the Model Code and the Model Rules
indicate that lawyers should avoid bringing fee disputes
to court and instead should use other means at their
disposal to collect their fees.

(b) E.C. 2-23 provides: "A lawyer should be zeal-
ous in his efforts to avoid controversies over fees with
clients and should attempt to resolve amicably any differences on the subject. He should not sue a client for a
fee unless necessary to prevent fraud or gross imposition
by the client."

(c) The Comment to Model Rule 1.5 states:

> If a procedure has been established for resolution of fee
> disputes, such as an arbitration or mediation procedure
> established by the bar, the lawyer should conscientiously
> consider submitting to it. Law may prescribe a procedure
> for determining a lawyer's fee, for example, in representa-
> tion of an executor or administrator, a class or a person
> entitled to reasonable fee as part of the measure of dam-
> ages. The lawyer entitled to such a fee and a lawyer
> representing another party concerned with the fee should
> comply with the prescribed procedure. [ABA/BNA
> 41:2001.]

(d) If the trustee proceeds in ignorance of these
ethical principles, may the client avoid having to pay? In
answering this question, consider that unethical conduct by an attorney is grounds for denial of a fee. Esser v.
A.H. Robins Co., Inc., 537 F. Supp. 197 (D. Minn.
1982); compare Kizer v. Davis, 369 N.E.2d 439 (Ind.
App. 1977).

TABLE OF CASES

TABLE OF THE UNIFORM
PARTNERSHIP ACT

The Uniform Partnership Act is reproduced in Appendix A.

TABLE OF RESTATEMENTS OF THE LAW

TABLE OF ABA ETHICS CODES

Select provisions of the Model Rules of Professional Conduct and the Model Code of Professional Responsibility are reproduced in Appendices B and C.

Canons of Professional Ethics (1908)

In general	2.1; 2.1 nn.2, 5, 6, 9; 2.2.1; 2.3.2; 4.4 n.3
Canon 7	2.3 n.14

Model Rules of Professional Conduct (1983)

In general	2.1, 2.1 n.4, 2.2.3.1; 2.2.3.2; 2.2.4; 2.3; 2.3 n.21; 2.3.1; 2.3.2; 2.3.4; 2.4 n.21; 2.4.3; 3.1.3; 3.1.4; 3.4; 3.4 n.6; 4.6.3; 4.4 n.3;

	5.4 n.19; 5.4.3
Rule 1.1	3.4 n.6
Rule 1.5(e)	4.4 n.4
Rules 1.6-1.10	2.2 n.44
Rule 1.6	3.4 n.6
Rule 1.7	3.4 n.6
Rule 1.8	3.4 n.6
Rule 1.9	2.2 n.44; 2.4.3; 3.4 n.6
Rule 1.9(a)	2.2 n.44
Rule 1.9(b)	2.4 n.21
Rule 1.9(c)	2.2 n.44; 2.4 n.21
Rule 1.10	2.4.3; 3.4 n.6
Rule 1.10(a)	2.4 n.22
Rule 1.10(b)	2.4 n.23
Rule 1.10(c)	3.4 n.6
Rule 1.16	3.4 n.6
Rule 1.16(a)(3)	2.3 n.4
Rule 5.1	5.1 n.3
Rule 5.6	2.3 n.21

TABLE OF ETHICS OPINIONS

Opinions in italics are reproduced in Appendix D.

ABA Formal Opinions

Formal Op. 300	*2.3 nn. 12, 13, 15; 2.3.2; 3.4 n.5*
Formal Op. 303	5.1 n.3

ABA Informal Opinions

Informal Op. 428	*2.4.2 n.17*
Informal Op. 521	*2.3 nn. 16, 17*
Informal Op. 522	*2.1 n.6*
Informal Op. 1072	*2.3 nn. 18–20; 2.3.2*
Informal Op. 1428	3.4 n.6
Informal Op. 1457	2.2 n.26
Informal Op. 1466	2.2 n.27

State Bar Association Opinions

D.C.: Op. 65	2.3 nn. 22, 26
D.C.: Op. 181	2.3 n.26
D.C.: Op. 194	2.3 n.26
Ill.: Op. 86-16	2.2 nn. 28, 30; 2.3 n.22
Ill.: Op. 628 (1978)	2.3 nn. 22, 26
Ky.: Op. 317	2.2 n.28
Ky.: Op. 326	2.3 nn. 22, 26, 36
Mich.: Op. CI-1133	2.2 nn. 28, 30
Tex.: Op. 459	2.3 n.26
Va.: Op. 880	2.3 n.37
Va.: Op. 985	2.3 n.30

INDEX

291